D1521891

The Unprecedented 2016 Presidential Election

Rachel Bitecofer

The Unprecedented 2016 Presidential Election

Rachel Bitecofer
Department of Political Science
Christopher Newport University
Newport News, VA, USA

ISBN 978-3-319-61975-0 ISBN 978-3-319-61976-7 (eBook)
https://doi.org/10.1007/978-3-319-61976-7

Library of Congress Control Number: 2017948256

Printed on acid-free paper

This Palgrave Macmillan imprint is published by Springer Nature
The registered company is Springer International Publishing AG
The registered company address is: Gewerbestrasse 11, 6330 Cham, Switzerland

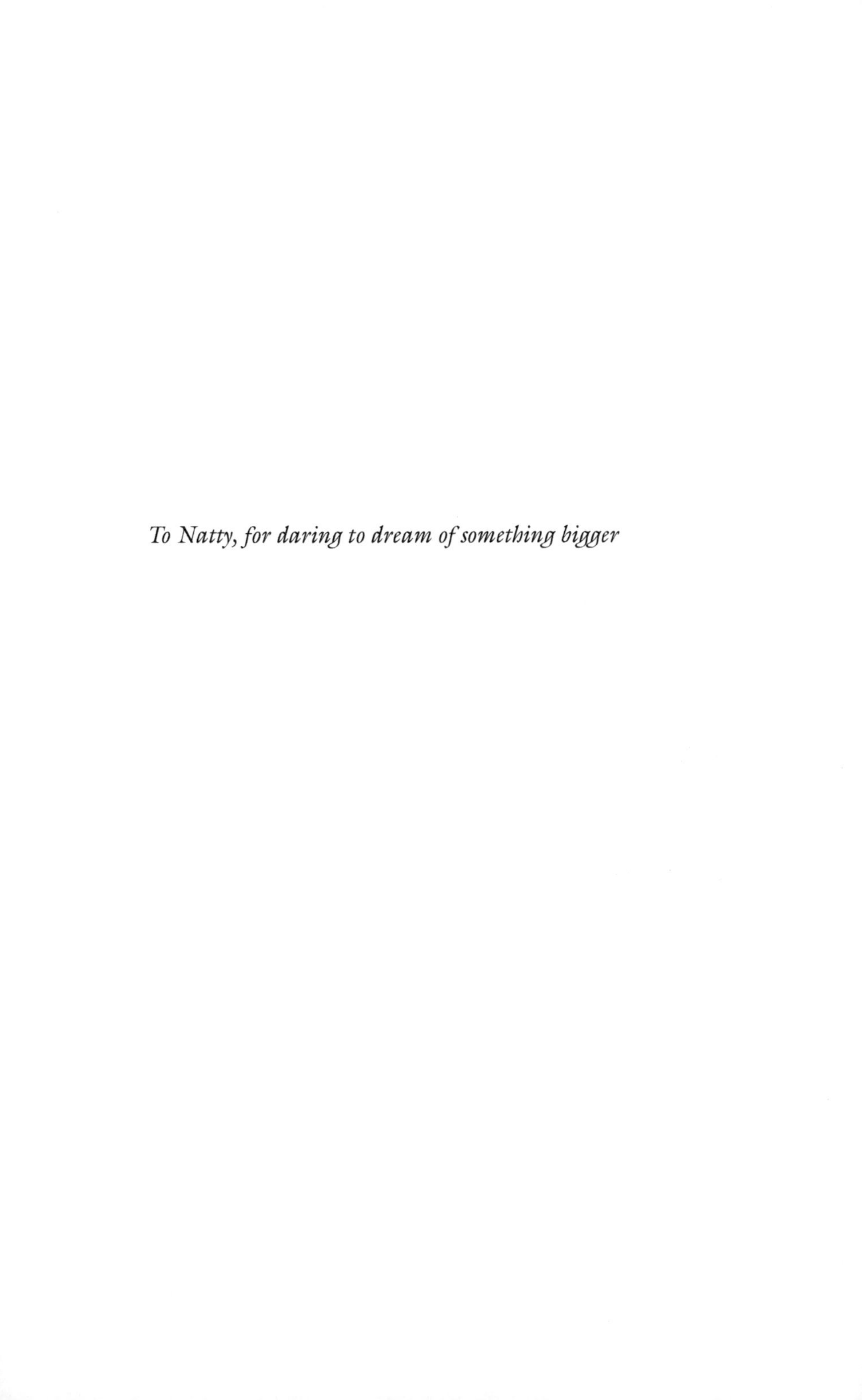

To Natty, for daring to dream of something bigger

Preface

The roots of this work stretch to the 2000 presidential election. Although I was always a political junkie, that election, and all the controversy that came after it, sparked my interest in presidential campaigns. Upon enrolling in my doctoral program at the University of Georgia 9 years later, I was lucky to find my mentor and friend Paul-Henri Gurian, who inspired me to focus my doctoral research on presidential elections. Paul's passion for presidential campaigns led him to host a weekly meeting each election cycle that brought faculty and graduate students together for a nerd fest where we would use our collective knowledge of campaigns and voter behavior to dissect the latest campaign events.

Paul was protective of these meetings, wishing it to remain an academic exercise free of the partisanship and superficiality that governs so much of the so-called analysis of elections. Over the course of the last few decades, the amount of coverage given to presidential elections, particularly presidential nominations, has increased exponentially. Yet what hasn't changed much is the *way* presidential campaigns are analyzed. The focus is always on what happened rather than on why it happened that way. This book endeavors to shed some light on the "why."

This book would not be possible without the support and inspiration I receive from my colleague Quentin Kidd, who is probably the most selfless person I have ever met. Quentin has given me an opportunity of a lifetime by allowing me to join him in the Wason Center for Public Policy here at Christopher Newport University. The Wason Center was established by Judy and Harry Wason to change lives, and it has definitely changed mine.

The creation of this book would not have been possible without my family, some of whom sacrificed a great deal so I could immerse myself in this work. I hope it makes you proud.

At that, I'll leave you with a famous quote from H.L. Mencken. Mencken became famous satirizing the Scopes Trial, dubbing it the Monkey Trial. On democracy, Menken once said, "Democracy is the theory that the common people know what they want, and deserve to get it good and hard." Indeed good sir. Indeed.

Newport News, USA Rachel Bitecofer

Contents

1	Introduction	1
2	Pitchforks and Torches	11
3	The 2016 Presidential Nominations	31
4	Donald J. Trump: The Making of a Media Event	39
5	The Party Decides?	59
6	The 2016 Presidential Election	81
7	Everybody Sucks 2016	93
8	A Tale of Two Campaigns	105
9	What (Really) Happened	141
Index		187

List of Figures

Fig. 2.1	Ideological distribution of the 88th Congress	14
Fig. 2.2	Ideological distribution of the 114th Congress	14
Fig. 2.3	Party unity in Congress 1950–2013	15
Fig. 2.4	Party sorting in the electorate: 1980 vs. 2016	16
Fig. 2.5	Change in self-identified ideology: 1980 vs. 2016	16
Fig. 2.6	Ideological distribution of the American electorate, by party: 1987	18
Fig. 2.7	Ideological distribution of the American Electorate, by party: 2012	18
Fig. 2.8	Decline in ideological moderates since 1987	19
Fig. 2.9	Hillary Clinton approval ratings	27
Fig. 3.1	Declared presidential primary candidates, by cycle	32
Fig. 3.2	Relationship between poll standings and fund-raising in the 2016 Republican primary	33
Fig. 4.1	*Politifact's* "Pants on Fire" scorecard for the 2016 primary candidates	43
Fig. 4.2	Donald Trump's daily domination of the 24 hour news cycle	48
Fig. 4.3	Trump's percent of media attention: June 2015	49
Fig. 4.4	Trump's percent of media attention: July 2015	49
Fig. 4.5	Trump's percent of media attention: August 2015	50
Fig. 4.6	Trump's percent of media attention: September 2015	50
Fig. 4.7	Trump's percent of media attention: October 2015	51
Fig. 4.8	Trump's percent of media attention: November 2015	51
Fig. 4.9	Trump's percent of media attention: December 2015	52
Fig. 4.10	Trump's percent of media attention: January 2016	52
Fig. 4.11	Trump's percent of media attention: February 2016	53

Fig. 4.12 Trump's percent of media attention: March 2016 53
Fig. 4.13 Trump's percent of media attention: April 2016 54
Fig. 4.14 Trump's percent of media attention: May/June 2016 54
Fig. 4.15 Percent of Trump candidate mentions with poll standings 55
Fig. 5.1 Clinton vs. Sanders pledged delegates in early contests 68
Fig. 5.2 Clinton vs. Sanders total delegates in early contests 69
Fig. 5.3 Clinton vs. Sanders: pledged delegates 70
Fig. 5.4 Clinton vs. Sanders: total delegates 70
Fig. 5.5 Clinton vs. Sanders pledged delegates through March 1st 71
Fig. 5.6 Clinton vs. Sanders total delegates through March 1st 71
Fig. 5.7 2016 Republican primary delegate allocation 73
Fig. 5.8 Iowa and New Hampshire with Republican super delegates 74
Fig. 5.9 Early contests with Republican super delegates 75
Fig. 7.1 Donald Trump favorability ratings 94
Fig. 7.2 Hillary Clinton favorability ratings 95
Fig. 7.3 Hillary Clinton word cloud 95
Fig. 7.4 Donald Trump word cloud 96
Fig. 7.5 Trump vs. Clinton candidate characteristics 97
Fig. 7.6 Emotions toward 2016 nominees 98
Fig. 7.7 Partisan assessments of own nominee 99
Fig. 7.8 Candidate qualifications 100
Fig. 8.1 Total fund-raising in the 2016 presidential election 118
Fig. 8.2 Donald Trump campaign events (8/1/16–11/7/16) 121
Fig. 8.3 Hillary Clinton campaign events (8/1/16–11/7/16) 122
Fig. 8.4 Donald Trump and Mike Pence campaign events (8/1/16–11/7/16) 123
Fig. 8.5 Hillary Clinton and her "Super Surrogates" campaign events (8/1/16–11/7/16) 123
Fig. 9.1 Personal attack ads by cycle 152
Fig. 9.2 Battleground state polls 158
Fig. 9.3 Hillary Clinton campaign appearances (final 10 days) 165
Fig. 9.4 Hillary Clinton and super surrogates campaign events (final 10 days) 165
Fig. 9.5 Donald Trump and Mike Pence campaign events (final 10 days) 166
Fig. 9.6 Party loyalty in Presidential Elections 170
Fig. 9.7 Independent voters nationwide 171
Fig. 9.8 Independent voters by swing state 172
Fig. 9.9 Swing state independent voters, by gender 172
Fig. 9.10 Vote choice of those with unfavorable views of both candidates 173
Fig. 9.11 White vote, by party 174

Fig. 9.12	Vote choice of white college-educated women	175
Fig. 9.13	General election defection Clinton vs. Sanders states	179
Fig. 9.14	2016 Vote choice of Sanders supporters	180
Fig. 9.15	Reason Sanders supporters voted for Clinton	180
Fig. 9.16	Most important reason for defection	181
Fig. 9.17	Effect of progressive Vice President pick on defection	181

List of Tables

Table 4.1	Donald Trump's "Pants on Fire" statements in the 2016 presidential election	44
Table 8.1	Donald Trump's evolving campaign team	107
Table 8.2	The Clinton campaign organization	115
Table 8.3	Campaign mistakes	127
Table 9.1	Major newspaper endorsements 2012 vs. 2016	154
Table 9.2	Third party defection rates 2012 vs. 2016	163
Table 9.3	Third party defection in the democrat's blue wall	176
Table 9.4	Effect of Sanders primary support on defection rate	178

CHAPTER 1

Introduction

Abstract Bitecofer documents the many unprecedented aspects of the 2016 presidential primaries and general election. The historic candidacies of Donald Trump, Hillary Clinton, and Bernie Sanders broke barriers and redefined our understanding of American presidential campaigns. Bitecofer analyzes the 2016 presidential election through the eyes of a political scientist. Drawing on decades of political science research on presidential campaigns, voting behavior, and political polarization, Bitecofer examines the strategic considerations made by the candidates and their campaigns as they battled first for their party's nomination and then for the White House.

Keywords Presidential election · Presidential primaries · Hillary Clinton Bernie Sanders · Donald Trump · Republican · Democrat

According to searches of *LexisNexis* and the *TV News Archive*, the word unprecedented appears in American media coverage of the 2016 presidential election, 2505 original times by television outlets and 1005 times by major newspapers. From Donald Trump unlikely nomination to Clinton's stunning loss on Election Day, the 2016 cycle was one for the record books.

The universal support that Hillary Clinton had from the Democratic Party's establishment was unprecedented. Not even Al Gore, who ran for the party's nomination in 2000 as the incumbent vice president,

R. Bitecofer, *The Unprecedented 2016 Presidential Election*,
https://doi.org/10.1007/978-3-319-61976-7_1

received as many early endorsements as Clinton. Her first elite endorsement came from Senator Claire McCaskill in 2013. A year out from the Iowa Caucus she had already amassed commitments from 60 Democratic Party super delegates, including 18 sitting senators, 40 members of the House of Representatives, and 2 governors.[1]

The size of the Republican field was also unprecedented. At seventeen declared candidates, the Republican field was by far the largest to ever compete for a party's nomination. The field was not only large, it was talented. The field included four current governors, five former governors, four current senators, one former senator, two celebrities, and a former CEO of a Fortune 500 company. There were so many Republican candidates that the Republican National Committee (RNC) made a controversial decision. Rather than try to cram seventeen candidates onto one debate stage, they would host two separate debates and use national poll standings to determine which candidates would be invited to participate in the main event.

Some of the candidates' campaign announcements were unprecedented. Bernie Sanders' official announcement came in the form of a ten-minute press conference on the lawn of the Capital Building. After brusquely stating his reasons for challenging Hillary Clinton for the Democratic Party's nomination, he took only one question from an eager press pool before abruptly cutting them off to attend a vote on the Senate floor.[2] Although Bernie Sanders' announcement was a no-frills affair, Ben Carson's campaign announcement was ostentatious. Carson's announcement in Detroit featured a full gospel choir singing an Eminem song (both Carson and Eminem are from Detroit).[3] Not to be outdone by Carson on musicality, Mike Huckabee's announcement featured Tony Orlando singing a rousing rendition of "Tie a Yellow Ribbon."[4]

Fearing blowback from an over-the-top announcement, Hillary Clinton elected to announce her candidacy completely online. The announcement video's theme was "I'm getting ready." It showed average (but notably diverse) Americans discussing things they were getting ready to do before revealing Clinton, in her trademark pantsuit, announcing she was "getting ready to do something too, I'm running for president."[5] Louisiana Governor Bobby Jindal also used an online video for his campaign announcement. The video showed the Jindal family, obstensibly gathered around a table on the back porch of the governor's mansion, discussing his decision to run for president.[6]

Donald Trump staged his announcement speech in the opulence of Trump Tower. With former super model wife Melania by his side and throngs of supporters crowded around the surrounding balconies, Trump descended down the Trump Tower escalator from his penthouse apartment[7] to the tune of Neil Young's "Rockin' in the Free World" to begin his forty-seven-minute announcement speech, the likes of which had never been seen before. With no teleprompter Donald Trump's announcement speech meandered between politics and self-promotion and included lines such as "I will be the greatest jobs president that God ever created."[8] The media had never seen anything like it and were immediately transfixed. They figured that Trump's candidacy wouldn't last long but while it did he'd be ratings gold. Of course, they couldn't have known then that they were looking at the next President of the United States of America.

Donald Trump's capture of the Republican Party's nomination made history; an achievement only overshadowed by his even less likely victory in the general election. Trump's candidacy adds many unprecedented elements to the 2016 cycle. He boycotted the final presidential debate in Iowa over a Twitter feud with a *Fox News* anchor and was the target of a movement to derail his candidacy financed by his own party's biggest donors. On his way to the White House, Donald Trump didn't just defy convention wisdoms he blew them apart, breaking almost every rule governing presidential campaigns along the way. And he did it without earning a single endorsement from a Republican member of Congress or Republican governor until three weeks after the Iowa Caucus. Over the entirety of the Republican primary, Trump earned just forty-eight elite endorsements total.[9]

Although more conventional, the Democratic primary was also unprecedented. Despite not being a Democrat and being a self-described socialist, Bernie Sanders earned more than 13 million votes and won 23 states, not bad for someone whose main motivation to run was to hold Hillary Clinton accountable to the party's progressive wing. At times, Sanders seemed awed by the throngs of fans crowding into sold-out arenas and concert halls to hear him speak. Despite a significant disadvantage in fund-raising, name recognition, and elite support, Bernie Sanders came less than 1% away from beating Clinton in Iowa, won New Hampshire handily despite a full court press by the Clinton campaign, and was competitive in the Nevada Caucus. Although ultimately unsuccessful, Sanders won 23 contests, 43.1% of the Democratic Party's primary votes, collected 39% of the total delegates, and raised more than $235 million dollars; an impressive feat for any candidate let alone one that doesn't even belong to the party whose nomination he sought.

The 2016 general election would offer more unprecedented elements. For the first time in history, a presidential nominee struggled to find a running mate. Several prominent Republicans took their names out of the running, including Senator Rob Portman of Ohio, Senator Marco Rubio of Florida, Governor Nikki Haley, Governor John Kasich of Ohio, Senator Bob Corker of Tennessee, and Governor Susana Martinez of New Mexico.[10] The Republican National Committee struggled to find high-profile Republicans to take on speaking roles at the party's convention in Ohio in July; a position that is usually coveted because of the stature and national exposure it brings.[11] Both former presidents Bush and Ohio's Sitting Governor John Kasich announced they would not even attend the convention. Neither would Mitt Romney nor Senator John McCain, both former Republican nominees.[12] The media indulged in breathless speculation about a brokered convention. Although that didn't come to pass, Ted Cruz used his convention speech to implore conservatives to "vote your conscious," eliciting raucous boos from the convention hall.[13]

The Democratic Party's convention was also mired in controversy. Despite endorsing Hillary Clinton two weeks earlier, the Bernie or Bust delegates still wanted a revolution. Working together, the Sanders and Clinton teams just barely contained an insurgency on the opening night of the convention. Passions had been stirred by the release of emails stolen from the Democratic National Committee on the eve of the convention, leading to the resignation of the DNC's chair just hours before the start of the convention. The attacks on the Clinton campaign by the Russian government in the 2016 election were unprecedented. Never before had a hostile foreign government interfered in an American presidential election.

The general election continued to deliver unprecedented aspects and events. Most presidential elections produce parity between the two campaigns. Both parties nominate experienced candidates with public service backgrounds who have robust support of the party's establishment. Both campaigns raise and spend hundreds of millions of dollars and once outside spending is factored in, usually come within just a few million dollars of each other in total spending. Both campaigns court favorable media attention and are loathe to do something that might invoke bad headlines.

Both candidates sequester themselves for days before the first presidential debate and undergo extensive preparations. No candidate would dream of insulting the Pope or accusing a federal judge of bias due to his ethnicity, or spending a week waging a war against a Gold Star family. And no candidate would ever urge the Russian government to hack their opponent's email, threaten to lock up their opponent if they win the election, or question the legitimacy of America's electoral system. Until 2016, no candidate could ever win the American presidency after being outraised, outspent, and out-organized by their opponent. Yet Donald Trump did all of that and more on his improbable path to Pennsylvania Avenue: unprecedented.

An election that broke all the rules and defied all of the conventional wisdoms deserves to be fully dissected. To that end, the work presented here does not provide the traditional overview of what happened in the 2016 election. There are several excellent works by fellow political scientists that offer these analyses and do so far better than I ever could. Those books have been critical to my understanding of presidential campaigns and if you have not already done so, I urge you to read at least one of them prior to reading the research presented here. These books tend to explain the results of the latest presidential election by using what is known about how campaigns operate; their rules, norms, and best practices, to show how the better executed campaign triumphed on Election Day. As such, I expect their authors are having some trouble writing them this election cycle. Nor is this book one of the salacious "tell-all" books put out by political journalists and pundits with inside access to the campaigns. Those works capture all the intrigue of presidential elections, bringing the reader down into the political trenches, but they are not all that useful in terms of explaining why things happened the way they did.

Instead, this book analyzes the 2016 presidential election by focusing on the strategic decisions made by the candidates and their campaigns. Rather than focusing on what happened, this book focuses on explaining *why* things happened the way they did. Why was Donald Trump able to win the Republican Party's nomination despite having the entire party establishment working against him? How did Hillary Clinton survive her 2016 primary challenge from Bernie Sanders but lose in similar circumstances against Barack Obama in 2008? Why did Clinton lose what many consider to be the most winnable presidential election in the modern era?

The research presented here answers these questions by drawing on decades of political science research on presidential campaigns, voting behavior, and political polarization. Chapter 2 sets the context of the

2016 presidential election. Rather than a singular event, the 2016 presidential election is best understood as the most recent chapter of a story that began decades ago. Over the past fifty years, America has undergone dramatic cultural, political, demographic, and technological transformations leading to an era of polarized politics. With one party immersed in a civil war and the other facing an emerging revolution, the stage was set for the unlikely candidacies of Donald Trump and Bernie Sanders.

Chapter 3 recaps the paths that Hillary Clinton and Donald Trump took to win their party's nomination. For Clinton, an unexpected primary challenge forced the campaign to compete for a nomination that was once inevitable. Coming from nowhere, Bernie Sanders' campaign tapped into the anti-establishment and populist sentiment of the progressive wing of the Democratic Party transforming his candidacy from a symbolic exercise into a powerful social movement. Meanwhile, despite being outspent and out-organized, Donald Trump won the Republican Party's nomination by giving voice to rising right-wing populism and nationalism in the Republican base.

Chapter 4 examines the role that Donald Trump's manipulation of the media played in his success in the Republican primary. Via controversial statements and policy positions, Trump starved his competitors of earned media coverage. Trump dominated the 24-hour news cycle. In a cycle with twenty-one candidates, Donald Trump received more than 50% of all candidate mentions on eighty-nine days and exceeded 60% on twenty-one more. Every time attention waned Donald Trump would say or do something to draw it back to himself; proving the adage that any attention is good attention, at least for Donald J. Trump. In the eyes of the Republican electorate, he could do no wrong. The more critical the media coverage the higher his poll standings went.

Chapter 5 demonstrates how the institutional structures of the two party's nominating systems affect the outcome of the 2016 presidential primaries. Despite a full frontal assault Republican Party elites had limited influence on the party's nomination process. It was not from a lack of trying; Donald Trump did not pick up a single elite endorsement until three weeks after the Iowa Caucus. Over the course of the entire primary, he earned just forty-eight. Despite the fact that Republican Party insiders were lined up against him, they were unable to derail the Trump Train because of their limited influence. In the Republican nominating system, elite endorsements are merely symbolic, they do not carry substantive weight. Unlike the Democrat's system which provides party insiders a tool to exert direct influence in the party's nomination process via super delegates, the Republican rules left the party vulnerable to a hostile takeover.

Chapter 6 recaps the major events of the 2016 general election starting with the party conventions and ending with Donald Trump's unexpected victory on Election Day. Both party conventions begin mired in speculation about brokered conventions and delegate revolts. Both parties face internal divisions over their party nominee's. Although Democratic Party elites are solidly behind Hillary Clinton, the Democratic base is divided. With Sanders' loss, the progressive wing of the party is angry and deeply suspicious about Hillary Clinton. The Republican Party faced the opposite problem. Although the Republican base is solidly behind the party's controversial nominee, Republican Party insiders are deeply divided. Many prominent Republicans boycotting the convention and refuse to join the ticket. As the general election moves on, the Trump campaign is plagued by scandals, most of which are unforced errors by their nominee. Heading into Election Day, Hillary Clinton's victory is all but guaranteed until the polls close in Florida, and the state's 29 Electoral College votes are added to Donald Trump total. With one candidate earning 3 million more popular votes and the other candidate winning the Electoral College, the 2016 presidential election ended with one final unprecedented act.

Before turning to the general election Chap. 7 uses public opinion data to analyze voters' evaluations of Clinton and Trump: the two most disliked candidates to ever run for president. When asked for the one word that best described Hillary Clinton, voters overwhelmingly chose the word liar. Top words for Donald Trump include racist, idiot, and crazy. Even partisans were wary of their own party's nominee. About 50% of Democrats said that Hillary Clinton made them feel angry at least some of the time while 54% of Republicans reported being afraid of their own nominee at least some of the time. The only way either of these nominees were competitive to win the White House was by running against each other.

Chapter 8 dissects the two campaigns in terms of their campaign organization and resources. The analysis of the campaigns' organizations reveals a significant talent gap between the two campaign's management teams. Just two weeks before Labor Day, Donald Trump hired his third campaign manager. Although a longtime GOP consultant Kellyanne Conway had never run a major campaign and now found herself to be the first woman to ever run a Republican presidential campaign. The analysis then shows during the general election, the Trump campaign trailed the Clinton campaign in every metric: fund-raising, television ad buys, talent, endorsements, and infrastructure. The chapter continues by analyzing the major mistakes made by each campaign and the impact they had on the race.

Chapter 9 explores the strategic considerations Donald Trump and Hillary Clinton made in terms of selecting their running mates. With the selection of Senator Tim Kaine, the Clinton team embraced a persuasion strategy to win the general election. They would make the entire race a referendum on Donald Trump. They would win the White House, and even perhaps control of the Senate, by bringing in Independents and disaffected Republicans. In the end, the Clinton campaign conducted the nearly perfect execution of the wrong campaign strategy. Political polarization and partisan acrimony have left very little of the electorate persuadable. Despite structuring the entire campaign around them, the Clinton campaign makes virtually no in-roads among Independents. And without a progressive running mate on the ticket to mobilize Bernie Sanders supporters, many defect to third-party candidates or write-in candidates leaving Hillary Clinton just 77,000 votes over three states shy of becoming the first female President of the U.S.

Notes

1. For endorsement data see https://projects.fivethirtyeight.com/2016-endorsement-primary/.
2. To watch Sanders' announcement see https://www.youtube.com/watch?v=dOIirPta4h4.
3. To see Carson's gospel choir perform Eminem see https://www.youtube.com/watch?v=kz5e1w4Q6Ik.
4. To see Tony Orlando perform at Huckabee's announcement see http://www.stereogum.com/1799521/mike-huckabee-sees-ben-carsons-gospel-eminem-cover-and-raises-tony-orlando-in-the-flesh-at-presidential-campaign-announcement/video/.
5. To see Clinton's announcement video go to https://www.youtube.com/watch?v=8V-_4-vFinM.
6. To watch Bobby Jindal's announcement see https://www.youtube.com/watch?v=WSDqJexwWok.
7. To watch Trump's entrance go to https://www.youtube.com/watch?v=Ab9AnZaLL1U.

8. Adam B. Lerner, "The 10 best lines from Donald Trump's announcement speech," *Politico*, http://www.politico.com/story/2015/06/donald-trump-2016-announcement-10-best-lines-119066.
9. For endorsement data see https://projects.fivethirtyeight.com/2016-endorsement-primary/.
10. Steve Benen,"As contenders quit, Trump's challenge is finding a willing VP," *MSNBC*, http://www.msnbc.com/rachel-maddow-show/contenders-quit-trumps-challenge-finding-willing-vp.
11. Alex Isenstadt, "Hardly anybody wants to speak at Trump's convention," http://www.politico.com/story/2016/06/hardly-anybody-wants-to-speak-at-trumps-convention-224815.
12. Jessica Taylor, "Dumpster Fires, Fishing And Travel: These Republicans Are Sitting Out The RNC," *NPR*, http://www.npr.org/2016/07/18/486398726/dumpster-fires-fishing-and-travel-these-republicans-are-sitting-out-the-rnc.
13. Peter Schroeder, "No Trump endorsement from Cruz: 'Vote your conscience,'" *The Hill*, http://thehill.com/blogs/ballot-box/presidential-races/288607-no-trump-endorsement-from-cruz-who-tells-gop-vote-your.

CHAPTER 2

Pitchforks and Torches

Abstract Bitecofer sets the context of the 2016 presidential election. Rather than a singular event, the 2016 presidential election is best understood as the most recent chapter of a story that began decades ago. Over the past 50 years, America has undergone dramatic cultural, political, demographic, and technological transformations leading to an era of polarized politics. With one party immersed in a Civil War and the other facing an emerging revolution, the stage was set for the unlikely candidacies of Donald Trump and Bernie Sanders.

Keywords Presidential election · Presidential primaries · Hillary Clinton Bernie Sanders · Donald Trump · Republican · Democrat

The 2016 presidential primaries and general election didn't occur in a vacuum. In order to understand these unprecedented elections, it is necessary to examine the context in which they occurred. Rather than a singular event, the 2016 presidential election cycle is best understood as the most recent chapter of a story that began decades ago. Over the past fifty years, America has undergone dramatic cultural, political, demographic, and technological transformations leading to an era of polarized politics. Starting in the 1960s, a series of landmark pieces of legislation and judicial rulings in the federal courts began to fundamentally alter the country's political and cultural landscape. *Brown v. Board of Education*, the *Civil Right Acts of 1964*, and the *Voting Rights Act of 1965* all used

R. Bitecofer, *The Unprecedented 2016 Presidential Election*,
https://doi.org/10.1007/978-3-319-61976-7_2

the power of the federal government to force an end to the Southern Jim Crow system of segregation and finally enfranchised southern blacks, who registered to vote en masse starting in the 1968 presidential election. Delivered by an alliance of northern liberal Democrats and liberal Republicans in Congress, and signed into law by a former Texas senator Democratic President Johnson, the *Civil Rights Act* and the *Voting Rights Act* tore apart the Democratic Party's New Deal Coalition; the longstanding alliance of liberal and conservative Democrats that had dominated Congress since the Great Depression. Over the course of the next few decades, southern Democrats began to disappear as ideological conservatives either party switched into the Republican Party or were replaced by Republicans challengers. The South enjoyed a brief period of party competition before moving back to one-party dominance; this time by an ideologically conservative Republican Party.

At the same time, other major cultural and political shifts were occurring. The women's liberation movement began to dramatically alter the role of women at home and at work. Women used the federal courts to challenge state-level obstacles to reproductive freedom such as access to birth control and later, abortion via the famous *Roe v. Wade* decision. The Vietnam War and then the Watergate scandal eroded the public's trust in government, redefined the ability of the press to access and publish classified information, and turned an entire generation into a counterculture movement. Over the same time period, America's public sphere underwent a transition to secularization. In the Supreme Court, a series of decisions under Chief Justice Warren presiding over the Court's last liberal majority ushered in a wall of separation between church and state from cases such *Engel v. Vitale 1962* where the Supreme Court ruled that recitation of prayer in public schools was unconstitutional and the *Abington School District v. Schempp 1963* decision where the Court ruled that the use of the Bible in public school classrooms presented unconstitutional violations of the First Amendment's *Establishment Clause*. More recently, the landmark Supreme Court decision *Obergefell v. Hodges 2015* struck down as unconstitutional state bans on same-sex marriage, legalizing same-sex marriage in all fifty states. The *Obergefell* decision was celebrated by civil rights activists and liberals but maligned by religious conservatives. Finally, the liberalization of America's immigration laws allowed for an influx of non-European immigrants and the emergence of multiculturalism, which challeges the notion of one dominant American identity. All of these changes occurred by federal intervention via judicial fiat, legislative fiat, or both.

These changes occurred over the same time period in which the country was in the midst of a technological revolution. Cable television, initially used to connect rural Americans to network television, was deregulated leading to pronounced growth. With growth came innovations such as premium networks like *Home Box Office* (HBO), *Music television* (MTV), and later, pay-per-view stations including stations showing pornography. Cable news channels were launched as well as conservative radio programs. American civic discourse began to change. Of course, cable television wasn't the only major innovation affecting civic life; as computer technology improved the internet began to emerge as the new center of the political universe; first with partisan blogs and later via social media sites.

The America that entered the twenty-first century was dramatically different. Children born after the 1970s knew only an egalitarian society in which sexism and racism were no longer openly tolerated and the role of religion in the public sphere had been dramatically reduced. These changes led to the so-called culture war in which the Republican and Democratic parties came to symbolize opposing factions. The Republican Party's center of power had once been concentrated in the North East but was now concentrated in the South and the Mountain West. The Democratic Party's power had been centered in the South, but the Democratic Party of the new millennium was concentrated in the North East and the West Coast. Once ideologically diverse, the parties had sorted into ideologically homogenous camps: Liberals into the Democratic Party and conservatives into the Republican Party in a phenomenon known as party sorting (Levendusky 2010; Abramowitz 2013). The modern Republican Party became a demographically homogenous ideological movement guided by a few key principles; small government, free market economics, and cultural conservatism. The Democratic Party's coalition became racially and ethnically diverse; representing a coalition of interest groups operating under the umbrella of the Democratic Party (Grossman and Hopkins 2016).

Ideological homogeneity allowed the parties to polarize politically. Moderates were purged via party primaries, especially within the Republican Party. Congress became ideologically polarized and fell into gridlock (McCarty et al. 2016). Figs. 2.1 and 2.2 show the massive ideological change that has occurred in Congress since the 1960s. In the 88th Congress, which began in 1963 and ended in 1965, Congress had many ideologically conservative Democrats and ideologically liberal

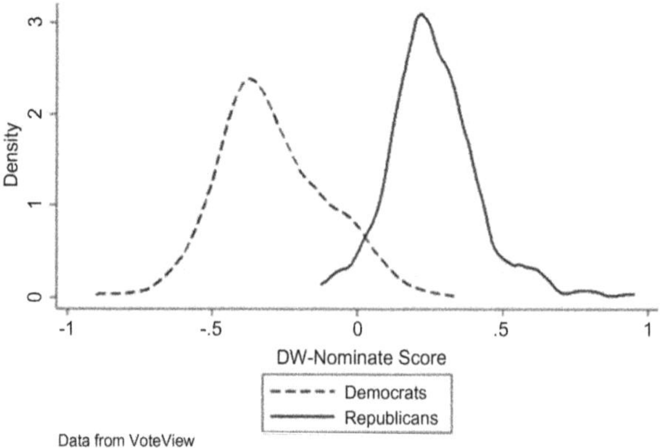

Fig. 2.1 Ideological distribution of the 88th Congress

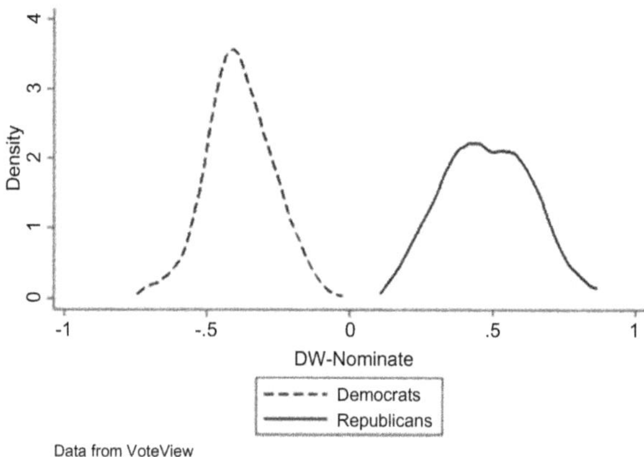

Fig. 2.2 Ideological distribution of the 114th Congress

Republicans who were able to form bipartisan coalitions to pass controversial legislation. By the 114th Congress, there were few liberal Republicans and conservative Democrats left; the last of the so-called Blue Dog, Democrats were wiped out in the 2014 congressional midterms. The number of ideologically moderate members in both parties decreased dramatically.

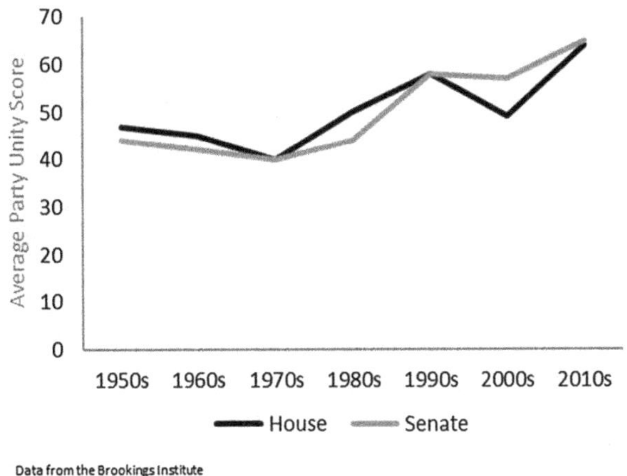

Fig. 2.3 Party unity in Congress 1950–2013

In today's Senate, the most conservative Democrat (Joe Manchin of West Virginia) is still more liberal than the most liberal Republican (Susan Collins of Maine). Party unity voting has also increased dramatically. Fig. 2.3 shows party unity scores from the 1950s until 2013 compiled by the *Brookings Institute for their Vital Statistics on Congress* report. Party unity scores consider how often a member is voting with their own party on partisan votes. Since the 1950s, scores have been increasing, especially in the Senate. Averaging party unity scores for each chamber for each decade reveals a sharp increase in party unity voting since the 1950s.[1]

Like their elite counterparts, American voters have become less moderate, more ideological, and more allegiant to their preferred political party. As Fig. 2.4 shows the ideological composition of the electorate has changed significantly since the 1980s. Although liberals always identified with the Democratic Party at high rates, conservatives were more nuanced. Between 1980 and 2016, the percent of conservatives identifying themselves as Republicans has increased significantly, rising from 59% in 1980 to 83% in 2016. Party sorting has caused the Republican and Democratic parties to adopt increasingly divergent party platforms, much of which is composed of culture war issues such as abortion, gay rights, and gun control.

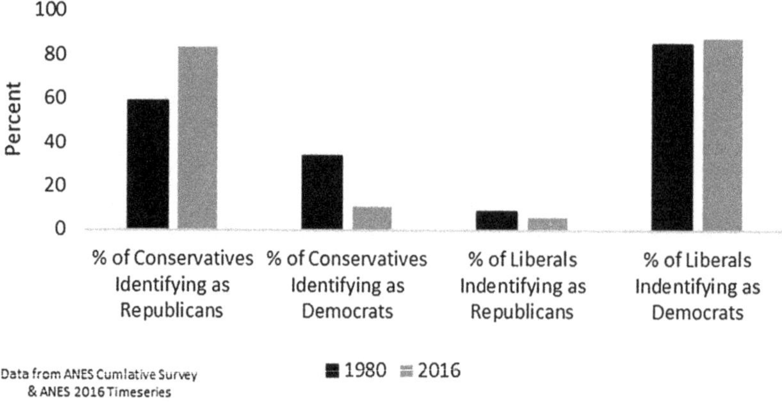

Fig. 2.4 Party sorting in the electorate: 1980 vs. 2016

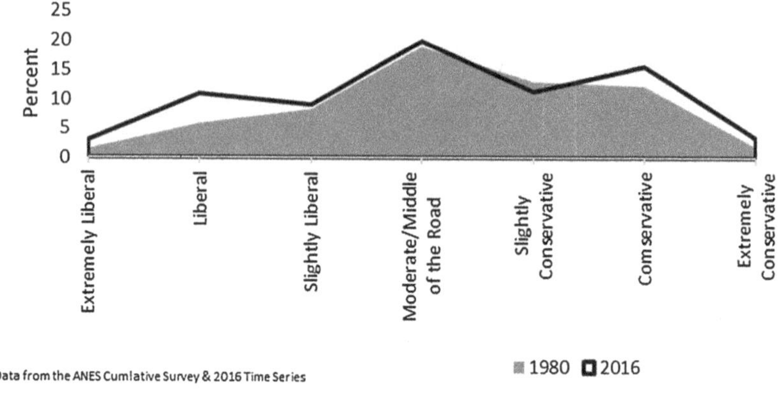

Fig. 2.5 Change in self-identified ideology: 1980 vs. 2016

Party sorting has led to increasing ideological extremism in the electorate. As conservatives and liberals sorted into their respective parties, their members became more ideologically homogenous. Ideological homogeneity allows the outer bounds of the ideological spectrum to stretch. Figure 2.5 shows the ideological distribution of Republicans and Democrats in both 1980 and in 2016. Respondents were asked to identify their ideology on a seven-point scale. Comparing the distributions reveals a very little change in the number of people who identify as moderates over the thirty-five year period. However, the number of respondents who identify as either liberal or conservative has increased significantly; as has the number of people who identify themselves as extremely conservative and extremely liberal.

The change in the ideological distribution of the electorate is even more profound when policy preferences are used as a proxy to measure ideology. While useful, self-identified ideology can be vulnerable to estimation bias because of the negative connotations that "liberal" and "conservative" have. People over report moderation in the same way that people over report being an Independent until they are pushed as to whether they lean toward one party or the other. Once so-called leaners are removed the "true" Independent rate is often cut in half. Another method of estimating ideology is to use voters' policy preferences as a proxy for self-identified ideology. As survey respondents express preferences along policy dimensions, they are telling us something about their ideological dispositions. Using longitudinal data from the *Pew Research Center* called the *American Values Survey*, I am able to recover policy preferences of American voters over three decades to examine if there is observable differences in policy preferences over time. The Pew data contain eight policy questions that have been asked consistently since 1987. Each respondent's responses on the eight policy questions are recoded into a numeric value ranging from 1 (the most conservative response) to = 1 (the most liberal response). Doing so allows their responses to be combined into one variable that provides an ideology score for each respondent. The ideology scores can be used to look for changes in the distribution of the electorate over time. Figs. 2.6 and 2.7 show changes in the ideological distribution of Republican and Democratic voters in 1987 and in 2012. The distribution of the electorate has changed significantly over the past few decades. The mean Democrat and the mean Republican have moved further apart, and there are less voters holding policy preferences that represent some conservative and some liberal preferences.

Combining all voters into one distribution for each year reveals a sharp decline in the number of moderates between 1987 and 2012, something that is not found in self-reported ideology (see Fig. 2.8). The difference suggests that there is more polarization in the electorate than previously thought when an indirect measurement is used. Also of note is the increase in the size and length of the tails of

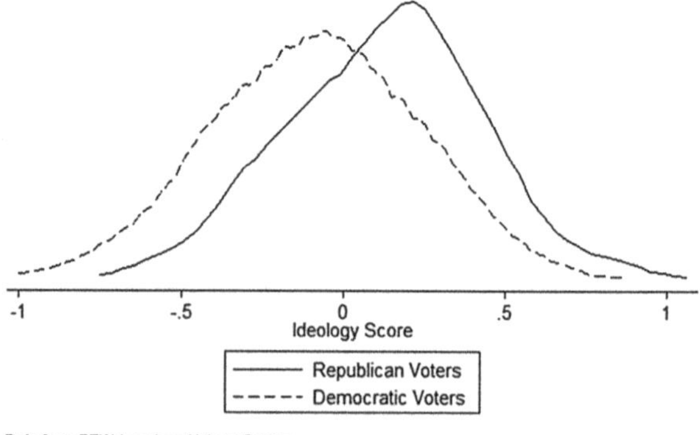

Fig. 2.6 Ideological distribution of the American electorate, by party: 1987

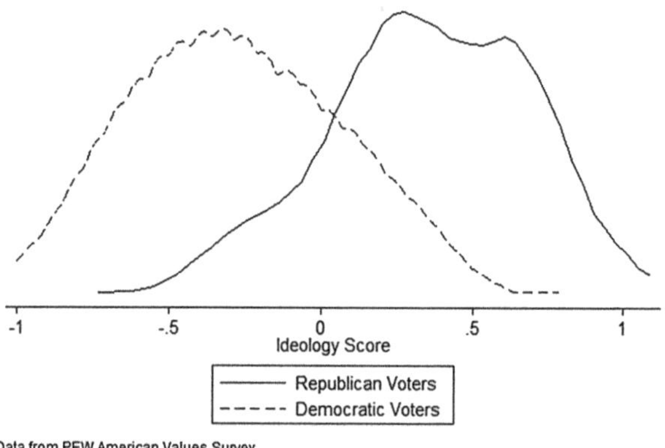

Fig. 2.7 Ideological distribution of the American Electorate, by party: 2012

the distribution. More voters are taking ideologically extreme positions in 2012 than were in 1987. Not only has policy moderation decreased, there has been a significant increase in the number of voters who display partisan policy preferences suggesting that party sorting has also led to an increase in ideological extremism.

As the ideological distance between partisan voters has increased, so too has partisan acrimony. In a report titled "Partisanship and Political Acrimony in 2016," the *Pew Research Center* finds that 55% of Democrats profess to being afraid the Republican Party, while 49% of

Fig. 2.8 Decline in ideological moderates since 1987

Republicans say the same about the Democratic Party. The findings are even more concerning when only regular voters are considered. When non-voters are removed 72% of Democrats and 62% of Republicans report being afraid of the opposition party. When asked whether members of the opposition party are more closed-minded, lazy, dishonest, and unintelligent, 70% of Democrats report that Republicans are more close-minded than other Americans and 46% of Republicans report that Democrats are lazier than other Americans. Republicans and Democrats are almost evenly split about whether talking to people they disagree with politically is stressful and frustrating or interesting and informative. Strong majorities (65% of Republicans and 63% of Democrats) report that those conversations reveal they have less in common with their partisan counterpart than they thought.[2]

Ideological polarization and high levels of partisan acrimony have increased the stakes of elections for partisans. These voters place a higher premium on winning control of government because the policy stakes are significant and because large portions of each party's base views the other party as a tangible threat to the survival of the Republic. *Pew Research Center* also asked partisan voters why they identify as a Republican or a Democrat and the results find that motivation is strongly grounded in policy terms. Both Democratic voters and Republican voters recognize the policy stakes that come with each party's label because of party sorting and issue polarization. Voters know that a Democratic administration will support one set of policies while Republican administrations will advance another and that increasingly, these policies represent entirely separate world views. Partisans now see each election as a clash of civilizations.

Due to changes in technology, Americans are increasingly living in their own realities; relying on partisan cable news networks, partisan radio programs, and partisan blogs to get their news and information. Republicans became skeptical of most media outlets; relying almost exclusively on *Fox News* for their political news and information. In a 2014 report called "Political Polarization and Media Habits," *Pew Research Center* found that 47% of "consistent conservatives" identified *Fox News* as their primary news sources, whereas "consistent liberals" reported a variety of sources including *CNN* (15%), NPR (13%), *MSNBC* (12%), and the *New York Times* (10%). Reliance on *Fox News* by conservatives was largely motivated by an increasing belief among Republicans that all other mainstream media outlets have a liberal bias. Trust in media had been on the decline in the U.S. for decades. According to *Gallup,* 53% of American said they had a great deal or fair amount of trust in the media in 1997. By 2015 that number had collapsed to 32%, fueled mostly by Republicans but certainly not limited to them.[3]

In the late summer and early fall of 2008, in the heat of that year's presidential election, the American economy crashed. If September 11, 2001, defined the first decade of the new century, the economic collapse in the fall of 2008 defined the second one. By the time, President Obama was sworn into office on January 20, 2009, the economy was hemorrhaging half a million jobs a month, and Congress had already enacted a $700 billion dollar bailout of the banking industry in the form of the *Troubled Asset Relief Program*, more commonly known as TARP. The Great Recession (as it came to be called) could easily have turned into the country's second Great Depression and almost certainly would have without the safe guards put into place after the Great Depression such as unemployment insurance, FDIC insurance, and food stamps as well as massive government intervention. Even before the economic collapse, the American middle class was slowly shrinking, and the working class was struggling. Household income growth since the 1980s was largely stagnant. Instead, much of the growth in consumer spending was being fueled by a massive expansion of credit powered by deregulation. Although wages remained flat and overall inflation low, inflation in critical areas such as housing, college tuition, and medical insurance was hyper-inflated. Americans were paying their bills, but doing so increasingly via credit such as home equity loans. Free trade policies supported by both parties had led to massive gains in wealth on Wall Street and cheap consumer products, but they had also combined with automation and technology to decimate American manufacturing. When the credit bubble burst so did the financial illusion most Americans had been living under for the past two decades. Credit became scarce and jobs even more so. The government had to step into stimulate the economy and to expand social welfare benefits such as food stamps and unemployment insurance. Cracks in the American political system turned into cleavages.

During the economic recovery over-the-top political rhetoric exploded. If political discourse had coarsened during the Clinton and Bush years, it became downright nasty in the Obama years. Republican politicians quickly learned there was a political price to pay if they pushed back on the rhetoric feeding the Tea Party rebellion (Libby 2014). By the time the so-called bitherism movement got going full steam in 2010 (a movement that would sow the seeds for Donald Trump's 2016 presidential run) most Republican leaders had worked out a way to avoid agreeing with the outlandish claims of their constituents and conservative media allies why simultaneously not discrediting it. Those who didn't or who appeared willing to compromise with the president were targeted for electoral extinction by conservative media figures like Rush Limbaugh and Glenn Beck. Republicans that were deemed too moderate were labeled as RINOs (Republican in name only) and were challenged in party primaries and some such as Representative Bob Inglis of South Carolina and House Majority Leader Eric Cantor of Virginia lost their party's nomination to Tea Party-backed challengers.

Heading into the 2012 Republican primary there was a full-blown civil war in the GOP, and the 2012 Republican nomination was the first major battle. The 2012 field had a clear front-runner in establishment favorite Mitt Romney; who in long-standing GOP tradition was "next in line" having been the runner-up for the party's 2008 nomination. Although Romney maintained his front-runner status throughout most of the invisible and formal primary seasons, there was historic instability throughout the race as Tea Party Republicans tried to settle on an alternative to Romney who they saw as not only ideologically moderate (bad), but also party of the party's establishment (worse). The right-wing populism that emerged in the wake of the Great Recession differed from traditional conservatism because it sought to reign in free trade and liberal immigration policies long championed by business conservatives. Romney was the quintessential business Republican. He was overtaken in the polls four times during the invisible and formal primary by four different candidates: Rick Perry in the early fall of 2011, followed by Herman Cain in late fall, then by Newt Gingrich twice (December of 2015 and then again during the South Carolina primary) and finally by Rick Santorum in the middle of February. Not only was Romney being challenged by a series of conservatives, he was also facing a surprising challenge from Libertarian candidate (and sitting Republican House member) Ron Paul. Paul had been a constant presence throughout the primary period polling at between 10% and 15% throughout and shocked the nation when he came in third in Iowa earning 21.43% of the vote.

Although Republican voters eventually coalesced around Mitt Romney, it had been a close call for the party's establishment; which had fought viciously to steer the nomination to Romney. In the end, they held off the insurgency. Many base Republicans felt that Romney had been helped along by the party's establishment, and Ron Paul supporters were furious over the way the media treated the candidate, consistently leaving him out of media coverage as a viable candidate despite his strong performance in Iowa. Romney's loss to Obama in the general election did nothing to heal the growing ideological cleavages appearing in the Republican Party's coalition. Base Republicans argued that had the party nominated a "real" Republican, they would have won the election.

By now, the Tea Party members of Congress had rebranded themselves into the Freedom Caucus. The Freedom Caucus in the House of Representatives was large enough to disrupt the legislative process for then-Speaker of the House John Boehner. The Republican congressional leadership was locked in a two-front war. They were battling President Obama and his Democratic counterparts in the Senate, but the real battle was internal. In 2013, the Freedom Caucus flexed their political muscle in the House and derailed a comprehensive immigration reform bill that had miraculously overcome the filibuster in the Senate and was certain to be signed into law by President Obama. The GOP's willingness to come to the table to pass comprehensive immigration reform was a product of the Republican Party's so-called autopsy report put out after Romney's loss to Obama in the 2012 election. The report, titled the

"Republican National Committee's Growth and Opportunity Report," called for the party to moderate on the issue of illegal immigration[4] and reembrace comprehensive reform that offered some type of opportunity for illegal immigrants already in the country to apply for legal status as well as provide a pathway to citizenship for Dreamers, children who were brought into the country illegally by their parents and then raised as Americans.

The Republican Party's establishment saw triangulation on the issue of immigration reform as a necessary move if they hoped to be competitive in national elections moving forward because of projected growth of Latino voters and their sharp turn away from the GOP since George W. Bush's reelection in 2004. In the Senate, the "Gang of Eight" senators formed to draft up the legislation.[5] Mitch McConnell worked hard behind the scenes to keep enough of his caucus together to overcome the filibuster. When the bill was passed by the Senate by a vote of 68–32 on June 27, 2013, it made national headlines because it was the first piece of major legislation passed in the Senate since the *Affordable Care Act* (Obamacare) was passed in 2010, and because it had managed to receive support from an astounding fourteen Senate Republicans, eight more than was required to the overcome the filibuster.

Fearing massive reprisals from the Freedom Caucus in the House as well as a revolt within the Republican Party's base Speaker Boehner refused to bring the bill up to the House floor for a vote, where it almost certainly would have passed with robust bipartisan support. Citing the "Hastert Rule," an unofficial Republican rule in the House that requires legislation receive a "majority of the majority." Boehner shelved the bill fearing that passing it would cost him his speakership. Despite killing the bill Boehner's #2 in the House, Majority Leader Eric Cantor was challenged in his primary by a Tea Party Republican challenger who used the immigration bill to paint Cantor as a moderate. Cantor's improbable defeat was one of the biggest upsets in political history; it sent shockwaves through the rest of the Republican Party, especially those serving partisan gerrymandered districts.

By the conclusion of the 2014 midterms, the Republican Party saw the ranks of their Freedom Caucus swell to more than sixty members in the House of Representatives, and they had an agenda: challenge the political establishment and advance a hardline conservative agenda no matter the cost. Speaker Boehner found himself in a constant battle against his own caucus. After nine months and facing another coup attempt Speaker Boehner announced suddenly that he was retiring.[6] The relief in the Speaker's demeanor was palpable; after more than three years fighting his own party members he was free. The aftermath of Boehner's unexpected retirement revealed just how deep the fissures in the Republican Party had become. Cantor had long been considered to be Boehner's heir apparent to the speakership, but was purged the year before. Boehner's new #2 was Kevin McCarthy, a representative from California. Almost immediately there was a sharp backlash to McCarthy. After driving Boehner out, the Freedom Caucus was not about to replace Speaker Boehner with another mainstream Republican. Facing a loss, McCarthy abruptly removed his name from the running just moments before the vote was scheduled to be held.[7]

The month that followed was remarkable. The one consensus candidate for the job, a fiscal hawk and former vice presidential nominee Paul Ryan, initially rejected it out of hand. After seeing what happened to John Boehner and Eric Cantor, Ryan worried that taking on the speakership would hurt him politically among the party's base by making him the new target of the Freedom Caucus. Representatives Darryl Issa and Jason Chaffetz both put their names into consideration but with caveats; both were willing to withdraw if Paul Ryan decided he wanted the job after all.[8] On October 20, 2015, after a month of uncertainty and chaos, Paul Ryan called a press conference where he agreed to consider running for the speakership provided House Republicans agreed to certain conditions. Ryan said he would agree to run only because it was a "dire moment," but in exchange, he demanded endorsements from all of the Republican caucuses; including the Freedom Caucus. No doubt thinking of John Boehner's experience, Ryan said: "I'm willing to take arrows in my chest but not in the back."[9] On October 29, 2016, Paul Ryan was confirmed as the new Speaker of the House earning the support of most, but not all of the members of the Freedom Caucus.[10] Boehner's resignation after a career spent coveting the speakership and Paul Ryan's hesitation to take the third most powerful position in American politics would foreshadow the tumultuous Republican primary that was already beginning to spin out of control of the party's establishment with the surprising status of an unexpected front-runner: Donald J. Trump.

Despite controlling the White House and achieving major legislative accomplishments early in the Obama Administration, the base of the Democratic Party was also growing frustrated with the status quo. Although most still approved of the President, many progressive

Democrats saw Obama's failure to enact immigration reform and other progressive policies as a lack of will rather than a product of the unprecedented obstructionism he faced by congressional Republicans. Like their Republican counterparts, the economic recession had pushed the base of the party further toward economic populism. President Obama found himself fighting his own party's base to pass the Trans-Pacific Trade deal, more commonly known as the TPP. Despite initially calling it the "gold standard" for trade deals, Hillary Clinton back-tracked on her support for the trade deal as backlash within the Democratic base grew. Clinton was also taking flack for her relationship with Wall Street, which she established while serving as a New York Senator.

Although short-lived, the economic crisis had also given rise to a populist movement on the left: Occupy Wall Street. Emerging in September of 2011, OWS emerged to draw attention to economic inequality which had been significantly exasperated by the financial collapse. For several months, protestors had occupied Zuccotti Park in the financial district of Manhattan and staged a series of protests. Where the Tea Party movement moved quickly from protest to infiltration of Republican politics at the local, state, and federal level, Occupy Wall Street did not identify themselves as part of the Democratic Party and after the initial energy dissipated the movement collapsed. However, anti-establishment sentiment remained in the progressive wing of the party. Hillary Clinton was the poster child for everything progressives hated about the Democratic Party. She was an insider, an elitist, a pragmatist, and ideologically moderate; the antithesis of the kind of president progressives sought to succeed Obama.

In the meantime, Hillary Clinton was also under attack by the Republican Party who saw her 2016 candidacy as all but evitable. Although there were legitimate concerns regarding the attacks on the U.S. embassy in Libya following the overthrow of long-term dictator Muammar Gaddafi, the Republicans intentionally politicized Benghazi with the goal of eroding Clinton's popularity coming off of her tenure as Secretary of State which ended in 2013 shortly after President Obama's second term began.

The Benghazi attacks occurred on September 11, 2011, right as the 2012 Republican primaries were beginning in earnest. Initially, Republicans raised legitimate concerns over public statements by the administration regarding the motivations for the attacks as well as the State Department's response as the attacks unfolded. The embassy attacks led to the deaths of Ambassador Chris Stevens as well as three other Americans working at the embassy. Although U.S. embassies had been attacked dozens of times over the past decade leading to twenty deaths of embassy personnel,[11] the Benghazi attack was the only one to lead to the death of an ambassador since the 1970s.[12]

After an internal State Department investigation ruled the event an accident and suspended four State Department officials for negligence; the House launched the first of what would become seven congressional probes into the matter. From the beginning, it was clear that congressional Republicans hoped to find negligence on Clinton's part. Although each investigation focused on particular aspects of the attacks and identified weaknesses in the State Department's security measures none produced evidence of culpability for Clinton.[13] However, after the conclusion of the sixth investigation, a *Freedom of Information Act* request (FOIA) from a conservative group revealed that for part of Clinton's tenure she had used a private email address hosted on a separate server. The revelation allowed the investigation to be reopened, this time with the private email server and potential mishandling of classified information as the focus. Despite failing to produce evidence of criminality by Secretary Clinton, the investigations eventually eroded the public's confidence in Clinton and tarnished what had been up until then a well-received tenure as Secretary of State.

In what *Washington Post* reporter E.J. Dionne called a "truthful gaffe" House Majority Leader Kevin McCarthy told *Fox News* host Sean Hannity in an interview that the repeated investigations into Clinton were a "strategy to fight and win." The majority leader went on to say, "Everybody thought Hillary Clinton was unbeatable, right? But we put together a Benghazi special committee, a select committee. What are her numbers today? Her numbers are dropping. Why? Because she's untrustable [sic]. But no one would have known any of that had happened, had we not fought."[14] In context, McCarthy's comments came when he was under consideration to assume the speakership position after Boehner stepped down. McCarthy was on the defensive; being hammered by Hannity about whether congressional Republicans were doing enough to thwart President Obama's agenda. McCarthy offered the comment as evidence that House Republican leadership would better meet the demands of the party's base under his tutelage.[15]

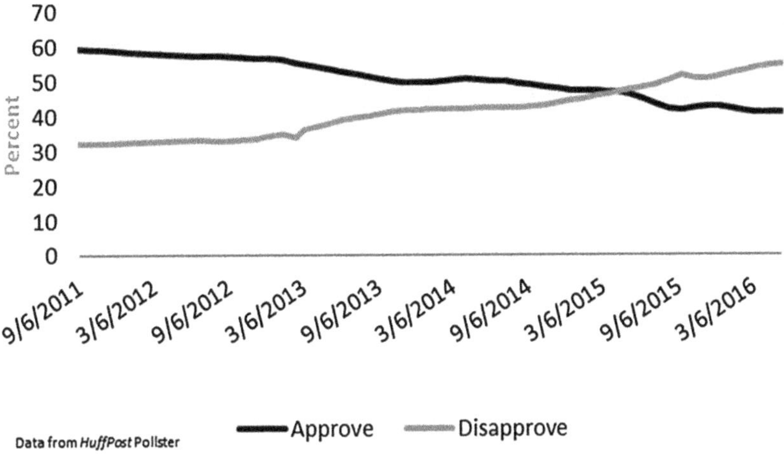

Fig. 2.9 Hillary Clinton approval ratings

Examining Clinton's approval rating over time reveals the effect that sustained investigations had on her favorability ratings. As Fig. 2.9 shows when the Benghazi attacks happened in late 2011, Clinton had a very high favorability rating of 59%. Two years after the attacks, Clinton's rating still remained positive despite already undergoing several investigations as well as a high-profile testimony in front of the Senate Foreign Relations Committee in January of 2013 as she prepared to leave office. Clinton's favorable/unfavorable ratio didn't inverse until the end of April 2015; nearly four years after the attacks. It would never return to positive territory. Whether by strategic design or by pure luck, the effect was the same: Four years of sustained investigations turned Clinton from one of the most popular political figures in the country into one of the least popular and neutralized one of Clinton's strongest assets: her tenure as Secretary of State.

Clinton's history as an economic centrist, combined with increasing fallout from the Benghazi investigations made her ripe for a challenge from the progressive wing of the party for the Democratic nomination. There was virtually no dissention in the party's establishment as to who should be the party's nominee, even after Clinton's popularity began to erode in late 2014. Democrats saw the later Benghazi committees as a partisan witch hunt and a poorly disguised attempt by the Republicans to derail her candidacy. Even as the public was beginning to move away from Clinton, partisan Democrats were digging in their heels—a decision they would later come to regret.

After the death of his son from brain cancer, Vice President Joe Biden decided to sit out. His decision was almost certainly helped along by the clear signals being sent by Democratic superdelegates, who had begun lining up behind Clinton as early as 2013. The progressive wing of the party saw her candidacy as a coronation but didn't show any appetite for other candidates considering runs like the former governor of Maryland Martin O'Malley. Despite the growing populism in the Democratic base, Massachusetts Senator and progressive firebrand Elizabeth Warren declined to run, being far too shrewd a politician to go up against the Clinton machine. But Bernie Sanders, an Independent Senator from Vermont, had no such inhibitions. Wanting to pressure Clinton from the left, he threw his hat into the ring hoping to give progressives a voice in the process. He almost certainly never expected to see his candidacy explode, turning from an advocacy campaign to a viable contender for the Democratic Party's nomination. The Democratic Party, like their Republican counterparts, had seriously underestimated the strength of the anti-establishment sentiment in the electorate. And like Donald Trump, Bernie Sanders offered voters the chance for a political revolution.

Notes

1. Vital Statistics on Congress, The Brookings Institute, https://www.brookings.edu/multi-chapter-report/vital-statistics-on-congress/.
2. "Partisanship and Animosity in 2016," Pew Research Center, http://www.people-press.org/2016/06/22/partisanship-and-political-animosity-in-2016/.
3. Art Swift, "Americans' Trust in Mass Media Sinks to New Low." *Gallup*, http://www.gallup.com/poll/195542/americans-trust-mass-media-sinks-new-low.aspx.
4. "Growth and Opportunity Report," Republican National Committee, https://www.gop.com/growth-and-opportunity-project/.
5. "Gang of Eight" Senate Proposal to Overhaul the Immigration System, *Washington Post*, https://www.washingtonpost.com/apps/g/page/politics/gang-of-eight-senate-proposal-to-overhaul-the-immigration-system/106/.

6. Jake Sherman, Anna Palmer, John Bresnahan, and Lauren French, "John Boehner Heads for Exits," *Politico*, http://www.politico.com/story/2015/09/speaker-john-boehner-retiring-from-congress-at-the-end-of-october-214056.
7. Susan Davis, "Paul Ryan Doesn't Want to be Speaker But These Republicans Do," *NPR*, http://www.npr.org/sections/itsallpolitics/2015/10/14/448408383/paul-ryan-doesnt-want-to-be-speaker-but-these-republicans-do.
8. Bill Hoffman, "Rep. Paul Ryan 'Seriously Considering' Speakership Bid," *Newsmax*, http://www.newsmax.com/Headline/paul-ryan-considers-house-speaker/2015/10/09/id/695457/.
9. Robert Costa and Mike DeBonis, "Paul Ryan will run for House speaker, under certain conditions," *The Washington Post*, https://www.washingtonpost.com/news/powerpost/wp/2015/10/20/scenes-from-the-house-gop-conference-meeting-where-everyone-is-waiting-on-paul-ryan/?utm_term=.e1686eee3828.
10. Mike DeBonis and Robert Costa, "'Supermajority' of House Freedom Caucus to back Paul Ryan's speaker bid," The *Washington Post*, https://www.washingtonpost.com/politics/supermajority-of-house-freedom-caucus-to-back-paul-ryans-speaker-bid/2015/10/21/d7411964-781e-11e5-a958-d889faf561dc_story.html?utm_term=.b13764e1e48a.
11. "A List of Deadly Terrorist Attacks on U.S. Diplomatic Targets Under President George W. Bush, 2001–2009," *Politifact*, http://www.politifact.com/embassyattacks/.
12. "Attacks on U.S. diplomatic facilities," *Wikipedia*, https://en.wikipedia.org/wiki/Attacks_on_U.S._diplomatic_facilities.
13. *Politifact*, http://www.politifact.com/truth-o-meter/statements/2015/oct/12/hillary-clinton/clinton-there-have-been-7-benghazi-probes-so-far/.
14. "Kevin McCarthy's truthful gaffe on Benghazi," *The Washington Post*, https://www.washingtonpost.com/opinions/kevin-mccarthys-truthful-gaffe/2015/09/30/f12a9fac-67a8-11e5-8325-a42b5a459b1e_story.html?utm_term=.b6776a929d9d.
15. *Politifact*, http://www.politifact.com/truth-o-meter/article/2015/oct/07/context-what-kevin-mccarthy-said-about-hillary-cli/.

References

Abramowitz, Alan I. *The Polarized Public? Why our Government is so Dysfunctional*. Upper Saddle River, NJ: Pearson, 2013.

Grossmann, Matt, and David A. Hopkins. *Asymmetric Politics: Ideological Republicans and Group Interest Democrats*. New York: Oxford University Press, 2016.

Levendusky, Matthew. The Partisan Sort How Liberals Became Democrats and Conservatives Became Republicans. Chicago, IL: University of Chicago Press, 2010.

Libby, Ronald T. *Purging the Republican Party: Tea Party Campaigns and Elections*. Lanham, MD: Lexington Books, 2014.

McCarty, Nolan M., Keith T. Poole, and Howard Rosenthal. Polarized America: The Dance of Ideology and Unequal Riches. Cambridge, Massachusetts: London, England: The MIT Press, 2016.

CHAPTER 3

The 2016 Presidential Nominations

Abstract Bitecofer recaps the paths that Hillary Clinton and Donald Trump took to win their party's nomination. For Clinton, an unexpected primary challenge forced the campaign to compete for a nomination that was once inevitable. Coming from nowhere, Bernie Sanders' campaign tapped into the anti-establishment and populist sentiment of the progressive wing of the Democratic Party transforming his candidacy from a symbolic exercise into a powerful social movement. Meanwhile, despite being outspent and out-organized, Donald Trump won the Republican Party's nomination by giving voice to rising right-wing populism and nationalism in the Republican base.

Keywords Presidential election · Presidential primaries · Hillary Clinton Bernie Sanders · Donald Trump · Republican · Democrat · Super delegates Endorsements

Right from the start the Republican Party's 2016 presidential nomination contest was unusual. Not since the 1968 Democratic convention had a party selected a presidential nominee while immersed in an ideological civil war. Ideological factionalism and prime conditions for a Republican victory in the general election created a large, fractured field of candidates. With 17 declared candidates, it was the largest field ever to compete for a party's presidential nomination (see Fig. 3.1). There were so many candidates that for the first time ever, two separate debates needed

R. Bitecofer, *The Unprecedented 2016 Presidential Election*,
https://doi.org/10.1007/978-3-319-61976-7_3

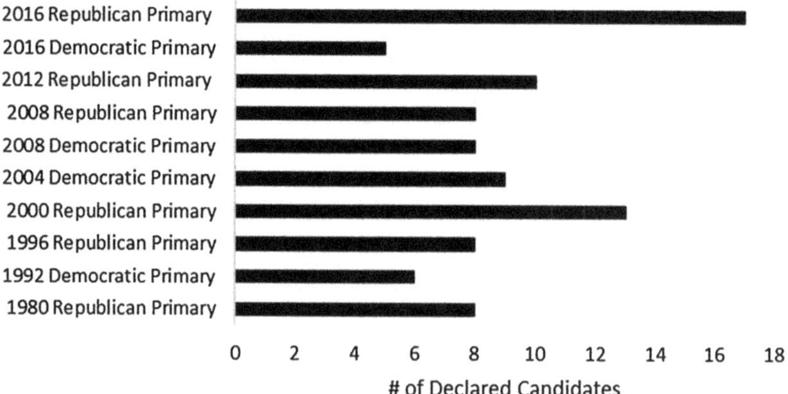

Fig. 3.1 Declared presidential primary candidates, by cycle

to be held in order to be able to accommodate everyone with national poll standings used to determine who would be given access to the main debate.

In addition to being a large field, it was also an experienced field, including eight current or former governors and five current or former senators. The field also offered a few well-known outsider candidates including Dr. Ben Carson, a pediatric neurosurgeon and bestselling author, and Donald J. Trump, a real estate magnet and reality television celebrity. Although the invisible primary produced some winnowing of the field before the formal primary began in February 2016 (Rick Perry on September 11, 2015 followed by Scott Walker on September 21, 2015), the Iowa Caucus ballot featured twelve candidates and only produced three exits (Mike Huckabee, Rand Paul, and Rick Santorum). Nine candidates competed in the New Hampshire primary with six staying in the race through South Carolina.

Another reason the 2016 Republican field grew so large was the emergence of SuperPACs, which can alter the traditional relationship between a candidate's poll standing and their ability to attract the financial resources needed to actively campaign (Wayne 2016). As Fig. 3.2 shows, there is little relationship between fundraising and poll standings in the 2016 Republican primary. According to data compiled by *The New York Times*, Jeb Bush, Ted Cruz, and Marco Rubio each more than doubled Donald Trump's fundraising. Even Ben Carson out-raised

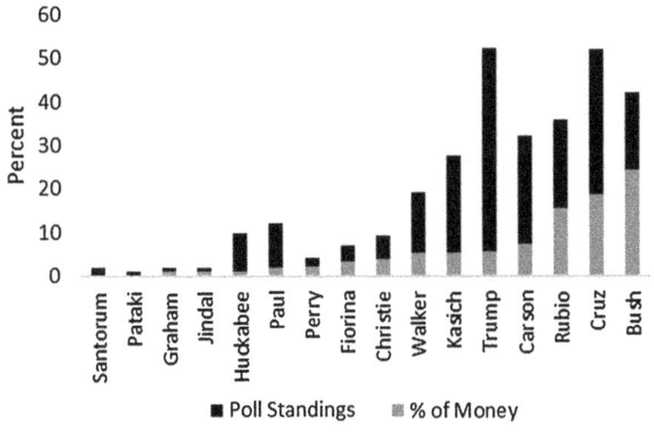

Fig. 3.2 Relationship between poll standings and fund-raising in the 2016 Republican primary

Donald Trump despite the fact that he stopped campaigning right before the Iowa Caucus. With SuperPAC money factored in Bush had four times the resources as Trump, yet never moved within striking distance in the polls; maxing out at 18% in the early period of the invisible primary. According to the *RealClear Politics* poll aggregator, Jeb Bush spent the entirety of the formal primary below 10% in the aggregate of national polls and earned only 3% of the vote in Iowa and 11% in New Hampshire. Despite this fact, Jeb Bush continued to have the financial resources to compete through the South Carolina primary.

The Trump Train

In mid-July of 2015, Donald J. Trump first emerged as the front runner for the Republican nomination. Throughout the remainder of the invisible primary period only Ben Carson polled close to Trump, tying him in November until a series of gaffes and shaky debate performances sent his campaign into a tailspin. Once Ben Carson's campaign collapsed, Ted Cruz began to rise in the polls as the social conservatives who had been backing Carson realigned in Cruz's camp. Still, despite his biography as a devout Catholic with extremely conservative views on social issues important to evangelical voters such as abortion and gay marriage, Cruz failed to pull enough evangelical voters from Donald Trump in Iowa to give him a decisive victory and lacked any support outside of the party's most socially conservative base.

Entrance polls taken at the Iowa Caucus show that Trump pulled in 33% of the evangelical Christian vote, compared to Cruz's 21%.[1] Trump's performance shocked Republican Party leaders who began to realize that Donald Trump was primed to win the nomination. Despite his consistent lead in the national polls, Trump's polling in Iowa had been erratic, partially in response to a series of controversies that disturbed some evangelical voters. At times he had strong leads only to be overtaken first by Ben Carson and then by Ted Cruz. Then, in the middle of January and about two weeks out from the Caucus, Trump took the lead. His decision to sit out of the final Iowa debate didn't appear to hurt him in the Iowa polls, and Trump took his strong polling numbers as a sign that he was headed for a win and he began to promise his voters an Iowa victory.

Ultimately, Trump lost the Iowa Caucus to Ted Cruz by about 6000 votes, coming in second. Had he not set expectations so high, his second place showing in Iowa would have been viewed differently. This decreased the amount of momentum he might have normally earned from a strong showing in a state that demographically should have been a struggle for Trump. Instead, the momentum went to Marco Rubio, whose third place result exceeded the modest expectations set by his campaign. Although both Ted Cruz and Marco Rubio were electorally competitive with Trump coming out of Iowa, it didn't last long. They both got trounced by Trump in New Hampshire. Donald Trump ended up taking 35% of the vote, beating both Rubio and Cruz by 25 points.

The last hope for the Republican Party to derail Trump's path to the nomination came eleven days later, in the South Carolina primary. Trump's polling in South Carolina was consistent throughout the entire invisible and formal primary periods. Heading into Election Day, Trump led his opponents by 13 points with 31% of the vote. The splintering of the rest of the field prevented any other candidate from becoming competitive but no one was willing to drop out of the race and throw their support behind another mainstream candidate. Heading into Election Day in South Carolina, Ted Cruz was polling at 18%, Rubio at 18%, Jeb Bush at 10%, John Kasich at 9%, and Ben Carson at 6%. Combined, the other Republican candidates held 37% of the vote, more than enough to topple Trump if the non-Trump vote was consolidated behind one candidate. Any effort to coordinate behind one alternative candidate was complicated by the deep-seated belief by most Republican elites, most pundits, and by this author, that Donald Trump was certain to do something at any moment that would be enough to end his candidacy and each candidate wanted to be in the race when that moment came.

Either the Republican Party failed to understand they had a problem in time or they simply couldn't coordinate to counteract it. Either way there was little the party could do to stop Donald Trump's nomination after the South Carolina primary. Due to the delegate allocation system in South Carolina, which awards their 60 delegates via a winner-take-all formula, a Trump win in South Carolina would all but ensure Trump's eventual victory. With his victory in South Carolina Trump's delegate lead wasn't insurmountable (at least mathematically) but it was substantial; having won two of the three early primaries, momentum was clearly on his side. Even though the party would fight Donald Trump through May the contest really was over by March 15. Against all odds, Donald J. Trump, a political novice who broke every norm and rule governing candidates had just crushed the best political machine in the free world: the Republican Party.

Feel the Bern

The 2016 Democratic primary had long been assumed to be a mostly symbolic exercise, leading some Democrats to complain that it would be a "coronation" of Hillary Clinton. Frustrations at the inevitability of a Clinton nomination prompted an Independent Senator from Vermont Bernie Sanders to launch his improbable bid for the Democratic nomination. The self-described Democratic-Socialist announced his candidacy on April 30, 2015; about two weeks after Hillary Clinton formally entered the race. Sanders announced his candidancy on the lawn of the Capital Building, during a no-frills ten-minute press conference that Sanders ended abruptly. During his statement, Sanders cited the importance of giving Democratic voters a choice at the ballot box and framed his candidacy as an effort to keep Hillary Clinton accountable to the progressive wing of the party.

The day Sanders formally entered the race his national polling average was 5.6%, compared to Clinton's commanding 62.2%. His polling average in Iowa, the first contest of the primary, was more competitive. Entering the fall of 2015 as the invisible primary was gaining steam Bernie Sanders was polling at about half of Hillary Clinton's average of 53%; earning support from about 21% of likely Caucus participants.

By the time of the first Democratic debate on October 13, 2015, Sanders was in striking distance of Clinton in Iowa, although the race opened back up in Clinton's favor for the rest of the fall period. Heading into the Iowa Caucus on February 1, 2016, the polls in Iowa had narrowed again and it was clear the contest could go either way. Political pundits began to speculate how a loss in Iowa to Sanders would impact Clinton's bid for the Democratic Party's nomination. If Clinton lost Iowa, it would mirror 2008 when Barack Obama ended up beating her for the nomination.

Ultimately, Clinton squeezed out the narrowest of victories in Iowa, saving her from an embarrassing loss. Although Sanders won the New Hampshire primary decisively, the win's value was lessened by the fact that New Hampshire borders Sanders' home state of Vermont. For Clinton, the loss in New Hampshire made a win in the Nevada Caucus on February 20, 2016 critical. A win for Sanders in Nevada would mean he was capable of extending his support beyond that of the party's progressive wing, mostly comprised of white voters. Latino voters comprise 28% of the population of Nevada, and as such, would play a decisive role in determining the winner of the state's contest.

Outside of the Iowa Caucus, which is a long-standing institution in the presidential nomination system for both parties, polling for caucuses is a tricky endeavor because it is not easy to estimate participation rates for caucuses and the demographic composition of the electorate. Heading into the contest, Clinton had on average a 2.5% advantage, well within the margin of error. She went on to win Nevada by 5%, helped by robust support in Clarke County, where Las Vegas is.[2] While exit polling showed that Sanders carried the Latino vote by 8 points, Clinton's performance in Clarke County makes this unlikely.[3] In any case, Clinton carried black voters in Nevada by more than 50%, which suggested that Sanders would struggle in the South Carolina primary and other racially diverse states, which was exactly what happened. Clinton won South Carolina decisively, bringing in 73% of the state's vote. By the conclusion of the South Carolina primary, Clinton was well on her way to securing the Democratic Party's nomination. Her growing delegate lead was further strengthened by super delegates, who were breaking for Clinton 40–1.

In terms of the delegate count, the race was over by mid-March but in the media and among Sanders supporters, it was just heating up. Sanders' populist, anti-establishment message found an eager audience among the Democratic Party's progressive wing. Like their Republican counterparts in the Tea Party, progressive voters have become more ideological over the past few decades and increasingly skeptical about institutions, mainstream media outlets, and political elites. This, combined with residual economic pressures from the Great Recession meant that progressive populism was a spark just waiting for a fire. That the fire would come in the form of a 72-year-old Brooklyn native with wispy white hair took everyone, including the candidate himself, by surprise. If there were two candidate characteristics the 2016 primary electorate wanted in a candidate it was outsider status and authenticity, and Sanders had those two characteristics in spades. His far-left progressive platform was especially attractive to millennial voters, who in the 2016 election found themselves, all 80 million of them, fully enfranchised for the first time.

A viable Democratic primary candidate running on a platform of a \$15 national minimum wage, free public college for everyone, single-payer health care, and a significant roll back in free trade economic policies would have been unthinkable in Democratic politics even just four years before. When Barack Obama challenged Clinton from the left in the 2008 nomination, he did so by advocating for modest changes in the healthcare system (Clinton actually offered the more progressive plan). Obama campaigned on an increase in Pell Grants and federal financial aid, and a barely mentioned endorsement of civil unions for gay Americans. Overall, Obama positioned himself only slightly to the left of Clinton and to the center-left for the general election campaign. Staying close to Clinton ideologically helped him attract support from super delegates who saw Obama as just as electable as Clinton. Sanders was no Obama. If he won the nomination, he would be by far the most ideological nominee ever put forth on the Democratic Party's ticket; a fact that was not lost on Democratic super delegates who worried about Sanders' electability.

Although the Sanders' campaign was ultimately unsuccessful, by its conclusion it reached milestones that exceeded all expectations. The Sanders campaign raised \$229.1 million dollars, compared to Clinton's \$334.9 million dollars[4] and had transformed the perception of the capabilities of an ideologically driven, grassroots campaign strategy aimed at the party's progressive wing. Of course, it is important to place the Sanders campaign into context. The success of the Sanders campaign may have been a product, at least in part, of the small Democratic field of candidates in which he competed, as well as the lack of a viable alternative to Hillary Clinton. Had Vice President Biden entered the race it is doubtful that Bernie Sanders' campaign would have unfolded the way it did.

Early into the invisible primary, it became clear that the Democratic primary electorate was divided into two distinct camps: the pro-Hillary camp and the anti-Hillary camp. With Biden in the race, it is possible that most of the anti-Hillary Clinton vote would have gone to him rather than Bernie Sanders, despite Biden's membership in the Democratic establishment. Unlike Hillary Clinton, Joe Biden is universally loved and seen as better aligned with progressives. And unlike Sanders, Biden would have had support from Democratic elites. In Chap. 5, you'll see how important that is in the Democratic system but first, a closer look at the primary campaign of Donald J. Trump is warranted.

Notes

1. Iowa Entrance Polls, *The New York Times*, https://www.nytimes.com/interactive/2016/02/01/us/elections/iowa-republican-poll.html.
2. Nevada Results, *The New York Times*, https://www.nytimes.com/elections/2016/results/primaries/nevada.
3. Nate Cohn, "No, the polling doesn't prove Bernie Sanders won the Hispanic Vote in Nevada", The Upshot, *The New York Times*, https://www.nytimes.com/2016/02/22/upshot/why-clinton-not-sanders-probably-won-the-hispanic-vote-in-nevada.html.
4. "Which Presidential Candidates Are Winning the Money Race," https://www.nytimes.com/interactive/2016/us/elections/election-2016-campaign-money-race.html?_r=0.

Reference

Wayne, Stephen J. The Road to the White House 2016. 10th ed. Boston, MA: Cengage Learning, 2016.

CHAPTER 4

Donald J. Trump: The Making of a Media Event

Abstract Bitecofer examines the role that Donald Trump's manipulation of the media played in his success in the Republican primary. Via controversial statements and policy positions, Trump starved his competitors of earned media coverage. Trump dominated the 24-hour news cycle. In a cycle with twenty-one candidates, Donald Trump received more than 50% of all candidate mentions in eighty-nine days and exceeded 60% on twenty-one more. Every time attention waned, Donald Trump would say or do something to draw it back to himself; proving the adage that any attention is good attention, at least for Donald J. Trump.

Keywords Presidential election · Presidential primaries · Hillary Clinton Bernie Sanders · Donald Trump · Republican · Democrat · Mainstream media · Media · Media bias

Although Bernie Sanders' improbable campaign tested conventional wisdom governing presidential nomination campaigns, Donald Trump's successful takeover of the Republican Party blew them apart. To say that Trump's primary campaign was unconventional is an understatement. Trump won the Republican Party's nomination despite the fact that he spent a fraction of the money spent by his competitors, ran few television campaign ads, and boycotted the final debate before the Iowa Caucus. Instead, Donald Trump's campaign strategy relied on using his celebrity

R. Bitecofer, *The Unprecedented 2016 Presidential Election*,
https://doi.org/10.1007/978-3-319-61976-7_4

status and penchant for controversy to dominate the 24-hour news cycle—a strategy never seen before in presidential politics.

In real time, watching Donald Trump careen from one controversy to the next during the Republican primary appeared haphazard. But underlying all of the chaos was a brilliantly executed strategy by a candidate that understood two things very well: the superficiality of America media and the ideological changes within the Republican base. Recounting an interview with Donald Trump in his essay in Larry Sabato's collaboration on the 2016 presidential election *Trumped: The Election That Broke All The Rules* veteran Washington reporter Robert Costa reveals that from the very beginning, Trump's strategy was to tap into the growing populist, antiestablishment sentiment within the Republican base that first emerged with the rise of the Tea Party in 2010. Not only would he run as a Washington outsider, he'd run as a Republican Party outsider.

Breaking with long-standing Republican orthodoxy on free trade and neoconservative foreign policy, Trump taps into the antiestablishment zeal that helped propel Ron Paul's bid for the 2012 Republican nomination from a long-shot issue advocacy campaign to an actual contender in the Iowa Caucus. That energy may have been unsuccessful in 2012, but it hadn't disappeared. It had a long simmer over Obama's second term. At a time when establishment Republicans sought to moderate their rhetoric on illegal immigration, Trump tracked even further to the right, advocating for a mass deportation force and a 2000-mile-border wall to be paid for by Mexico. The Republican base wanted more strident anti-immigration rhetoric, not less, and Trump was willing to give it to them.

Trump also separated himself from traditional Republican Party positions on the economy: rejecting the free trade orthodoxy that had been a centerpiece of Republican economic policy for decades. His populist messaging on trade allowed him to cast his mainstream Republican rivals as "elites" and "insiders" bent on maintaining their economic dominion over regular Americans. To illustrate this point, Trump said he was heading to D.C. to "drain the swamp," never making a distinction between his Democratic Party opponents and his Republican Party peers. Trump's populist messaging strategy tapped right into the economic anxieties of the white working class, an increasingly reliable and influential constituency in the Republican base. Economic populism combined with unabashed nationalism proved to be a powerful platform for the Republican primary because it tapped into long simmering tension between business conservatives and working-class whites, for whom

Republican policies on free trade and trickle-down economics had failed to yield prosperity.

Costa also writes that from the onset, Trump planned his campaign strategy around capitalizing on his celebrity status and drumming up regular controversy in order to dominate the news cycle and starve his competitors of media attention. What appeared to journalists, political analysts, and political scientists (including this author) as one disastrous gaffe after another hid a marketing strategy that hinged on the assumption that the Republican base was hungry enough for change, and angry enough at the status quo, that norms governing the conduct of presidential candidates would be forgiven. Trump's strategy evolved around the adage that any attention is good attention, a risky calculus for any political candidate to make. But Trump believed the normal rules would not apply to him because of his celebrity status and immense wealth as long as he did not behave like a normal candidate. He would do what he's always done, never apologize, never back down, and constantly stay on the offensive.

Underlying Trump's earned media strategy was an uncanny understanding of how the American media system operates, especially the 24-hour news cycle. Trump recognized the influence that media coverage has on campaigns. Although risky, a media dominance via controversy strategy offered two advantages for Trump. It would allow him to keep the conversation focused squarely on his own candidacy while simultaneously depriving his competitors of any opportunity to gain media attention for themselves. He would do this primarily in two ways. He would say and do things to his Republican rivals that no one has ever said or done before, and he would wage war against the media, whom Republican voters already distrusted.

A 2014 *Pew Research Center* analysis of American media habits reveals that Republicans have a deep distrust for so-called mainstream media outlets. More than half of Republicans identified *Fox News* as their main source of news and compared to liberals, conservatives tend to rely on a more narrow selection of media outlets.[1] Liberal media bias has been a consistent theme in Republican politics for decades, so much so that the assumption that the major networks and most major newspapers have a liberal bias is taken as gospel on conservative talk shows like Rush Limbaugh, television shows like *Hannity*, and on conservative blogs such as *Breitbart*. Of course, there *is* a liberal bias in mainstream media, just not the type that is alleged in conservative circles. Liberal media bias manifests in the way the media frames some events and issues. Other than *PBS, NPR* and the *BBC* traditional media outlets are profit-maximizing corporations subject to the same types of market forces other corporate entities are subject to. As such mainstream media coverage tends to be framed to attract larger audiences and support multiculturism, diversity, equality, and political correctness: all elements of the liberal worldview. Major elements of conservative ideology such as moral traditionalism are largely absent from mainstream media coverage. For the same profit-centric reasons, mainstream media outlets also have structural bias which frames coverage in ways that favor the establishment over outsiders and American exceptionalism and capitalism (Flanigan et al. 2015) which often lead to allegations of conservative and elite media bias from Democrats. If there is one thing both right- and left-wing ideologues can agree on it is that the mainstream media is biased.

Trump was certainly not the first Republican candidate on the national stage to make media bias and corruption a major theme in their campaign. Sarah Palin coined the phrase the "lame stream media" during her failed bid for the vice presidency in 2008. To varying degrees, most of the 2012 Republican primary field ran also against the mainstream media. Where Trump's media strategy differed from other Republicans was its confrontational nature and the scope of the allegations. Before long he was calling venerable news agencies such as *The Washington Post* and *The New York Times* "fake news"; a practice he has continued as president. Trump regularly accused the media of outright lying, even about things that were demonstrably true. All the while, fact checkers were having a hard time keeping up with Donald Trump. As Fig. 4.1 shows, Trump is an anomaly in the 2016 field of candidates. No other candidate even comes close to the twenty-five "pants on fire" statements made by Donald Trump during the primary, which ended at the beginning of June. All told, Donald Trump made fifty-two "pants of fire" statements during the 2016 presidential election which are documented in Table 4.1. Although Hillary Clinton only made one during the Democratic primary, she made four more during the general election. Donald Trump's "pants on fire" statements range from inconsequential misstatements of fact (America has never had a chess grandmaster) to over-the-top allegations (President Obama is working with Al Qaeda).[2]

By tapping into the Republican electorate's distrust of the mainstream media, Trump was able to discredit them and neutralize any damage that might have resulted from some of his more outlandish behaviors among

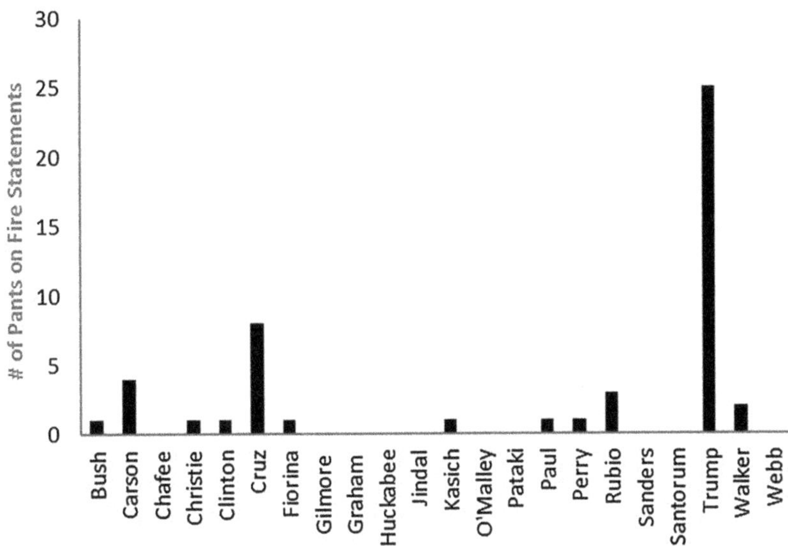

Fig. 4.1 *Politifact's* "Pants on Fire" scorecard for the 2016 primary candidates

the Republican base. Every time the media pushed back against his misstatements of fact or controversial statements, he used the negative media coverage as evidence that the mainstream media had it out for him. He frequently referred to the media as "the enemy." At rallies, Donald Trump goaded his audience into harassing members of the traveling press corp. One such episode involved *MSNBC*'s political correspondent Katie Tur. Recounting her experiences covering the Trump campaign for an article in *Marie Claire* magazine, Tur writes about her experience at a rally in Mount Pleasant, South Carolina, where Trump singled her out to the audience telling them, "|s|he's back there. Little Katy. She's back there." She required a Secret Service escort from that event writing that the crowd "seemed to turn on me like a large animal, angry and unchained."[3] What followed was months of harassment, both in person and on social media. Tur highlights some of the tweets she received from disgruntled Trump supporters calling for her to be murdered.

In her interview, Tur also points out how different the Trump campaign's relationship with the media is from that of other political candidates. Candidates, especially presidential primary candidates, covet media

Table 4.1 Donald Trump's "Pants on Fire" statements in the 2016 presidential election

Date	*Statement*
6/16/2015	"The last quarter, it was just announced, our gross domestic product … was below zero. Who ever heard of this? It's never below zero"
7/9/2015	"The Mexican government forces many bad people into our country"
7/28/2015	"The number of illegal immigrants in the United States is 30 million, it could be 34 million"
8/9/2015	"The Mexican government … they send the bad ones over"
9/30/2015	The unemployment rate may be as high as 42 percent
10/20/2015	Says Bernie Sanders is going to "tax you people at 90 percent"
10/28/2015	"I never said that" Marco Rubio was Mark Zuckerberg's personal senator
11/12/2015	The Trans-Pacific Partnership "was designed for China to come in, as they always do, through the back door and totally take advantage of everyone"
11/18/2015	"The federal government is sending refugees to states with governors who are Republicans, not to the Democrats"
11/22/2015	"I watched in Jersey City, N.J., where thousands and thousands of people were cheering" as the World Trade Center collapsed
11/23/2015	Says crime statistics show blacks kill 81 percent of white homicide victims
12/1/2015	President Barack Obama "wants to take in 250,000 (people) from Syria"
1/4/2016	A Trump television ad shows Mexicans swarming over our southern border
2/11/2016	"Don't believe those phony numbers when you hear 4.9 and 5 percent unemployment. The number's probably 28, 29, as high as 35. In fact, I even heard recently 42 percent"
2/23/2016	Says that in the Philippines more than a century ago, Gen. John Pershing "took 50 bullets, and he dipped them in pigs' blood," and shot 49 Muslim rebels." "The 50th person, he said, 'You go back to your people, and you tell them what happened.' And for 25 years, there wasn't a problem"
3/2/2016	Says Ted Cruz "said I was in favor in Libya. I never discussed that subject"
3/2/2016	"I don't know anything about David Duke"
3/24/2016	"Out of 67 counties (in Florida), I won 66, which is unprecedented. It's never happened before"
3/30/2016	Says that when Michelle Fields "found out that there was a security camera, and that they had her on tape, all of a sudden that story changed"
4/1/2016	The 2016 federal omnibus spending bill "funds illegal immigrants coming in and through your border, right through Phoenix"
5/2/2016	"Frankly, (Hillary Clinton) doesn't do very well with women"
5/3/2016	Says Ted Cruz's father "was with Lee Harvey Oswald" before the assassination of President John F. Kennedy

(continued)

Table 4.1 (continued)

Date	*Statement*
5/25/2016	"Look, we are at war with these people and they don't wear uniforms. … This is a war against people that are vicious, violent people, that we have no idea who they are, where they come from. We are allowing tens of thousands of them into our country now"
5/26/2016	It "is Hillary Clinton's agenda" to "release the violent criminals from jail. She wants them all released"
5/31/2016	"I wanted to keep it private, because I don't think it's anybody's business if I want to send money to the vets"
6/9/2016	"Crime is rising"
6/15/2016	"The Obama administration was actively supporting Al Qaeda in Iraq, the terrorist group that became the Islamic State"
6/22/2016	"For the amount of money Hillary Clinton would like to spend on refugees, we could rebuild every inner city in America"
6/23/2016	Says Hillary Clinton "has even deleted this record of total support (for the Trans-Pacific Partnership trade agreement) from her book"
6/24/2016	Says Ted Cruz "never denied" his father was photographed with Lee Harvey Oswald
6/24/2016	On gift taking, "Bob McDonnell took a fraction of what (Tim) Kaine took"
8/1/2016	"As usual, Hillary & the Dems are trying to rig the debates so 2 are up against major NFL games"
8/3/2016	"We have a fire marshal that said, 'Oh we can't allow more people' … And the reason they won't let them in is because they don't know what the hell they're doing"
8/5/2016	"I'm beating (Kelly Ayotte) in the polls by a lot"
8/5/2016	"Hillary Clinton says she wants to raise taxes on the middle class"
8/11/2016	Says Barack Obama "founded ISIS. I would say the co-founder would be crooked Hillary Clinton"
8/15/2016	Says the U.S. election system is "rigged"
8/30/2016	"Inner-city crime is reaching record levels"
9/1/2016	The number of illegal immigrants "could be 3 million. It could be 30 million"
9/9/2016	Says Hillary Clinton has "not answered a single question" about her immigration plan
9/14/2016	"My opponent has no child care plan"
9/16/2016	"I finished" the controversy about where President Barack Obama was born
9/22/2016	"Our African-American communities are absolutely in the worst shape they've ever been in before. Ever. Ever. Ever."
10/9/2016	Says a tweet he sent out "wasn't saying, 'check out a sex tape.' It was just 'take a look at" the background of Alicia Machado"
10/12/2016	Says he won the second debate with Hillary Clinton "in a landslide" in "every poll"

(continued)

Table 4.1 (continued)

Date	*Statement*
10/14/2016	"We don't have any" chess grandmasters in the USA
10/17/2016	"Of course, there is large scale voter fraud happening on and before election day"
10/19/2016	"It's possible that non-citizen voters were responsible for Obama's 2008 victory in North Carolina"
10/20/2016	When Hillary Clinton "ran the State Department, $6 billion was missing. How do you miss $6 billion? You ran the State Department, $6 billion was either stolen—they don't know"
10/25/2016	"Wikileaks also shows how John Podesta rigged the polls by oversampling Democrats, a voter suppression technique"
10/31/2016	Says Hillary Clinton "wants to let people just pour in. You could have 650 million people pour in and we do nothing about it. Think of it. That's what could happen. You triple the size of our country in one week"
11/6/2016	Says that at a campaign rally President Barack Obama "spent so much time screaming at a protester, and frankly it was a disgrace"

attention. Campaigns try to make it as easy as possible for the media to cover them by providing a campaign-sponsored media bus and itineraries that allow the media to plan their coverage in advance (Polsby et al. 2016, 69). But the Trump campaign had an asset usually reserved for sitting presidents and vice presidents in primaries: a private plane. Media was rarely invited to join the candidate on his plane. Unlike other candidates, Trump didn't need to accommodate the media to continue to receive attention. As he pointed out several times during the course of his campaign, the media needed him more than he needed them: His antics were a ratings bonanza for them.

For most of the primary, media outlets clamored to book Trump for interviews. More than 24 million viewers tuned into watch the first Republican debate, earning it the distinction of the most-watched non-sports cable program ever.[4] To put that into perspective, the first Republican debate for the 2012 primaries had only 3.3 million viewers.[5] The public's fascination with Donald Trump remained high through the general election as well. Nearly 84 million viewers tuned into watch the first debate between Clinton and Trump, the most-watched debate in American history.

Trump's controversial media strategy was implemented the moment the campaign was officially launched in the lobby of Trump Towers in New York

City on June 16, 2015. His announcement speech made headlines, particularly the section in which he said "|w|hen Mexico sends its people, they're not sending their best. They're not sending you. They're not sending you. They're sending people that have lots of problems and they're bringing those problems with us [sic]. They're bringing drugs, they're bringing crime, they're rapists, and some, I assume, are good people."[6] The announcement speech was the first in what would become a long series of expertly staged media events disguised as campaign events. The Trump campaign were masters at staging these events, holding them at opulent Trump properties and on the deck of the *U.S.S. Wisconsin*. The candidate made a grand entrance at the Iowa State Fair flying in on his Trump-branded helicopter to give rides to Iowan children.[7] He staged events in airport hangers with his Boeing 757, nicknamed T-Bird strategically placed in the background,[8] and then later, in sold-out arenas filled with raucous crowds chanting "build the wall" and towards the end of the primary calender "lock her up!"

All told, Donald Trump held 183 campaign rallies during the primary where he spoke to an estimated 765,000 attendees.[9] Because of Trump's antics, most of these rallies were covered live by the cable news networks, translating into over a 1000 hours of free media coverage. According to a *The New York Times* analysis, as of March 15, 2016, Trump amassed at least $2 billion dollars of free media coverage.[10] Trump also spent more than $2 million dollars on his trademark Make America Great Again hats.[11] Pundits derisively dismissed the efficacy of Trump's hat strategy, categorizing it as another foolish element of Trump's haphazard campaign. But the pundits missed that the campaign hats were a manifestation of a sophisticated branding strategy that had one goal: market the Trump brand of rough and tumble politics. Along with the powerful political imagery of thousands of red hats bobbing up and down in agreeance with their candidate, the hats also turned individual Trump supporters into a community rallying around a simple but powerful message: Make America Great Again! Symbolism in political campaigns can be a powerful thing. Think of Barack Obama's "Yes We Can" slogan in 2008 which invoked in his supporters a belief that they could bring about change by banding together. Trump's Make America Great Again slogan, borrowed from Ronald Reagan's 1980 change campaign against incumbent President Jimmy Carter, was the perfect message for a Republican electorate resentful of the changes ushered in under a liberal president.

Just how well did Donald Trump's unconventional media strategy work? Using a filter created by the GDELT Project to search media data

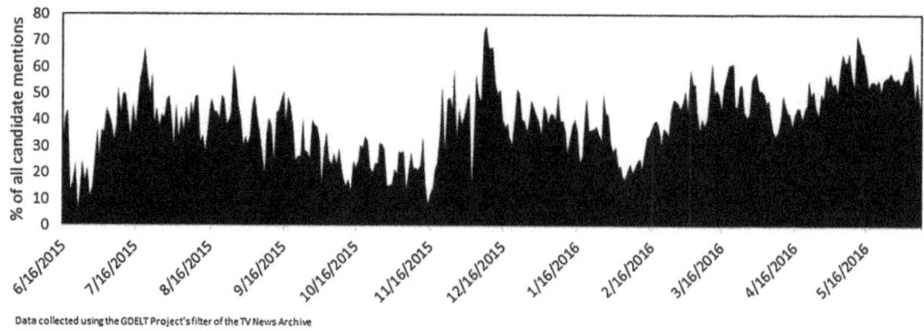

Fig. 4.2 Donald Trump's daily domination of the 24 hour news cycle

from the *Television News Archive* I collected data on the media attention Donald Trump received over the course of the presidential primaries. The data presented in Fig. 4.2 show the percent of candidate mentions Donald Trump received on a daily basis as a percent of all candidate mentions that day, including the rest of the Republican field as well as the Democratic candidates. The analysis shows that Donald Trump absolutely dominated media coverage. Of the 359 days in the invisible and formal primary periods, Donald Trump received at least 50% of all candidate mentions on 89 days. On 21 days, his percent of all candidate mentions met or exceeded 60%. Keep in mind that is at least half of all candidate mentions going to one candidate out of twenty-one candidates during the invisible primary and out of about seven candidates during the height of the formal primaries. Once the Republican field winnowed to just Cruz, Trump, and Kasich and Bernie Sanders and Hillary Clinton on the Democratic side Donald Trump's received more than half of all candidate mentions (52%).

Figures 4.3, 4.4, 4.5, 4.6, 4.7, 4.8, 4.9, 4.10, 4.11, 4.12, 4.13 and 4.14 show the percent of candidate of mentions Donald Trump earns for each day over each month of the invisible and formal primary. Days when his coverage spikes correspond with some of the Donald Trump's most controversial moments. On July 20, 2015, the day that Trump said that John McCain should not be considered a war hero because he "got caught" in Vietnam, Trump dominated the news cycle, earning 67.5% of all candidate mentions on televised programs. On August 26, 2015, when Trump kicked *Univision* journalist Jorge Ramos out of a press conference and entered into his first, but not his last, Twitter tirade against

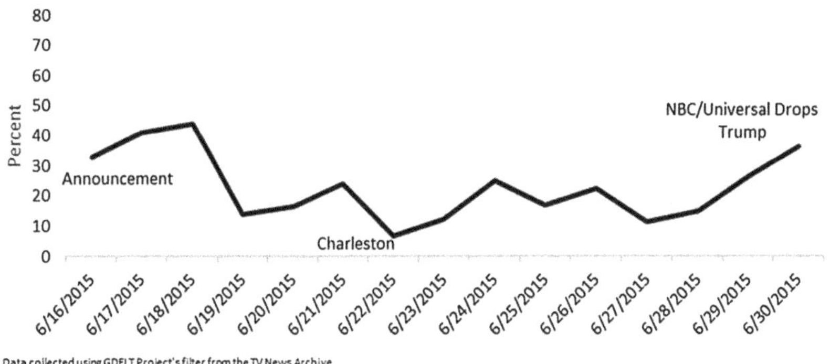

Fig. 4.3 Trump's percent of media attention: June 2015

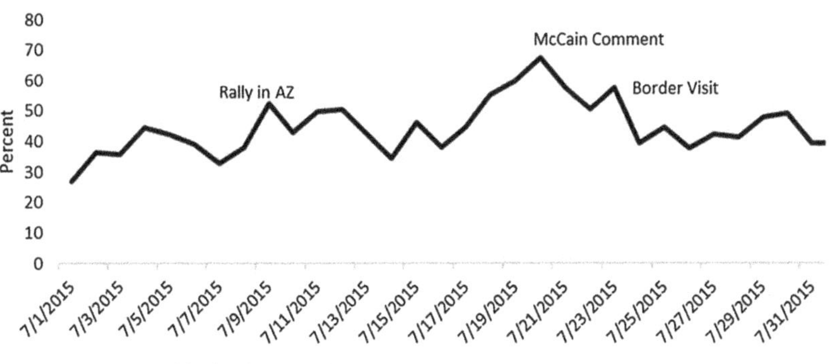

Fig. 4.4 Trump's percent of media attention: July 2015

Fox News host Megyn Kelly (he retweeted a follower's post calling Kelly a "bimbo"), he earned 61.1% of all candidate mentions.

Trump would go on to crack the 60% threshold twice more during the invisible primary. The first time was on November 26, 2015, when he made statements claiming he predicted the 9/11 attacks in his 2000 book, *The America We Deserve*. Trump cracked 60% of all mentions again on December 8, 2015, when in the wake of the San Bernardino terror attacks, Trump called a news conference and read this press statement: "Donald J. Trump is calling for a total and complete shutdown

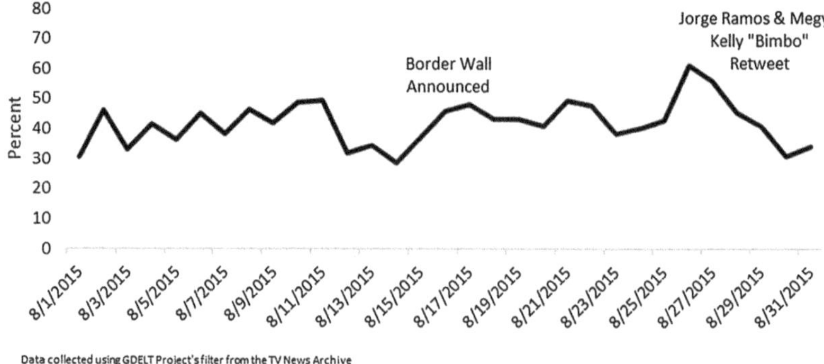

Fig. 4.5 Trump's percent of media attention: August 2015

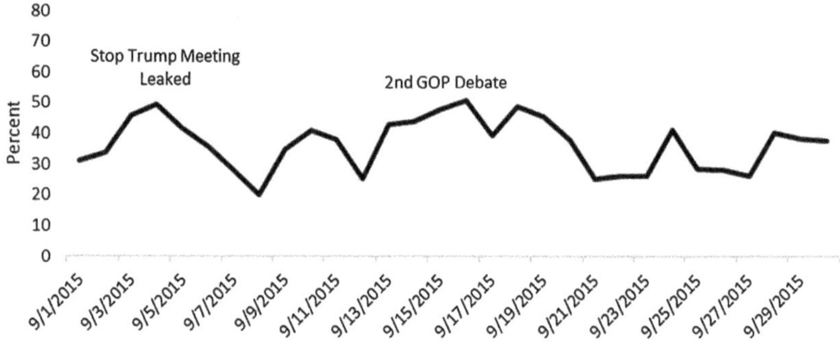

Fig. 4.6 Trump's percent of media attention: September 2015

of Muslims entering the United States until our country's representatives can figure out what the hell is going on." That kicked off a five-day stretch of days above 60% of candidate mentions on televised media, peaking to 75.9% on December 9th and closing out on December 12th, which was also the day that rumors of holding a brokered convention occurred at a secret meeting of RNC officials.

As Fig. 4.15 demonstrates, Trump's percent of candidate mentions tracks closely with his daily polling average from the *RealClear Politics* aggregator. Periods of heavy media attention are almost always followed

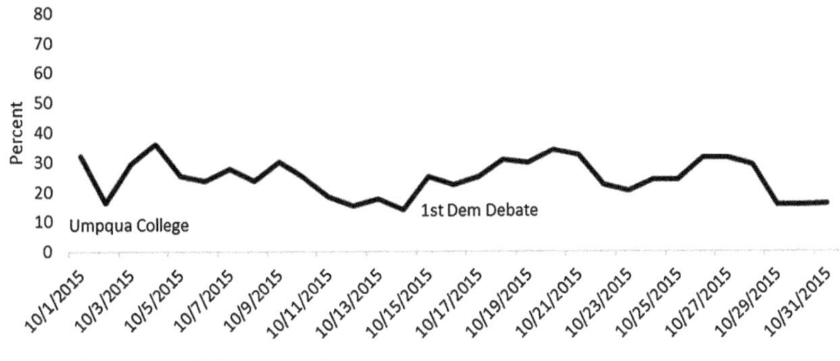

Fig. 4.7 Trump's percent of media attention: October 2015

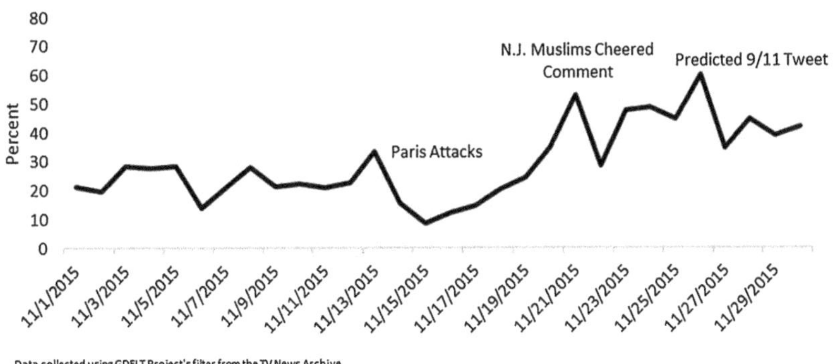

Fig. 4.8 Trump's percent of media attention: November 2015

by a sustained rise in the polls. After *NBC Universal* announced they were dropping Trump over his comments about Mexicans on June 30, 2015 (earning Trump 36.3% of candidate mentions), and Jeb Bush's July 4, 2015, admonishment of Trump over the same issue, Donald Trump rose in the polls from an average of 5% to an average of 6.5%. His polling continued its upward track in the wake of his July 12, 2015, rally in Phoenix, Arizona, where Trump continued to lay out a controversial immigration platform to a crowd so large they had to change venues to the Phoenix Convention Center. That rally, along with Trump's previous

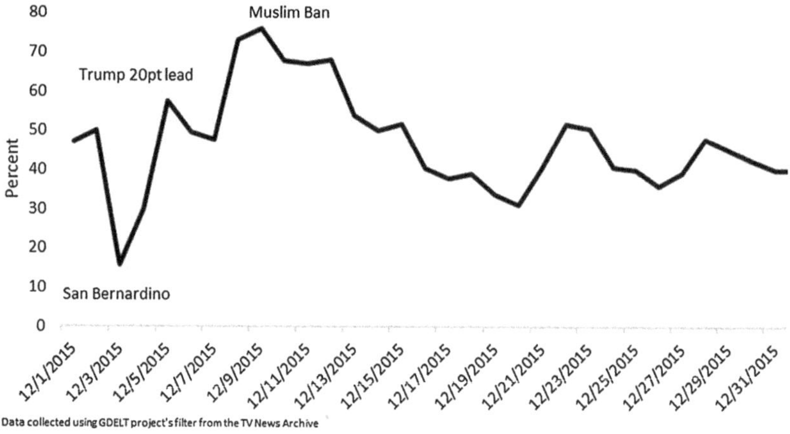

Fig. 4.9 Trump's percent of media attention: December 2015

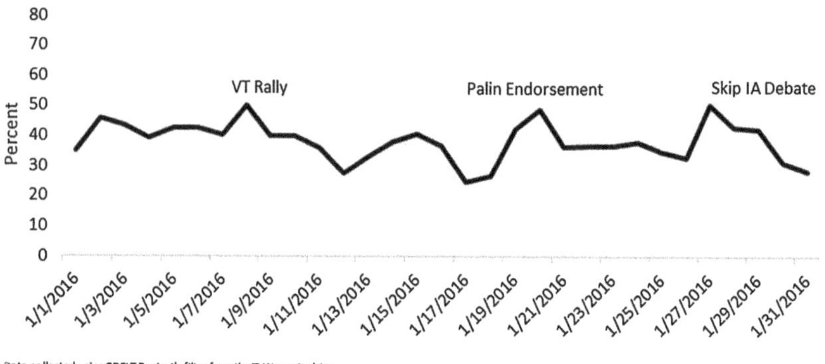

Fig. 4.10 Trump's percent of media attention: January 2016

statements about Mexicans, prompted Reince Priebus, then Chairman of the Republican National Committee, to issue a statement imploring Donald Trump to tone down his rhetoric. Trump seized on Priebus' comments to help build his case against Republican Party elites.

By the time Trump made his statements about John McCain's experience as a P.O.W. in Vietnam a week later, he had more than doubled his polling average, reaching 15% from about 7%. When pundits declared

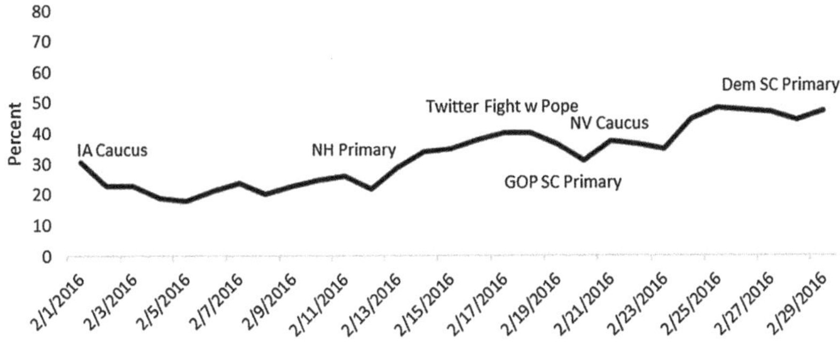

Fig. 4.11 Trump's percent of media attention: February 2016

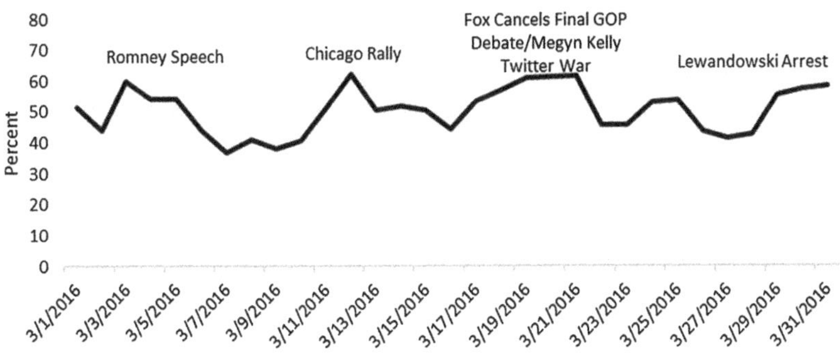

Fig. 4.12 Trump's percent of media attention: March 2016

his candidacy dead because of the McCain comments his poll standings increased instead. Three weeks after those comments, Trump's polling average had increased another seven points reaching a new high of 22.5%. On August 17, 2015, Trump announced his plans to build a full border wall, which became his signature immigration reform proposal. The wall proposal was met with condemnation from Democrats and skepticism from many Republicans, who pointed out the logistic difficulties of building a border wall and the billions of dollars in federal funding that would be needed to complete the project. Trump countered

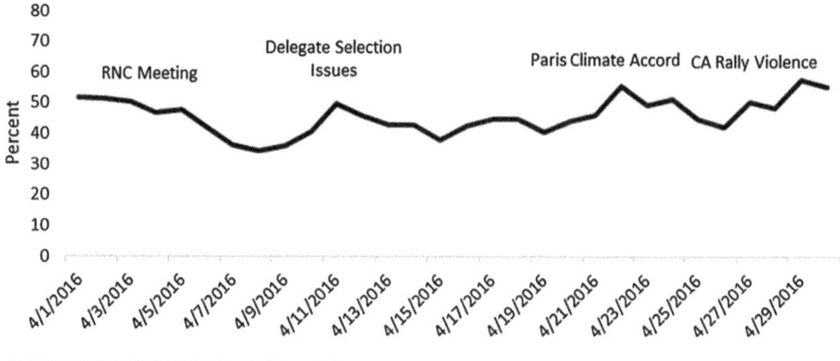

Fig. 4.13 Trump's percent of media attention: April 2016

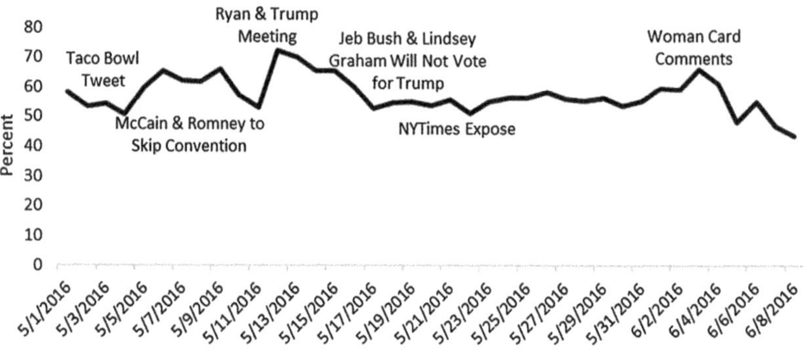

Fig. 4.14 Trump's percent of media attention: May/June 2016

the criticism from his fellow Republicans by adding that he would get the Mexican government to pay for the wall. After the Jorge Ramos and Megyn Kelly events at the end of August, Trump's poll numbers increased again, from 22 to 25% and then to 27% over the preceding two weeks. On September 4, 2015, the first reports of a clandestine meeting of Republican elites hoping to derail Donald Trump's campaign were leaked to the media. Trump raged against Republican Party elites and his polling average reached 30%, putting him 15% ahead of his closest competitor at the time, Dr. Ben Carson.

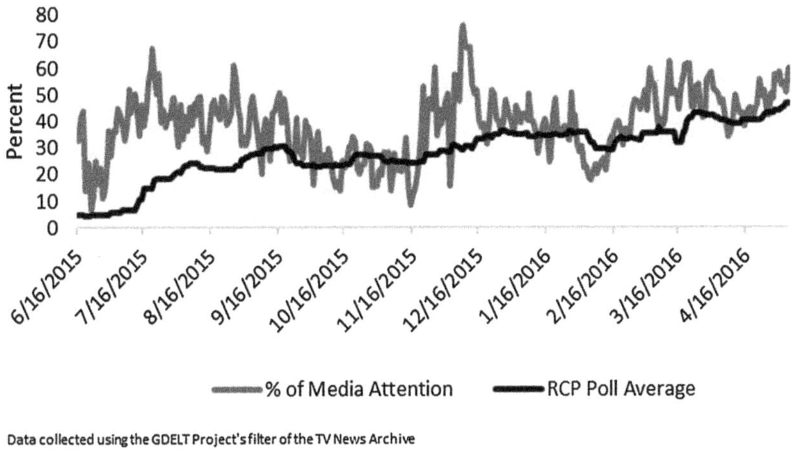

Fig. 4.15 Percent of Trump candidate mentions with poll standings

Over October and November of 2015, coverage of Donald Trump declined, and so too did his polling average. He went 59 days between September 16th (the day of the second GOP debate) and November 20th without a single day earning 50% of the candidate mentions. His average daily candidate mention for that time period was only 26%, far lower than his 44% total average. Lower rates of media attention continued until, in the wake of the Paris terrorist attacks, he alleged that he had seen footage of thousands of Muslims celebrating the 9/11 attacks from a rooftop in New Jersey; a claim swiftly and unequivocally debunked by the media. Those comments returned him squarely to the center of the media's attention, and he remained there for the rest of the invisible primary period, earning on average 46% of all daily candidate mentions and a total of 15 days above the 50% threshold.

By the beginning of December, Trump was back at 30% in the polls. The announcement of his proposal to enact a ban on Muslims entering the U.S. after the San Bernardino terrorist attacks and the five-day media frenzy that followed it led to a sharp increase in Trump's poll standings. Despite outcries of racism and bigotry, even from members of his own party, the Muslim ban proposal gave him an immediate 3% bump followed another 3% in the days following. After starting the month of December at a 28% average in the polls, Donald Trump closed the month out at 35%, holding a twenty point lead over his closest rival.

The formal primary period began with Donald Trump as the clear front-runner. During the formal primary, Trump received 60% or more of all candidate mentions on eighteen days. The first day was March 1, 2016, when he defended the size of his hands against attacks from Marco Rubio in the third GOP debate. The next time was just two days later on March 3rd when Mitt Romney gave his unprecedented speech imploring Republican voters to not support Donald Trump. On March 12, 2016, Trump dominated the news cycle again when escalating violence at his rallies prompted him to cancel a rally in Chicago, Illinois. Threats of violence at his rallies, both from protestors and from Trump supporters, attracted more media attention on March 20th when his rally in Tucson, Arizona, was delayed by protestors shutting down a highway. Around the same time, Trump reopened his ongoing feud with *Fox News* anchor Megyn Kelly. On March 30th, his campaign manager Corey Lewandowski was arrested for misdemeanor assault stemming from rough treatment of a member of the press pool at a rally in Florida. On May 5th, the media went crazy after he tweeted a picture of himself with a taco bowl stating "Happy #CincoDeMayo! The best taco bowls are made in Trump Tower Grill. I love Hispanics!"

The rest of the his 60%+ days are products of fights with fellow Republicans or intra-party fights such as on May 6th when John McCain, Jeb Bush, and Mitt Romney announced they would not attend Trump's nominating convention in Ohio and May 7th when Jeb Bush and Lindsey Graham announced they would not be voting for Trump in the general election. On May 12th, Trump dominated the news cycle with 72% of candidate mentions by holding a summit with Speaker Paul Ryan and continued the dominance over three days as stories broke about his butler being arrested by the Secret Service for threatening President Obama followed the next day by a *New York Times* expose chronicling allegations by several women of sexually abusive behavior. And through all of it, Trump's poll standings continued to climb, defying every conventional wisdom of campaigns.

To put Donald Trump's media dominance into perspective, it is useful to compare him to Hillary Clinton. Like Trump, Clinton was a focus of heightened media attention due to the investigation into her use of a private email server and as the front-runner in the Democratic primary. Hillary Clinton's best media coverage day was March 22, 2015, when she received 53.9% of all candidate mentions. That was the day she spent 22 hours testifying in front of the final Benghazi committee. Clinton's two other high coverage days were October 12, 2015, when President Obama called her decision to host a private email server a mistake and on December 3, 2015, when she renewed her call for increased gun control after the San Bernardino shooting, but neither day earned her more than 40% of mentions.

Never before in political history had a candidate gone out of the way to generate negative media coverage. At times, even Trump himself seemed surprised that his risky strategy was working. On January 23, 2016, at a rally in Sioux City, Iowa, Donald Trump commented on the durability of his lead in the polls saying, "I could stand in the middle of 5th Avenue and shoot somebody and I wouldn't lose voters."[12] Indeed. The more controversial Donald Trump became, the more Republican primary voters embraced him, especially when the controversies had him taking on the media, fellow Republicans, and later, his general election opponent he dubbed "Crooked Hillary."

Notes

1. "Political Polarization and Media Habits," *Pew Research Center*, http://www.journalism.org/2014/10/21/political-polarization-media-habits/.
2. For the running tally see http://www.politifact.com/personalities/donald-trump/statements/byruling/pants-fire/?
3. Katy Tur, "My Crazy year With Trump," *marie Claire*, http://www.marieclaire.com/politics/a21997/donald-trump-katy-tur/.
4. Brett Edkins, "Donald Trump's Election Delivers Massive Ratings For Cable News," *Forbes*, https://www.forbes.com/sites/brettedkins/2016/12/01/donald-trumps-election-delivers-massive-ratings-for-cable-news/#bcc1f87119e9.
5. Kim Bellware, "Fox Hosted The Most-Watched Presidential Primary Debate In History," *Huffpost*, http://www.huffingtonpost.com/entry/fox-gop-debate-ratings_us_55c4f019e4b0923c12bcbfe8.
6. "Here's Donald Trump's Presidential Announcement Speech," *Time*, http://time.com/3923128/donald-trump-announcement-speech/.
7. Jesse Byrnes, "Trump gives kids helicopter rides at Iowa State Fair," *The Hill*, http://thehill.com/blogs/ballot-box/presidential-races/251208-trump-gives-kids-helicopter-rides.
8. To see the plane, watch this: https://www.youtube.com/watch?v=w_CwuSkR7Ec.

9. Data from FairVote, https://docs.google.com/spreadsheets/d/14Lxw0vc4YBUwQ8cZouyewZvOGg6PyzS2mArWNe3iJcY/edit#gid=0.
10. Nicholas Confessore and Karen Yourish, "$2 Billion Worth of Free Media for Trump," The Upshot, *The New York Times*, https://www.nytimes.com/2016/03/16/upshot/measuring-donald-trumps-mammoth-advantage-in-free-media.html.
11. Phillip Bump, "How many hats has Donald Trump bought, anyway?" The Fix, *The Washington Post*, https://www.washingtonpost.com/news/the-fix/wp/2016/06/29/how-many-hats-has-donald-trump-bought-anyway/?utm_term=.6d1fe7a1b23f.
12. Jeremy Diamond, "Trump: I could 'shoot somebody and I wouldn't lose voters,'" *CNN Politics*, http://www.cnn.com/2016/01/23/politics/donald-trump-shoot-somebody-support/.

References

Flanigan, William H., Nancy H. Zingale, Elizabeth A. Theiss-Morse, and Michael W. Wagner. *Political Behavior of the American Electorate*. Los Angeles, CA: SAGE/CQ Press, 2015.

Polsby, Nelson W, Aaron B Wildavsky, Steven E Schier, and David A. Hopkins. Presidential Elections. 1st ed. Lanham, MD.: Rowman & Littlefield, 2016.

Sabato, Larry. Trumped: Inside the Election that broke all the rules. 1st ed. Lanham, MD: Rowman & Littlefield, 2017.

CHAPTER 5

The Party Decides?

Abstract Bitecofer shows how the institutional structures of the two party's nominating systems affected the outcome of the 2016 presidential primaries. Despite a full-frontal assault, Republican Party elites had limited influence on the party's nomination process. Even with the vast majority of Republican Party insiders lined up against him, they were unable to derail the Trump Train because of their limited influence in the nomination process. In the Republican nominating system, elite endorsements are merely symbolic, and they do not carry substantive weight. Unlike the Democrat's system which provides party insiders a tool to exert direct influence in the party's nomination process via super delegates, the Republican rules left the party vulnerable to a hostile takeover.

Keywords Presidential election · Presidential primaries · Hillary Clinton Bernie Sanders · Donald Trump · Republican · Democrat · Super delegates Endorsements · Establishment

In the 2016 presidential primaries, both parties saw their nomination contests hijacked by party outsiders riding waves of populist fervor in the electorate, yet only one party was able to successfully subvert their respective insurgent's candidacy. Despite a full frontal assault from the unprecedented Never Trump movement, the Republican Party establishment was unable to derail the Trump Train. In the end, he received 13,000,000 votes in the Republican primary, more than any other

R. Bitecofer, *The Unprecedented 2016 Presidential Election*,
https://doi.org/10.1007/978-3-319-61976-7_5

Republican primary candidate in history, and 62% of the pledged delegates; a fact not lost on party insiders as they decided to forgo a contested convention despite months of speculation.

Why was the Democratic Party able to subvert Bernie Sanders' candidacy while the Republicans were unable to stop Donald Trump? Research into presidential nominations finds that despite reforms to the nominating system after the tumultuous 1968 Democratic National Convention which transferred power away from party elites and into the hands of voters, party elites still influence the selection of nominees via elite endorsements (Cohen et al. 2008). Voters use elite endorsements as cues to a candidate's viability (ability to win the party's nomination) and voters are more likely to support a candidate that is supported by party officials such as governors and members of Congress. Contrary to the elite theory of presidential primary endorsements, Republican Party elites were unable to push voters away from Donald Trump. Meanwhile, overwhelming support of elites for Hillary Clinton in the Democratic Party helped her hold back a challenge from Bernie Sanders.

Why did the elite theory of endorsements hold for the Democrats, but not for the Republicans in the 2016 primary cycle? I argue the use of symbolic elite endorsements in the Republican's system rather than substantive elite endorsements in the Democratic Party's nominating system left the Republican Party, already fractured by an ideological Civil War, vulnerable to a hostile takeover. In the Republican Party, elite endorsements do not carry substantive implications as they do in the Democratic Party's system. In the Democrat's system, elite endorsements do more than send a signal to the electorate, they translate into super delegate votes. One year before the Iowa Caucus, Hillary Clinton has already amassed elite endorsements from 72 Democratic members of Congress and governors, all super delegates. No other Democratic candidate in history comes anywhere close to that robust a level of support that far out from the formal primary; not even Al Gore who was running as the incumbent vice president in the 2000 Democratic primary. After her announcement, Clinton's elite endorsements grew exponentially, hitting 199 the day before the Iowa Caucus. Although super delegates are officially distributed with their respective state's pledged delegates after the state's contest is complete (they are added to the candidate's share of the state's pledged delegates to produce a total delegate count) Clinton had a large lead in total delegates before a single primary or caucus ballot was cast.

Meanwhile, Republican Party elites were frantically pledging support to their own preferred candidates. Complicating matters was the presence of four establishment candidates coming out of the South Carolina primary. The two hundred and eight elite endorsements offered during the Republican primary were too divided to carry much symbolic value and had no substantive value. The party leadership was powerless to stop a voter revolt.[1] The Republican Party kept waiting for Donald Trump's candidacy to implode. It had been declared dead by the media multiple times after scandals only to emerge stronger than before. The GOP should be forgiven for what later looks like foolish optimism. Each of Trump's transgressions and missteps would have surely been terminal events for other candidates. In the 2004 Democratic primary, Howard Dean destroyed his chance at the Democratic Party's nomination with one overly enthusiastic "yee-haw" at a campaign event.[2] In the 2012 Republican primary, Herman Cain saw his candidacy end when he responded to a questions about "gotcha" questions "like who is the president of Uzbekistan" with this statement: "When they ask me who is the president of Ubeki-beki-beki-beki-stan-stan I'm going to say, "You know what I don't know…who is the head of these small insignificant states."[3] Having never held elected office, the answer was widely mocked and ended his candidacy.

Even in the 2016 cycle, the standard rules applied to everyone other than Donald J. Trump. After seeing his momentum coming into the New Hampshire primary disrupted by an artfully deployed attack by Chris Christie at the final debate before the New Hampshire primary and desperately needing wins in Super Tuesday states, Marco Rubio tried adopting Donald Trump's unique debate style of insulting his opponents. Rubio looked like he was conducting a "roast," hammering Trump on everything from his small hands and "fake university" to belittling his multiple bankruptcies.[4] Despite resonating well with Never Trumpers, the effort fell flat with the electorate. Rubio ended up having to apologize to his own children who were reportedly embarrassed by their father's behavior.[5] Rubio wasn't the only other candidate to face a double standard in the 2016 primaries. Despite a strong showing in the late fall, Ben Carson's poll numbers plummeted after he alleged the Egyptian Pyramids were created to store grain. But Trump was Teflon Don; the more outlandish his statements, the more unorthodox his behavior, the more his poll numbers rose. By the Iowa Caucus, Trump held a significant lead over the rest of the field. Only Ted Cruz and Marco Rubio had any hope of catching him, but even they were behind by more than 15 points in national polls.

Still, the remaining establishment candidates were sure that Trump's candidacy would implode and when the inevitable happened, they planned on being in the race to capitalize on it. The decisions of Jeb Bush, Marco Rubio, and John Kasich to stay in the race and divide up the mainstream component of the Republican electorate prevented any one of them from gaining enough momentum to truly challenge Donald Trump. Further complicating things for the GOP was the presence of Ted Cruz in the race, who was siphoning off the portion of evangelicals that were uncomfortable with Trump but lukewarm toward the moderates.

By the time the primary calendar moved into its second half, the unthinkable had happened: Ted Cruz was the only viable alternative to Donald Trump. Senate colleagues whose deep dislike of Ted Cruz was well known suddenly found themselves looking at endorsing him to help wrangle the nomination away from Donald Trump. In an interview, Senator Lindsey Graham likened to the choice between Trump and Cruz to choosing between being "shot or poisoned."[6] Coming out of the March 1st "SEC" primary, Trump had amassed 364 delegates compared to Ted Cruz's 284. Both Marco Rubio and John Kasich opted to stay in the race and compete in their home state primaries of Florida and Ohio. After losing Florida badly to Trump, Marco Rubio suspended his campaign. By the conclusion of the March 15th contests, Donald Trump secured 705 delegates to Cruz's 486, with John Kasich and Marco Rubio holding 162 and 143, respectively. Of Rubio's 162 delegates, 96 of them were bound to him until the first ballot at the convention in July as per state rules. However, with the Never Trump movement reaching a fever pitch in the wake of Mitt Romney's unorthodox appeal to Republican voters to support any Republican candidate other than Donald Trump, and with rumors of a contested convention swirling, Rubio made an unprecedented effort to keep *all* of his delegates in case a contested convention actually materialized. Kasich too refused to concede defeat, arguing that the 66 delegates picked up in his home state victory in Ohio signaled a new momentum for mainstream Republicans, and the party's last opportunity to thwart both Trump and Cruz. By the time the establishment wing of the party accepted the mathematical reality of their situation in April and finally coalesced behind Ted Cruz as the only alternative to Donald Trump, Trump's delegate lead was insurmountable.

Symbolic versus Substantive Elite Endorsements

Given the strength of the elite resistance to Donald Trump how might have the Republican primary unfolded differently if the party had super delegates like the Democrats? In the Democrats' system, super delegates are individuals vested with a full delegate vote to pledge to the candidate of their choice. There are no rules that curtail the autonomous power granted to these individuals; they are free to pledge or even repledge their delegate for whomever they choose (Kamarck 2009). They are also free to pledge their delegate as early in the primary process as they choose, regardless of factors such as the outcome of the vote in their state, the electoral viability of the candidate at the convention, or any other external factor.[7] Although super delegate support is factored into a candidate's support at every stage of the process, in general, they are officially distributed into the candidate's total delegate count at the conclusion of the super delegate's home state contest. As such, the Democratic Party's delegate count consists of the total of two different types of delegates: pledged delegates that are bound proportionally based on the state's vote share of each candidate exceeding 15% of the state's vote and super delegates whose one vote carries weight equal to thousands of primary voters (Polsby et al. 2016).

There were a total of 712 super delegates in the 2016 Democratic presidential nomination contest, and they comprised about 15% of the total voting power at the party's convention. Super delegates are made up of the 432 members of the Democratic National Committee, 20 distinguished party leaders, 193 Democratic members of the House of Representatives, 47 Democratic senators, and 21 Democratic governors.[8] Super delegates are able to informally pledge their support to a candidate at any stage of the primary and are allowed to recommit their support to another candidate at any time and for any reason. In the 2008 Democratic primary, some super delegates announced support for Hillary Clinton early, then withdrew their support and pledged their support to Barack Obama after Obama's surprise victories in Iowa and South Carolina established him as a serious contender for the nomination.

In the 2008 Democratic primary, Hillary Clinton started off with a two to one advantage over Barack Obama in super delegate support. However, as Obama began to pull ahead of Clinton with pledged delegates the super delegates began to switch their allegiance, moving from Clinton to Obama. By the most competitive part of the primary, they were virtually tied: Clinton with 273 and Obama 272. By June 3, 2008, when Barack Obama secured enough total delegates to be declared the party's presumptive nominee, he led Clinton by 100 super delegates and about 100 pledged delegates for a lead in total delegates of about 200.[9]

At the end of the primary contests, the total delegate count was 2272 for Barack Obama and 1978 for Hillary Clinton. Obama had carried 51% of the Democratic primary vote compared to Clinton's 49%. The total delegate count hid just how close the nomination contest really was: Obama had just 62 more pledged delegates than Clinton. What made his lead so commanding was the inclusion of the super delegates into the total delegate count. Heading into the convention where all delegates would be (graciously) pledged to Obama by acclamation by Hillary Clinton's release of her delegates, Obama had almost doubled Clinton on super delegates support, ending up with 478 to her 246. The majority of super delegates had put their fingers on the scale in favor of Obama but had they wished too; they could have easily thwarted his candidacy and used their power to prop up the equally competitive Clinton campaign. Instead, they broke for the insurgent outsider, a charismatic upshot first term Senator from Illinois challenging Clinton from the left.

Eight years later, the super delegates could have done the same for Bernie Sanders, but they didn't. Why not? In 2008, Barack Obama was a mainstream Democrat who carefully positioned himself just to the left of Hillary Clinton. The Democratic Party's establishment saw him as electable: someone who could compete against the centrist Republican nominee John McCain. In short, there was no incentive for the party elite to derail Obama's candidacy short of a sense of obligation to Clinton. As the first African American party nominee, Obama offered every advantage Clinton offered and without any of the political baggage of the Clinton machine. There was simply no reason for the party's establishment to push back against the party's base, who clearly favored Obama. In fact, the super delegates actually helped Obama win the nomination. As they defected from Clinton to Obama, they sent signals to Democratic primary voters about his viability to win the nomination, giving him additional momentum. As Obama's viability increased, Clinton's decreased. In the final month of the contest, adding super delegates to the delegate total made it seem as though the nomination was out of Hillary Clinton's reach.

If all of that sounds familiar it should. In many ways, the 2016 nomination fight between Hillary Clinton and insurgent candidate Bernie

Sanders played out similarly; only this time, Hillary Clinton was the beneficiary. The nearly universal preference of the super delegates for Clinton signifies the unease that most Democratic insiders felt at the prospect of a Sanders' nomination. Like Obama before him, Bernie Sanders came out of nowhere to challenge Clinton for the nomination. But unlike Obama, Sanders was an outsider, not even technically a Democrat. While Obama positioned himself left of center in 2008, Sanders took far left policy positions that most mainstream Democrats worried would be untenable in the general election such as support for a $15 federal minimum wage and free college tuition for everyone. As such, Democratic Party elites had little interest in using their influence to promote Sanders' candidacy.

Democratic elites were solidly behind Hillary Clinton because of the resume she would bring to the general election and the way she conducted herself after her 2008 loss to Obama. Despite the bruising loss, Hillary Clinton became a major asset to Obama. Starting with her gracious concession at the Democratic National Convention and her work on the campaign trail to help Obama win the White House and ending with her tenure as his Secretary of State, Hillary Clinton had worked hard to gain the trust of her Democratic peers and enjoyed robust favorability among Democratic voters. Combined with her experience as a senator from New York Clinton's tenure as Secretary of State would make her one of the best qualified candidates to ever run for president, an important asset for a female nominee to have. For many in the party Clinton's nomination provided an opportunity to continue building on Obama's legacy while breaking the gender barrier.

The inevitability of Clinton's nomination and the robust support she had within the Democratic Party was so powerful it had a depressing effect on the field. After Joe Biden decided to not enter the race, it was clear the Democratic Party's primary would be a largely symbolic exercise. In fact, that is what inspired Bernie Sanders to throw his hat into the ring. Unexpectedly, Sanders galvanized progressives and millennial Democrats, allowing him to ride a wave of support powered primarily through grassroots activism and small donations. For the Democratic Party's progressive base, Sanders represented an untainted alternative to the Clinton dynasty. Staunchly progressive, Sanders is far to the left of every Democrat in the Senate except Elizabeth Warren. Clinton, an ideological centrist and political pragmatist, was unable to connect ideologically with progressive voters, who were increasingly embracing Bernie Sanders' bold and unapologetic progressivism.

Clinton won the Iowa Caucus by the narrowest of margins, and Sanders beat her soundly in the New Hampshire primary, leading many pundits to wonder if Clinton's candidacy was doomed for a 2008 repeat. Fortunately for Clinton, the order of contests allowed her to bounce back with wins in the Nevada Caucus as well as in the South Carolina primary. This time she had the advantage with a core constituency: African American voters. Heading into the March 1st primaries, Clinton had 91 pledged delegates to Sanders' 65, a 26 delegate lead. However, once total delegates were factored in by including the super delegates from Iowa, New Hampshire, Nevada, and South Carolina, Clinton had 116 total delegates to Sanders' 67: nearly doubling her total delegate advantage.

Support from super delegates affects the public's perception of the competitiveness of the race and can add to, or subject from, a candidate's momentum. In presidential primaries, success begets success; each victory lays the groundwork for the next victory by bringing in more campaign resources, earned media attention, and increasing the candidate's poll standings (Kamarck 2009; Wayne 2016). In elections, momentum is critical. Victories produce momentum, especially unlikely ones such as Barack Obama's unexpected Iowa Caucus victory in 2008. Losses can also generate momentum *if* the candidate exceeds media expectations of their performance such as Marco Rubio's third place showing in the 2016 Republican Iowa Caucus. Because the media interpreted Rubio's loss as exceeding expectations, it gave him momentum heading into the New Hampshire primary and made him a contender for the nomination. News media outlets began to cover him as an alternative front-runner. However, Rubio stumbled badly in the New Hampshire debate, effectively ending his momentum before it really began.

Despite claims to the contrary, super delegates were not used to "steal" the Democratic Party's nomination for Hillary Clinton. By every metric, Clinton beat Sanders. She earned more popular votes and won more contests, and as a result, she earned more pledged delegates. In fact, the 2016 Democratic primary was far less competitive than that of the 2008 Democratic primary, whose results were universally accepted. But super delegates did influence the process in Clinton's favor, just as they had done in Obama's favor eight years prior. Had there been the will, super delegates certainly could have used their influence to prop up Bernie Sanders' candidacy and had enough of them done so, he almost certainly would have become the Democratic Party's nominee.

Like in 2008, the super delegates added to the perception of one candidate's viability at the expense of the other candidate's viability. In the 2016 Democratic primary, super delegates were united behind one candidate, Hilary Clinton, and used their collective weight to help steer the nomination her way.

By breaking for Clinton, super delegates influenced the nomination's outcome by blunting Sanders' momentum during the early primary. By greatly exceeding expectations, the Sanders campaign left Iowa with momentum. Clinton's narrowest of victories allowed her to meet expectations in Iowa and just barely avoid a repeat of the 2008 cycle. Because Vermont was Sanders' home state, the New Hampshire primary did not carry the impact it normally does. Sanders' win in New Hampshire was expected and although his margin of victory was higher than predicted, the win failed to produce any additional momentum for the senator.

The impact of Sanders' strong showing in Iowa and win in New Hampshire was further blunted by the addition of each state's super delegates to the total delegate count. Despite a virtual tie in Iowa and a lopsided victory in New Hampshire, the addition of super delegates allowed Clinton to maintain a solid lead in the overall delegate count. Unlike the complex system used by the Republican Party which includes a combination of proportional, winner-take-all, and hybrid delegate allocation rules, the Democratic Party allocates their pledged delegates through a proportional system for every contest (Kamarck 2009; Wayne 2016). As such, even the most convincing victories usually produce delegate gains for other candidates.[10] Because Iowa came down to less than a 1% advantage for Clinton, the two candidates split Iowa's 44 pledged delegates nearly equally, with Clinton earning 23 and Sanders earning 21. However, Clinton also picked up six super delegates in Iowa, so the total delegate count going into the New Hampshire primary was 29 total delegates for Clinton and 21 for Sanders. In the New Hampshire primary, Sanders took 60% of the vote to Clinton's 37%, and as such, he was awarded the majority of the pledged delegates: 15 pledged delegates to Clinton's nine. Without super delegates, Sanders would have actually led Clinton in delegates heading into the Nevada Caucus: 36 to 32. However, with the super delegates factored in Clinton left New Hampshire with 14 total delegates to Sanders' 15, virtually erasing the significance of Sanders' win there. And the delegate count given to the public on the nightly news showed Clinton leading Sanders with 44 total delegates to Sanders' 37. The importance of the super delegates on perceptions of the status of the

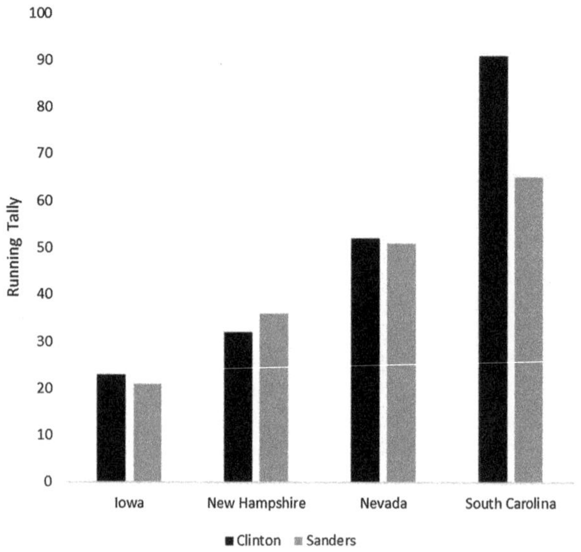

Fig. 5.1 Clinton vs. Sanders pledged delegates in early contests

race is illustrated in Figs. 5.1 and 5.2 which show the running tally of delegates for the first four contests. With super delegates, Clinton leads in all four of the early states. Without them, Sanders leads coming out of New Hampshire and remains tied coming out Nevada, only falling behind Clinton after the South Carolina primary.

Ultimately, it is not possible to know if the outcome of the Democratic nomination would have been any different had Sanders' held the lead coming out of the New Hampshire primary but the media narrative would have been different: Sanders, not Clinton, would have been the front-runner and the media would likely have been critical of Clinton's failure to have the lead. That being said, with or without super delegates, Sander faced another disadvantage in the primary, this time an entirely democratic one. Bernie Sanders lost the 2016 Democratic Party's nomination for the same reason Hillary Clinton lost the 2008 primary: African American voters. Whether the front-runner coming out of New Hampshire or not Sanders was always going to be facing a high hurdle in terms of winning over African American voters who favored

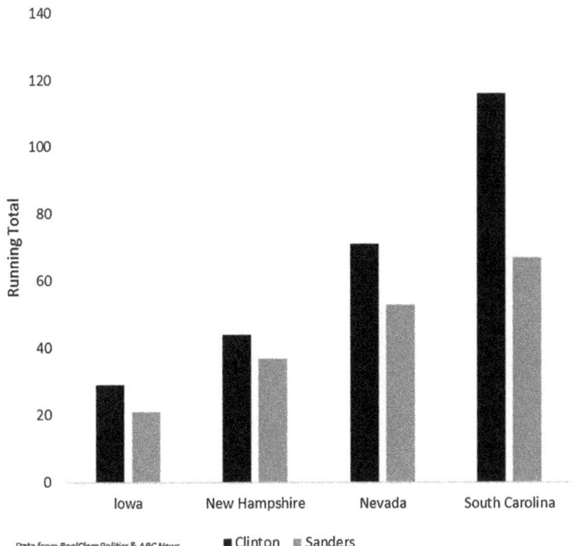

Fig. 5.2 Clinton vs. Sanders total delegates in early contests

Clinton at rates of 7–3. As the cycle played out, Clinton consistently outperformed Sanders in diverse states.[11] As seen in Figs. 5.3 and 5.4, Clinton's advantage over Sanders remains even when super delegates are not considered. Figure 5.3 shows the two candidates' delegate counts when only pledged delegates are considered, and Fig. 5.4 shows their total delegate counts which include super delegates. There is almost no difference in the two distributions; both systems show Clinton pulling ahead of Sanders early and maintaining her lead steadily. Ultimately, Sanders' issues with African American voters and failure to carry states with large populations caused him to lose the party's nomination just as it had caused Clinton to lose to Obama in 2008. As shown in Figs. 5.5 and 5.6, Clinton's pledged delegate lead grows after the early contests and by the conclusion of the "SEC" primaries on March 1st, she pulled out of reach of Sanders. Although Clinton did not need super delegates to beat Sanders, Sanders would have needed super delegates to beat Clinton: 390 of them to be exact.

Given the opposition to Donald Trump within the Republican Party, one must wonder whether the Republican National Committee was eyeing

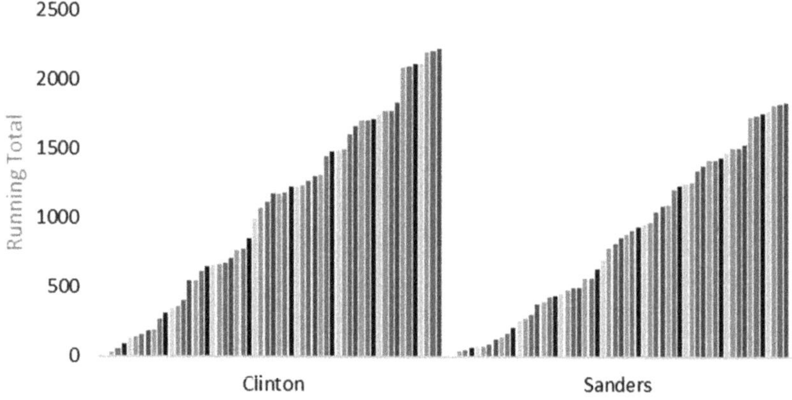

Fig. 5.3 Clinton vs. Sanders: pledged delegates

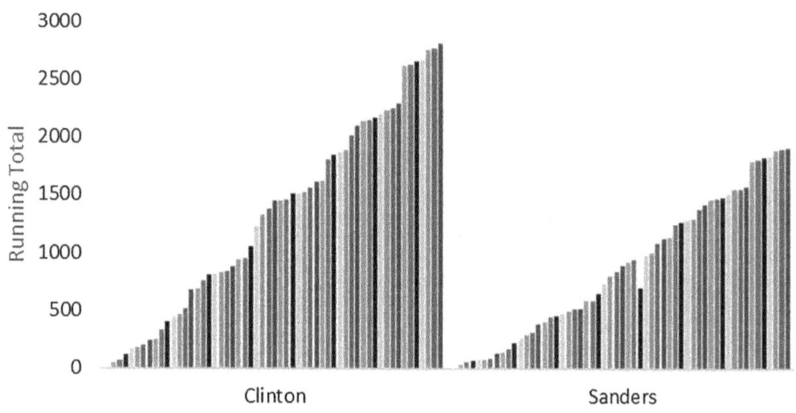

Fig. 5.4 Clinton vs. Sanders: total delegates

the Democratic Party's super delegates longingly, wishing their own party's rules allowed for something similar. The rationale for the inclusion of super delegates in the Democrat's nominating system is based on the idea that those serving the party with distinction should have some influence on the outcome of the nomination process. Rather than merely a signaling tool, the Democrats allow party insiders and committed activists' direct

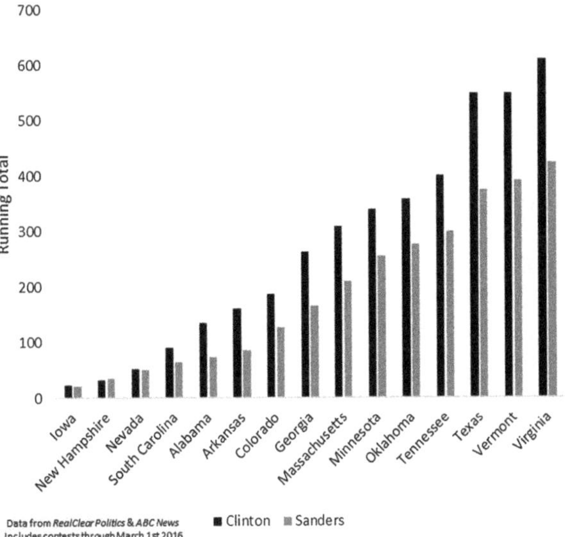

Fig. 5.5 Clinton vs. Sanders pledged delegates through March 1st

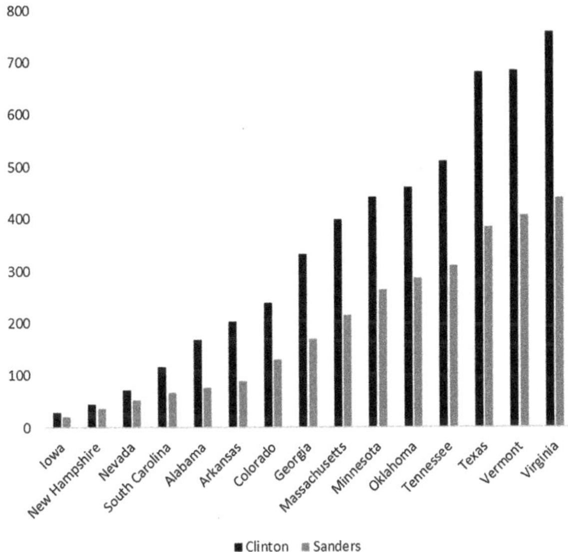

Fig. 5.6 Clinton vs. Sanders total delegates through March 1st

influence on the nomination process. As documented in the analysis of the 2008 and 2016, Democratic primaries super delegates can influence the nomination at all stages of the process. During the invisible primary, they can be used to signal party support of a favored candidate and to ward off challengers. They affect the way that media covers the primary, becoming one of the metrics the media uses to assess a candidate's viability. Once the formal primary season begins and elite endorsements translate into super delegates, they can be used to add to a candidate's momentum like with Obama in 2008 or to blunt a candidate's momentum like with Sanders in 2016. In 2016 they were used to the push the nomination towards the centrist candidate but in 2008 they proved pivotal in pushing the nomination towards the candidate preferred by progressives.

What might have happened had Republican Party elites been able to draw on substantive elite endorsements rather than merely symbolic ones to subvert Donald Trump's insurgent candidacy? Republican Party insiders certainly tried their best to use elite endorsements to move Republican voters away from Donald Trump. Despite becoming the Republican front-runner two months before the first contest, Trump did not earn his first elite endorsement until three weeks after the Iowa Caucus, when he picked up endorsements from two members of the House of Representatives: Duncan Hunter and Chris Collins. The failure of any Republican elites to endorse Donald Trump until he was already well underway to securing the party's nomination is yet another unprecedented element of the 2016 cycle. All told, Donald Trump would only receive just 15 elite endorsements over the course of the entire primary, just 11% of the 132 earned by Mitt Romney in the 2012 Republican primary. Most of the endorsements came in the closing days of the primary cycle, once Donald Trump had mathematically secured enough delegates to earn the title of "presumptive nominee." The extreme reluctance Republican office holders had to support Trump suggests that had the Republican Party had super delegates, few, if any, would have used them to support his candidacy.

What would a Republican super delegate system look like? If structured similarly to the Democrat's system, each elected Republican member of Congress (255), along with each Republican governor (33) would be given a delegate vote totaling 288 votes. In addition, the Democrats include 437 elected members of the Democratic National Committee, 150 of which are comprised of state chairs, as well as members of important constituency groups, and 75 at-large members.[12] Finally, the Democrats' allows for 20 votes to what they call their Distinguished

Party Leaders (DPLs) which include former presidents Clinton and Carter as well as other party dignitaries such as Al Gore and former party chairs such as Howard Dean.[13] Technically, the Republican Party already has some super delegates. Each state's party chair, along with two district-level committee members are automatically seated at the convention and are technically unbound. As such, it is safe to assume that a Republican super delegate system would include RNC leaders as well as party leaders. Using the Democrat's system this would create a pool of at least 778 potential Republican Party super delegates.

Assuming the 2016 Republican primary played out exactly as it did, super delegates would not have been enough alone to steer the party's nomination to an establishment Republican like Jeb Bush or Marco Rubio. Figure 5.7 demonstrates that Donald Trump absolutely dominated his competitors in the Republican primary. Coming out of Iowa, the race was tight: Trump seven delegates, Cruz eight, and Rubio seven. Then Trump's decisive win in New Hampshire gave him 12 more delegates for a total of 19 while Cruz gained just three for a total of 11 and Rubio gained just one giving him just eight total. If there was a place for super delegates to exert influence on the outcome to steer the contest to an establishment Republican, it would have had to have happened in Iowa and New Hampshire.

As Fig. 5.8 shows, if the Republican Party's system included super delegates than theoretically, Marco Rubio could have led the delegate

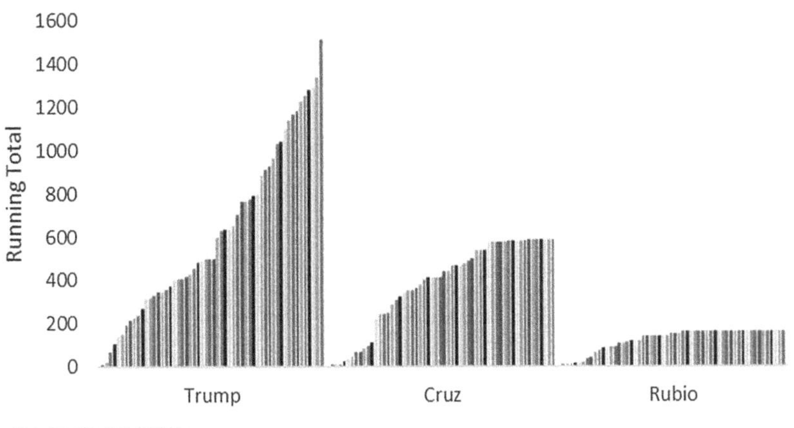

Fig. 5.7 2016 Republican primary delegate allocation

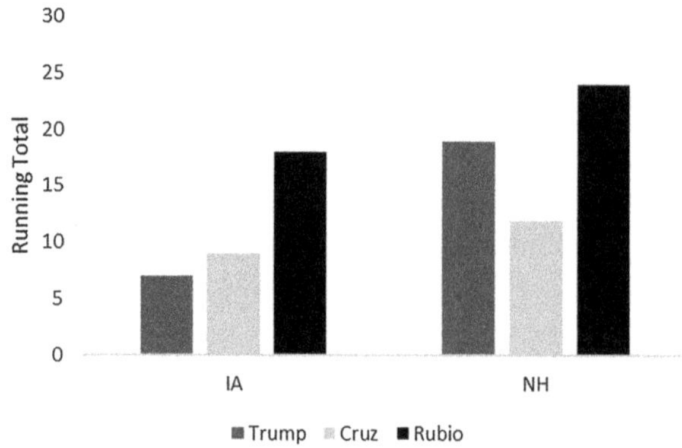

Fig. 5.8 Iowa and New Hampshire with Republican super delegates

count heading into the decisive South Carolina primary. Because of South Carolina's winner-take-all delegate allocation formula, whoever came out of that race victorious would take a commanding lead in the delegate total. With a 50 delegate winner-take-all cache to the top vote getter and a guaranteed third place in the primary calendar, South Carolina exerts considerable influence on the outcome of nomination as it did in 2016. This most likely contributes to their high rate of aligning with the eventual nominee 71% of the time.[14] In the 2016 Republican primary, Donald Trump won a plurality of the state's votes (32.5%) and took all 50 delegates. Although the Republican primary was still covered as competitive heading into the March 1, 2016 "SEC" primaries, Trump's win in South Carolina all but ensured he would capture the Republican nomination. Even if the Republican Party had super delegates, Trump's victory in South Carolina made his delegate lead insurmountable, especially because it was followed quickly by another dominate performance in Nevada (see Fig. 5.9).

Even with super delegates, the Republican Party's effort to steer the nomination to an establishment candidate like Marco Rubio would fail under the actual outcome of each state's contest in 2016 because of the presence of Ted Cruz in the race and the inclusion of Texas in the March 1st "SEC" primaries. The Texas primary offered 155 pledged delegates with a 20% threshold for awarding of any delegates. As a home state senator, it is doubtful that Ted Cruz would have withdrawn from the race until after the Texas primary, regardless of his performance in the early

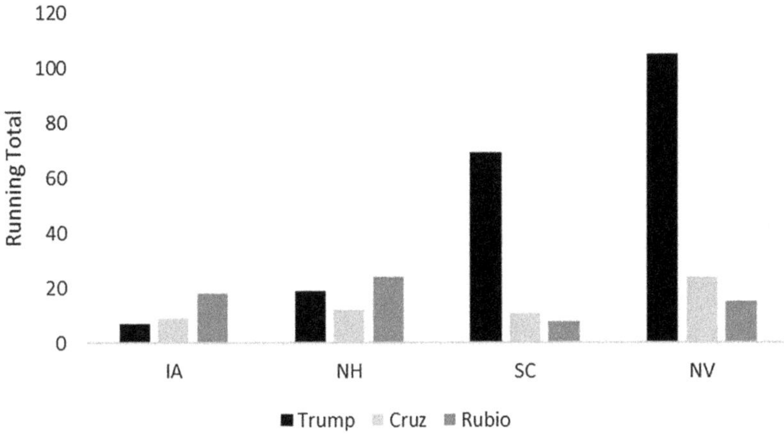

Fig. 5.9 Early contests with Republican super delegates

contests. After campaigning hard in his home state, Cruz carried 43.6% of the vote earning him 104 of the state's delegates. Texas was by far the largest cache of delegates in the early primary period. Thus, Cruz's strong showing there put him within reach of Donald Trump. Because of the Texas primary, it was Ted Cruz *not* Marco Rubio who emerged as the party's only alternative to Donald Trump. At the end of the March 1st, primaries Donald Trump had 346 pledged delegates while Ted Cruz had 284. By that point in the calendar, 116 super delegates would have been allocated. If they all threw their support behind Cruz, then he would have taken the lead from Trump with 400 delegates to Trump's 346. Under the actual 2016 Republican primary results, the party's establishment could have used super delegates to derail the Trump Train after the March 1st primaries, but they could not have done so by directing the nomination toward an establishment candidate. Instead, they would have needed to prop up the candidacy of a man they almost universally despised.

Of course, with super delegates in the Republican system, it is unlikely that the 2016 Republican primary would have unfolded in the same way did. One reason is the effect that super delegates have on the size of the candidate field and on the longevity of office-seeking candidates once they are shown to not be viable to win the party's nomination. Unlike policy-seeking candidates (candidate's whose presence in the race is geared toward setting the substantive agenda), office seekers are using their candidacies to advance their political careers. As such, they exit the race once they can no longer win to avoid embarrassing headlines and additional losses (Haynes et al. 2004).

The unusual size of the Republican field in 2016 is at least in part a product of the lack of super delegates in the Republican nomination system. On average Republican fields in the modern nominating system have averaged nine candidates when 2016 is excluded and ten candidates when 2016 is included. Meanwhile, Democratic fields average about seven candidates. On top of being smaller, Democratic fields also tend to winnow faster than Republican fields. As super delegates begin to align with their preferred candidate those that are failing to attract party support tend to withdraw from the race. For example, in the 2008 Democratic primary, once it became clear that the super delegates were split between Obama and Clinton almost exclusively, the other candidates withdrew. By January 30th, just after the South Carolina primary, the third place candidate Senator John Edwards withdrew from the race, leaving just Obama and Clinton to compete for the nomination. Support from super delegates becomes a major factor in a candidate's overall viability. As such, in a Republican system with super delegates, it is doubtful that the field would have remained as crowded for as long as it did. Additionally, Donald Trump's durability in the polls through the fall might have led the Republican establishment to put intense pressure on non-viable establishment candidates to withdraw and coalesce around one establishment candidate early, well before the formal primaries began. This scenario might produce a wildly different outcome because it would change the entire narrative of the campaign.

It is important to note that super delegates, both the real ones in the Democrat's nominating system and the hypothetical ones created for the purpose of simulating their use in the Republican's system are designed to allow party insiders to influence the nominating process, not override the will of the voters should the voters robustly support a candidate insiders do not. Remove every super delegate from Hillary Clinton's delegate count, and she still beats Bernie Sanders, due in large part to her robust support among minority voters. With 4051 pledged delegates and only 712 super delegates, the super delegates comprise just 15% of the total available delegates. If the electorate is united behind a candidate, there is nothing party insiders can do. The same would be true in our hypothetical system for Republicans. With 2420 total delegates, less than 800 party elites cannot subvert a unified electorate. The super delegates lack the mathematical weight to matter in a one-sided contest. They can only be influential when the electorate is closely divided between at least two candidates.

Lacking substantive elite endorsements, as the Never Trump movement picked up steam, some Republicans began to eye the rules governing the pledged delegates for loopholes that could be exploited to force a brokered convention. The party had a few different pathways available to derail Trump's nomination but all of them would involve an undemocratic coup to override the will a strong plurality of the Republican electorate. Republican Party insiders had only one option to stop Trump: they would have to literally steal the nomination. Party insiders felt they faced an impossible choice: stage a coup and destroy the Republican Party themselves or stand aside and watch Donald Trump destroy the party for them. Ultimately, the party's convention rules saved them from having to make a choice. Under the current rules of the Republican system, pledged delegates must cast their ballots for the winner of their state's contest (if a winner-take-all system is used) or in proportion (if a proportional allocation system is used). Because of Trump's commanding delegate lead, the party would have to find a way to free pledged delegates on the first ballot; a task made impossible due to the number of pro-Trump delegates seated at the convention. As rumors of a brokered convention began to spread, the Trump campaign made moves to shore up their defenses by electing Trump-friendly delegates at state conventions. Paul Manafort, a veteran Republican operative, was brought into oversee the delegate count, and staffers were hired to ensure the delegate selection process could not be used as a back door option to derail Trump. For all the speculation, a brokered convention was a mathematical impossibility.

Both the Republican and Democratic Party's 2016 presidential nomination campaigns produced insurgent outsiders who became serious contenders for their party's nomination. In the Democratic primary, elite endorsements carrying substantive weight via super delegates helped shore up the candidacy of Hillary Clinton whose candidacy enjoyed majority support among Democratic primary voters. In the Republican Party, symbolic elite endorsements were unable to derail the candidacy of Donald Trump. Nearly, every presidential primary cycle produces calls for reform and pressure for rule changes. Although Hillary Clinton won the nomination over Bernie Sanders through democratic means, super delegates did influence the process in Clinton's favor. Given the competitiveness of the race, had party insiders wanted Bernie Sanders to be the party's nominee, they could have used their substantive endorsements to advantage Sanders as they did in 2008 to advantage Barack Obama.

Given the high level of suspicion in the Democratic Party's base about super delegates and their role in the 2016 Democratic Party primary, there are already calls for the party to reform or perhaps even eliminate the use of super delegates in 2020. As part of the agreement struck by the Sanders and Clinton teams at the Democratic National Convention, a Unity Reform Commission has been created by the Democratic National Committee. Along with possible changes to the super delegate system, the commission will also examine the types of primary systems used (open versus closed) and the use of caucuses.[15]

After the hostile takeover of the Republican Party by Donald Trump, the Republican Party may consider adding super delegates or something similar to their nominating system so that the party's establishment gains some substantive influence in the selection of their party's nominee. Right now such a move would not be popular among Republican voters. The 2016 iteration of the *American National Election Survey* asks respondents how party nominees should be chosen: entirely by voters, mostly by voters with some say from party leaders, equally by voters and party leaders, or mostly by party leaders with some say from voters. 58% of Republicans indicate a preference that party nominees be chosen entirely by voters, compared to only 49% of Democrats and 51% of Independent voters. Voter support for reforms to the party's nomination system, especially those seeking to increase the influence of party leaders, may be contingent on the Trump Administration's performance in office. If successful calls for reforming the nominating system that produces his victory will probably die out. However, at the writing of this book, the Trump Administration has been plagued by scandal and controversies, most of which have been caused by Donald Trump himself. Should Trump's legacy be one of chaos and disorder it would not be surprising to see the Republican Party take steps to fortify their nomination process against similar candidates.

Notes

1. For endorsement data see https://projects.fivethirtyeight.com/2016-endorsement-primary/.

2. Kenneth T. Walsh, "The Battle Cry That Backfired on Howard "The Scream" Dean," *U.S. News & World Report*, https://www.usnews.com/news/articles/2008/01/17/the-battle-cry-that-backfired.
3. Ben Smith, "Uzbek (bek) outrage at Cain," *Politico*, http://www.politico.com/blogs/ben-smith/2011/10/uzbek-bek-outrage-at-cain-040069.
4. Kyle Cheney, "Rubio ambushes Trump at GOP debate," *Politico*, http://www.politico.com/story/2016/02/republican-debate-february-2016-219807.
5. Ben Kamisar,"Rubio regrets attacks: My kids 'embarrassed'," *The Hill*, http://thehill.com/blogs/ballot-box/272451-rubio-regrets-attacks-my-kids-embarrassed.
6. "Graham: Choice between Trump, Cruz like 'being shot or poisoned'," *Politico*, http://www.politico.com/story/2016/01/lindsey-graham-trump-cruz-choice-218069.
7. In the 2016 primary, facing public backlash from Sanders supporters, some Super Delegates (mostly current elected officials) elected to pledge their vote to the winner of their state's popular vote.
8. DeSilver, Drew. "Who are the Democratic superdelegates?" Pew Research Center (May 5, 2016).
9. "If you thought the democratic primary was close the one in 2008 was even tighter," *The New York Times*, https://www.nytimes.com/interactive/2016/06/07/us/elections/clinton-sanders-delegate-fight.html.
10. In the Democratic Party's system, a candidate must break a 15% threshold to earn any delegates from a contest.
11. Nate Silver, "Clinton Is Winning The States That Look Like The Democratic Party," *FiveThirtyEight*, https://fivethirtyeight.com/features/clinton-is-winning-the-states-that-look-like-the-democratic-party/.
12. A breakdown of the super delegates can be found here https://en.wikipedia.org/wiki/List_of_Democratic_Party_superdelegates,_2016.
13. "Who are the Democratic superdelegates?," *Pew Research Center*, http://www.pewresearch.org/fact-tank/2016/05/05/who-are-the-democratic-superdelegates/.
14. "How 50 Years of Data May Help Predict Party Nominations," Kogod School of Business, American University, https://onlinebusiness.american.edu/blog/presidential-primary-predictions/.
15. Daniel Marans,"DNC Announces Members Of Unity Reform Commission," *Huffpost*, http://www.huffingtonpost.com/entry/dnc-unity-reform-commission_us_58f50d1fe4b0b9e9848d92eb.

References

Cohen, Marty. *The Party Decides: Presidential Nominations Before and After Reform*. Chicago, IL: University of Chicago Press, 2008.

Haynes, Audrey A., Paul-Henri Gurian, Michael H. Crespin, and Christopher Zorn. "The Calculus of Concession: Media Coverage and the Dynamics of Winnowing in Presidential Nominations." *American Politics Research* 32, no. 3 (2004): 310–37. doi:10.1177/1532673x03260353.

Kamarck, Elaine Ciulla. *Primary Politics: How Presidential Candidates have Shaped the Modern Nominating System*. Washington, DC: Brookings Institution Press, 2009.

Polsby, Nelson W, Aaron B Wildavsky, Steven E Schier, and David A. Hopkins. Presidential Elections. 1st ed. Lanham, MD.: Rowman & Littlefield, 2016.

Wayne, Stephen J. *The Road to the White House 2016*. 10th ed. Boston, MA: Cengage Learning, 2016.

CHAPTER 6

The 2016 Presidential Election

Abstract Bitecofer recaps the major events of the 2016 general election starting with the party conventions and ending with Donald Trump's unexpected victory on Election Day. Both party conventions begin mired in speculation about brokered conventions and delegate revolts. As the general election moves on, the Trump campaign is plagued by scandals, most of which are unforced errors by their nominee. Heading into Election Day, Hillary Clinton's victory is all but guaranteed until the polls close in Florida and the state's 29 Electoral College votes are added to Donald Trump's total. With one candidate earning 3 million more popular votes and the other candidate winning the Electoral College, the 2016 presidential election ends with one final unprecedented act.

Keywords Presidential election · Presidential primaries · Hillary Clinton Bernie Sanders · Donald Trump · Republican · Democrat · DNC · RNC

The 2016 general election officially commenced with the Republican Party's nominating convention in Cleveland, Ohio on July 18, 2016. The Republican National Committee's selection of Ohio for their convention was strategic. Ohio is the ultimate bellwether state, picking the winner of the presidential election 95% of the time.[1] Ohio offered the Republican Party additional benefits. It was home to one of the most popular Republican governors in the country (John Kasich) as well as to a popular Republican Senator (Rob Portman). When the convention

R. Bitecofer, *The Unprecedented 2016 Presidential Election*,
https://doi.org/10.1007/978-3-319-61976-7_6

site was selected, it was assumed that both Kasich and Portman would play prominent roles in the convention, but in the end, Governor Kasich boycotted the event entirely and Senator Portman attended but turned down a speaking role, preferring to remain out of the limelight.

That John Kasich chose to publically boycott the Republican National Convention in his home state tells you everything you need to know about the status of the Republican Party heading into the 2016 general election. It was a party torn asunder, deeply divided over its presidential nominee. National party conventions are highly anticipated events, and speaking roles are normally coveted because of the reputational gains they bring. Barack Obama's unlikely political trajectory from little known Illinois state senator, to U.S. Senator, to president in just a little over 5 years began at the 2004 Democratic National Convention where he delivered the keynote address that became known simply as "The Speech."[2] The fact that the Republican National Committee was having a hard time finding talent to speak at the 2016 nominating convention was yet another unprecedented aspect of the 2016 presidential election.

Governor Kasich was not alone, several other prominent members of the Republican Party declined to even attend the convention, let alone speak at it. The list of convention boycotters includes both former presidents Bush, Senator John McCain, and 2012 nominee Mitt Romney. Other prominent Republicans also skipped the convention citing various reasons. Senator Ben Sasse's spokesman informed the media that he was "instead taking his kids to watch some dumpster fires across the state, all of which enjoy more popularity than the current front-runners." Representative Mario Diaz told *Politico* he had a hair appointment he couldn't miss. Senator Jeff Flake would be mowing his lawn. Representative Trey Gowdy went on a beach vacation. And a Kansas state senator reported having a hot date lined up "touring Kansas libraries, courthouses, and pharmacies."[3] All told six sitting governors, twenty-one sitting senators, and nine members of the House of Representatives did not attend their own party's national convention. To be sure, party officials skipping the national convention for political reasons isn't novel. It happens at every convention. But what is novel was the number of them doing so, nearly 50% of the GOP's Senate delegation did not attend. Unprecedented.

Rumors abound on who did, and who did not, actually receive offers for speaking roles but turned them down. The eventual line-up ended up producing few current office-holding Republican speakers with national profiles. One of those speakers was Texas Senator Ted Cruz who used his moment in the spotlight on a symbolic coup, extolling GOP delegates to "vote their conscious." The only thing Cruz's efforts got him was a cacophony of boos and jeers from the audience.[4] Cruz's speech only mentioned Donald Trump once, at the beginning when he congratulated him for winning the nomination but Cruz never gave Trump his endorsement. Given the events of the Republican primary and the ongoing feud between Ted Cruz and Donald Trump, the selection of Cruz for a speaking role was indicative of the struggle convention organizers faced presenting party unity, the centerpiece of all nominating convention's messaging strategy.

In accepting the Republican Party's nomination, Donald Trump made history, becoming the first presidential nominee without any public service experience in history. Trump delivered a 75-minute speech, one of the longest convention speeches ever given. The speech was dark for a convention speech, invoking an image of an America in decline, inundated by crime, threats of terrorism, and illegal immigration. Despite some rough patches from a plagiarism controversy involving Melania Trump and the disunity displayed by Ted Cruz's speech, the Republican National Convention ended on a high note, earning Trump a 5-point convention bounce in the polls. It would be the only time he would lead Clinton in the polls throughout the entire general election.

The Democratic Party's convention in Philadelphia a week later also opened with disunity. In what would later be revealed to be a planned attack by Russia, a cache of stolen emails from the Democratic National Committee was released to the public via WikiLeaks on the eve of the convention. Some emails showed DNC staff members deriding Bernie Sanders' and his supporters, giving more fuel to claims that the DNC had "interfered" in the primary process to advantage Hillary Clinton's candidacy. In the hours before, the convention officially commenced, then DNC Chair Debbie Wasserman-Schultz was forced to resign from the DNC and give up her role of formally opening the convention.

The Democratic National Convention kicked off with "Bernie or Bust" delegates in open rebellion. Speakers were booed, even Elizabeth Warren. Following the lead of their candidate eventually the protests died out and the convention took on a controlled tone. Where the Republican Party had struggled to find speakers, the Democratic Party's convention was stocked full of top-tier talent.

Elizabeth Warren, Bernie Sanders, and Michelle Obama on the first night, Bill Clinton the second night, President Obama and Vice President Joe Biden the third night: the party's leaders presented a unified front excited about their 2nd history-making nominee in a row.

But the party unity on display in the closing days of the each party's convention hid deep divisions. For the Republican Party, the base was united behind their contraversial nominee but the party's elites were fractured, unsure how much, if any, support they should give Donald Trump. For Democrats, the unity of party insiders obfuscated disunity and discontent within the progressive wing of the Democratic base. Progressives were deeply skeptical of Hillary Clinton, and some were downright hostile. Research into party disunity finds that division within the party's base from the primary can hurt the party's chances to win the general election. So too does division within the party's elites in which the national party cannot unite to support the party's nominee. (Gurian et al. 2016). The 2016 presidential election featured one campaign entering the general election suffering from a divided electorate and the other campaign entering the general election suffering from a divided national party. It would be the party that could best bridge their respective divide that would prevail in November.

On Thursday July 28, 2016, Hillary Clinton also made history, becoming the first woman to officially accept the nomination for President of the United States from one of the two major political parties. In general, the Democratic National Convention received good reviews buying Clinton a modest, 3-point convention bounce. However, the modest increase in Clinton's polling average from the convention was enhanced by Trump's rapid polling collapse after he went on the attack against the Khan family, who spoke on Clinton's behalf at the Democratic Party's convention. The Khans lost their son when he died in combat on a deployment to Iraq. As a Muslim family, they hoped sharing their story of service and loss would highlight the contributions that American Muslims make and humanize Donald Trump's proposal to ban Muslims from entering the U.S. Khirz Khan's convention speech resonated with the liberal audience but it ended up giving the Democrats much more than that after Trump lashed out at the family in a series of interviews and tweets. In an interview with *ABC News*, Donald Trump suggested that Khan's wife Ghazala Khan stood behind her husband silently because she was "not allowed to speak."[5] Facing furious backlash not only from Democrats but also from his own party members, Trump doubled down on his attacks. After less than two weeks of relative party harmony,

Trump quickly erased both his poll gains and the ground he'd made winning over reluctant Republican Party insiders.

The incident kicked off a troubled August for the Trump campaign which was struggling to develop a viable campaign infrastructure. Trump had been trailing Clinton in the polls for weeks and was under pressure to raise funds after a lethargic summer. The Trump campaign began to turn things around in late August. Paul Manafort was fired and replaced by veteran GOP operative Kelly Anne Conway. At the end of the month, the Trump campaign reported strong August fund-raising. Through September, the race began to narrow. By the middle of the month, Clinton's lead was down to just three points, within the margin of error.

Just when it looked like Donald Trump would be competitive against Clinton and had perhaps gotten a handle on his erratic behavior, signs of new trouble began to emerge. In the days before the first presidential debate reports began to surface that Trump was refusing to engage in traditional debate preparation. The idea was so preposterous that some political analysts (including your author) theorized the Trump campaign was leaking a false narrative about his debate preparation as part of a strategy to lower expectations. Clinton was known to be a skilled debater, so it seemed reasonable that the Trump team would work to lower expectations to mitigate what most recognized as a significant disadvantage for Donald Trump. Indeed, Trump's debate expectations were lower than even those of Sarah Palin's in the 2008 vice presidential debate against Joe Biden.

In the end, Donald Trump did exceed expectations at the first presidential debate; he managed to do even worse than expected. A scientific poll released after the debate showed Clinton beating Trump by an almost historic margin with 53% of respondents, identifying Clinton as the winner compared to just 18% selecting Trump. While more than half of respondents credit Clinton with getting most of her facts right, just 29% said the same about Trump.[6] Either never having been coached on debate etiquette or simply not utilizing any of his training, Donald Trump spent the entire 90-minute debate on rambling, nonsensical tirades. He committed innumerable physical gaffes such as rolling his eyes and sighing exasperatedly.

The debate culminated with Trump walking right into a trap laid by the Clinton team. The trap was so obvious that *Saturday Night Live* would go on to parody it by showing Clinton reeling Trump in with a fishing pole. In a well-rehearsed cadence, Hillary Clinton recounted Trump's comments about former Miss Universe Alicia Machado. Hillary Clinton recounted comments made by Donald Trump in which he allegedly called her "Miss Piggy" and "Miss Housekeeping" (referring to her Latina heritage).[7] The next morning on *Fox and Friends*, Donald Trump responded exactly the way the Clinton team hoped he would: by doubling down. Rather than apologizing for the statements and deflecting to other issues as any other candidate would do, Trump defended his treatment of Machado during her tenure as Miss Universe telling the panel she had gained a "massive amount of weight."[8] Subsequent interviews with Machado would reveal that during her tenure as Miss Universe, Trump had shamed her publically for her weight gain, even going so far as to force her to work out in front of cameras. Facing blowback, Trump kept on the offensive, turning to Twitter to continue to attack her for her weight and urging his followers to "check out |her| sex tape and past." Combined with his disastrous debate performance, the Machado scandal tanked Trump's poll numbers. By the beginning of October, the race had opened back up in Clinton's favor, giving her a six-point lead. Then on October 8, the *Access Hollywood* video dropped. The video footage showed Donald Trump and *Today Show* host Billy Bush engaged in lewd, at times predatory, discussion of women and a now-famous line from Trump in which he said that being a celebrity allows him "grab |women| by the pussy" if he wants to.[9]

The *Access Hollywood* video was damning, more so even than the famous 47% video that had badly hurt Mitt Romney's campaign in 2012.[10] Still, despite some polls showing a large decline in support for Trump, the *RealClear Politics* aggregate changed only modestly. At the state level, the effects were more evident. A poll my colleague and I ran after the video was released found Clinton leading Trump by 15 points in Virginia, effectively moving the state off of the battleground list. A week after the video's release, Clinton was leading Trump by four points in Florida, six points in Nevada, eight points in Colorado, six points in Pennsylvania, and eight points in Wisconsin, and the Trump campaign was in a free fall. Senator Rob Portman, up for reelection in Ohio, pulled his endorsement. South Dakota Senator John Thune called on Trump to withdraw from the race. New Hampshire Senator Kelly Ayotte, also in a tough reelection fight, reversed her commitment to vote for Donald Trump. All told more than three dozen Republicans called on Donald Trump to hand the ticket over to his vice presidential nominee Mike Pence.[11]

Speaker Paul Ryan held a conference call with his congressional caucus and told them they could do whatever was in their best interests electorally in regard to Trump.[12] He pulled himself out of a rally with Trump in Wisconsin and said he would no longer "engage" with the candidate although he did not retract his endorsement.[13] The move elicited a typical Trump Twitter response. Trump tweeted "|o|ur very weak and ineffective leader, Paul Ryan, had a bad conference call where his members went wild at his disloyalty" followed up by a second tweet that said, "despite winning the second debate in a landslide (every poll), it is hard to do well when Paul Ryan and other (sic) give zero support."

Although the second debate was better for Trump, scientific polls conducted after the debate again showed Clinton was the winner.[14] To rebut the *Access Hollywood* scandal, the Trump team devised a strategy to neutralize the issue at the second debate. They brought women from Bill Clinton's past, some of whom had accused him of sexual assault, to the debate and sat them prominently in the debate audience with the hopes of unsettling Clinton.[15] Trump spent the debate relentlessly attacking Hillary Clinton for her husband's infidelity and alleged sexual harassment. At one point, he threatened to imprison her over her use of a private email server if he won the presidency.[16] Trump also continually loomed closely behind Clinton when she spoke, so much so that at one point she stopped mid-point to glance over her shoulder.[17] The unconventional strategy delighted Republican base voters but unnerved other voters.

Heading into the third and final debate on October 19, the race had assumed a stasis of a six-point Clinton advantage. The third debate was the most substantive of the three and Donald Trump's best performance. That being said, Donald Trump continued his unorthodox rhetorical style and refused to commit to accepting the results of the November 8 election after a week making headlines asserting widespread fraud in the U.S. electoral system that some argued damaged the legitimacy of American democracy. Election forecasting models from *fivethirtyeight.com* and *Huffington Post's Pollster* showed the probability of a Clinton victory on Election Day at 70% or better. Although Trump had improved as a candidate, his performance was still well below that of traditional presidential candidates and although the campaign had managed to stop the bleeding, they had made virtually no progress in growing his portion of the electorate.

Then, on Friday, October 28, FBI Director James Comey sent a letter to Congress informing them that additional emails that may be related to the investigation of Clinton's email server had been uncovered and would need to be reviewed. The revelation set off a firestorm of media coverage and breathless speculation and put the controversy back on center stage. For the final two weeks of the campaign, Donald Trump used the reopened investigation to remind voters of what he characterized as Clinton's reckless disregard for national security during her tenure as Secretary of State. For most of the primary campaign, the email server scandal had hung on the Clinton campaign like an albatross. In July, in a controversial news conference, Comey announced the conclusion of the probe into Clinton's private email server and the decision by the FBI not to recommend charges against Clinton despite what he characterized a "reckless" handling of classified material. Although prominent on the stump at Trump campaign rallies, the email scandal had largely faded into the background. Now the skeptiscm voters had regarding Clinton's trust and honesty was back in the forefront of voters' minds. Whether or not the Comey letter actually pushed voters away from Clinton in the final days, it breathed new life into what was up until that point a deflated Trump campaign. Trump hit the stump with new vigor and more discipline, largely staying on the teleprompter and away from Twitter. Three days before the election, FBI Director Comey announced the additional emails contained no new relevant information pertaining to Clinton and the investigation was once again closed. But the damage had already been done. The polls had narrowed to within a few points, well within the margin of error in some swing states.

Despite the narrowing of the polls on Election Day, the Clinton team still felt confident that they would be ending the night by making history having elected the first female President of the United States. Forecasting models not only predicted a decisive Clinton win but also a strong performance for the Democratic Party in down ballot races. The victory party was to be held at the Javits Center in Manhattan. The Javits Center hosted an enormous glass ceiling; the symbolism would be breathtaking. It is the job of campaigns to express optimism about winning on election night, but inside the Clinton campaign, they were well aware that the Midwest had become a problem. The Comey letter hadn't moved Clinton voters away from Clinton but it did seem to be pushing disaffected Independent voters planning on voting third party to change their mind and vote for Trump (Allen and Parnes 2017, 366). Abandoning their strategy to expand the Electoral College map, the Clinton team shifted resources to Michigan and Pennsylvania. The final day of campaigning Clinton held an event in Michigan and two in Pennsylvania before wrapping up her campaign with a star-studded rally in North Carolina.

On Election night, the first signs of trouble came in Florida. Trump was outperforming Romney in the state's rural areas by big numbers, wiping out the modest gains Clinton had made improving Obama's turnout (Allen and Parnes 2017). By 11 p.m., Trump held modest leads in Michigan, Wisconsin, and Pennsylvania, and the realization that Clinton was probably going to lose the election had settled over the once jubilant crowd at the Javits Center. Footage from the room showed shocked disbelief which eventually turned into visible grief. The finger-pointing had already begun both internally within the campaign and across the nation's media outlets. It was the greatest upset in the history of American politics and everyone was scrambling to offer explanations.

In the end, Donald Trump won the presidency by carrying 30 states and 304 Electoral College votes. He hadn't just broken through the Democrat's Blue Wall, he'd shattered it. All told Trump flipped six states Obama had carried in 2012 and 2008: Michigan, Wisconsin, Ohio, Pennsylvania, Iowa, and Florida. He carried Michigan and Wisconsin by less than 1%. Remarkably, Hillary Clinton had carried the popular vote by nearly 3,000,000 votes but lost the election via the Electoral College. The last time that had happened was the controversial election of 2000, when Al Gore lost the presidency via the Electoral College while winning the popular vote by a half million votes. Election 2016 cemented its place in the history books by offering one final unprecedented event: the improbable victory of Donald J. Trump.

Since the election, many theories have been offered to explain why Hillary Clinton lost the most winnable campaign in the history of presidential elections. The Clinton team points to the Comey letter, combined with effects from the DNC and Podesta emails leaked by the Russians, as playing a decisive role in her loss. In *Shattered*, Allen and Parnes argue it was Clinton's failings as a candidate combined with a poorly run campaign plagued by internal power struggles, nepotism, and no clear chain of command. Because of its superficiality, the *Shattered* hypothesis is particularly popular in the media who need to explain complex problems via digestible soundbites.

Vice President Joe Biden argues Clinton's loss was a product of poor messaging that ignored white working-class voters and failed to incorporate enough populist angst. In an interview, Hillary Clinton argued that as a female candidate she is limited in the amount of anger it is advisable to show on the stump. A man might be able to stand up and give a fiery speech denouncing "the man" but if a woman did the same she would come off as too aggressive and unhinged.[18] The explanation offered in this research argues that Clinton's loss was a product of all of these things yet none of them, at least not individually. They are all effects, not causes. They are manifestations of a broader strategy the campaign adopted months before Election Day; a strategy that was the right one until the election results proved it to be the wrong one. To understand *why* Hillary Clinton lost the 2016 presidential election, one must look for the cause, not at effects. As such, the campaign must be examined holistically and from a wide strategic lens. The Clinton campaign made a key strategic decision at the beginning of the general election cycle that framed every other decision they made and dictated how the campaign played out on Election Day. But in order to understand why the Clinton campaign chose this particular strategy and why it ultimately failed, it is first necessary to take a deep dive into the minds of voters.

Notes

1. Kyle Kondik, Why Ohio Picks the President," *Sabato's Crystal Ball*, University of Virginia Center for Politics, http://www.centerforpolitics.org/crystalball/articles/why-ohio-picks-the-president/.
2. You can watch "The Speech" here: https://www.youtube.com/watch?v=eWynt87PaJ0.
3. Tessa Stuart, "27 Best Republican Excuses for Skipping Trump's RNC," *RollingStone*, http://www.rollingstone.com/politics/news/27-best-republican-excuses-for-skipping-trumps-rnc-w429467.
4. Peter Schroeder, "No Trump endorsement from Cruz: 'Vote your conscience'," *The Hill*, http://thehill.com/blogs/ballot-box/presidential-races/288607-no-trump-endorsement-from-cruz-who-tells-gop-vote-your.
5. Steve Turnham, "Donald Trump to Father of Fallen Soldier: 'I've Made a Lot of Sacrifices'," *ABC News*, http://abcnews.go.com/Politics/donald-trump-father-fallen-soldier-ive-made-lot/story?id=41015051.
6. Gary Langer, "Clinton Trounces Trump in Debate Reactions; Trump's Unfavorability Edges Up," *ABC News*, http://abcnews.go.com/Politics/clinton-whomps-debate-reactions-trumps-unfavorability-edges-poll/story?id=42498052.

7. "Trump and Clinton Discuss Alicia Machado," *Time*, https://www.nytimes.com/video/us/politics/100000004674290/trump-and-clinton-discuss-alicia-machado.html.
8. "Trump doubles down on former Miss Universe Alicia Machado: 'She gained a massive amount of weight'," *The Week*, http://theweek.com/speedreads/651452/trump-doubles-down-former-miss-universe-alicia-machado-gained-massive-amount-weight.
9. Ben Mathis-Lilley, "Trump Was Recorded in 2005 Bragging About Grabbing Women "by the Pussy"," *Slate*, http://www.slate.com/blogs/the_slatest/2016/10/07/donald_trump_2005_tape_i_grab_women_by_the_pussy.html.
10. David Corn, "SECRET VIDEO: Romney Tells Millionaire Donors What He REALLY Thinks of Obama Voters," *Mother Jones*, http://www.motherjones.com/politics/2012/09/secret-video-romney-private-fundraiser/.
11. Aaron Blake, "Three dozen Republicans have now called for Donald Trump to drop out," *The Washington Post*, https://www.washingtonpost.com/news/the-fix/wp/2016/10/07/the-gops-brutal-responses-to-the-new-trump-video-broken-down/?utm_term=.226dba5c8bdf.
12. Phillip Rucker and Robert Costa, "The GOP tumbles toward anarchy: 'It's every person for himself or herself'," *The Washington Post*, https://www.washingtonpost.com/politics/the-gop-tumbles-toward-anarchy-its-every-person-for-himself-or-herself/2016/10/10/31bc6d24-8f13-11e6-a6a3-d50061aa9fae_story.html?utm_term=.a3dada9526fd.
13. Lisa Mascro, "House Speaker Paul Ryan will not campaign with Trump, but still endorses him," *Los Angeles Times*, http://www.latimes.com/nation/politics/trailguide/la-na-campaign-2016-updates-morning-1476114008-htmlstory.html.
14. Neetzan Zimmerman, "Second poll declares Clinton winner of presidential debate," *The Hill*, http://thehill.com/blogs/blog-briefing-room/news/300166-second-poll-declares-clinton-winner-of-second-presidential.
15. Andrea Mitchell and Alastair Jamieson, "Trump Planned Debate 'Stunt', Invited Bill Clinton Accusers to Rattle Hillary," *NBC News*, http://www.nbcnews.com/storyline/2016-presidential-debates/trump-planned-debate-stunt-invited-bill-clinton-accusers-rattle-hillary-n663481.
16. Gregory Krieg, "Trump threatens to jail Clinton if he wins election," *CNN Politics*, http://www.cnn.com/2016/10/09/politics/eric-holder-nixon-trump-presidential-debate/index.html.
17. Meghan Keneally, Veronica Stracqualursi, Sushannah Walshe, Meredith McGraw, and Julia Jacobo, "2nd Presidential Debate: 11 Moments That Mattered," *ABC News*, http://abcnews.go.com/Politics/presidential-debate-11-moments-mattered/story?id=42687340.

18. Meghann Farnsworth, "Watch Hillary Clinton's full interview from our Code Conference," *Recode*, https://www.recode.net/2017/5/31/15716226/watch-live-hillary-clinton-code-conference-today.

References

Allen, Jonathan, and Amie Parnes. *Shattered: Inside Hillary Clinton's Doomed Campaign*. New York: Crown, 2017.

Gurian, Paul-Henri, Nathan Burroughs, Lonna Rae Atkeson, Damon Cann, and Audrey A. Haynes. "National Party Division and Divisive State Primaries in U.S. Presidential Elections, 1948–2012". *Political Behavior* 38 no. 3 (2016) 689–711. doi:10.1007/s11109-016-9332-1.

CHAPTER 7

Everybody Sucks 2016

Abstract Bitecofer uses public opinion data to analyze voters' evaluations of Clinton and Trump: the two most disliked candidates to ever run for president. When asked for the one word that best described Hillary Clinton voters overwhelmingly choose the word liar. Top words for Donald Trump include racist, idiot, and crazy. Even partisans were wary of their own party's nominee. 50% of Democrats said that Hillary Clinton made them feel angry at least some of the time while 54% of Republicans reported being afraid of their own nominee at least some of the time. The only way either of these nominees were competitive to win the White House was by running against each other.

Keywords Presidential election · Presidential primaries · Hillary Clinton Bernie Sanders · Donald Trump · Republican · Democrat

There's no sugar coating it: Voters hated both of the 2016 presidential nominees. Interspersed with Clinton and Trump lawn signs were Everybody Sucks 2016 signs, and one of the best-selling bumper stickers of the season was Giant Meteor 2016: Let's End it Already. According to *Gallup*, Donald J. Trump and Hillary Clinton are the two most disliked presidential nominees in history. Clinton ended the election with an unfavorable rating of 52%; Trump with an astounding unfavorable rating of 61%.[1] The only way either of these candidates could be competitive for the presidency was in a race against each other. Both candidates were

R. Bitecofer, *The Unprecedented 2016 Presidential Election*,
https://doi.org/10.1007/978-3-319-61976-7_7

negative on their favorable/unfavorable ratios throughout the entirety of the general election campaign, yet another unprecedented element of the 2016 presidential cycle. Clinton's average unfavorable rating between July and November was 54%, Trump's 59%. To illustrate just how bad those numbers are, President Obama's average favorable/unfavorable ratio through the same time period in his 2012 reelection was 50/45—nearly 10 points in the positive. His competitor Mitt Romney's average favorable/unfavorable ratio was 46/45. Through the entire general election cycle, Mitt Romney was negative on his net favorability in only 23 polls, Obama in just 5. As polling data from *RealClear Politics* Figs. 7.1 and 7.2 show, in the 120 days of the general election neither Hillary Clinton nor Donald Trump spent one single day positive in their net favorability.

In order to explore voters' perceptions about the two candidates, my colleagues and I administered a national survey at the start of the general election. The survey is a representative, web-based survey which includes 1504 respondents, fielded on August 28 and 29 of 2016. Along with voter preferences, the survey was designed to analyze how voters evaluated Donald Trump and Hillary Clinton in terms of their qualifications for office. As part of the survey, respondents were asked for the first word that popped into their heads when they thought of Clinton and Trump. The results are displayed as word clouds in Figs. 7.3 and 7.4. The word clouds display the top 100 words used to describe each candidate and illustrates the frequency of their use by the size of the font. The results demonstrate the overwhelmingly negative views voters had about both candidates as well as the uniformity of views regarding Hillary Clinton's character. Of the 1351 responses for Clinton, 190 of them were some variation of the word "liar." Another 105 responded with the

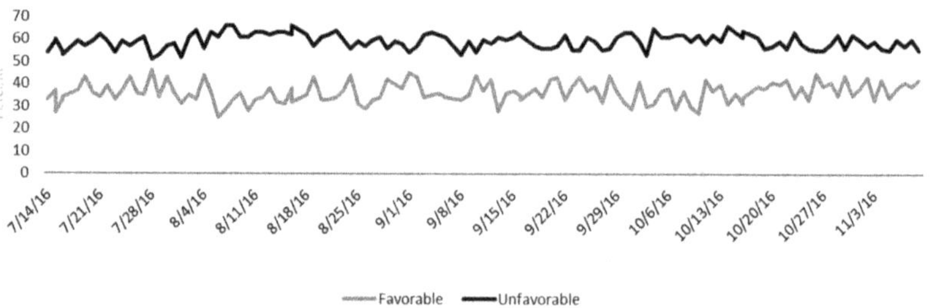

Fig. 7.1 Donald Trump favorability ratings

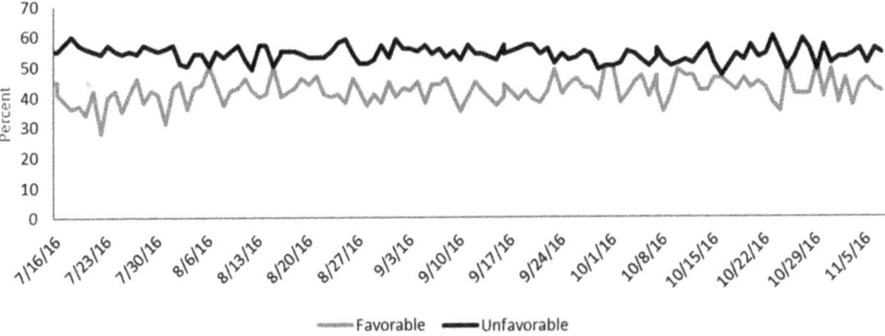

Fig. 7.2 Hillary Clinton favorability ratings

Fig. 7.3 Hillary Clinton word cloud

word "criminal." All told, 422 respondents produced words that negatively referenced Clinton's character and honesty.

Although responses for Donald Trump were more varied, they were also overwhelmingly negative with "idiot," "crazy," and "racist" all appearing in his top five mentions. The takeaway from the word cloud data is that many voters felt they faced a choice between voting for a well-qualified liar and voting for a crazy, perhaps even racist, idiot. As part of our series of presidential polls for Virginia, my Wason Center colleague and I asked Virginia voters to agree or disagree with the following

Fig. 7.4 Donald Trump word cloud

statements: Hillary Clinton cannot be trusted with classified information and Donald Trump is a racist. The results were astounding; 54% of voters said that Clinton couldn't be trusted with classified information and 53% of voters agreed that Donald Trump was a racist. Given the strong wording of the question about Trump (we asked voters to ascribe racism to the candidate not to his policies), the results were stunning.

Data from the 2016 *American National Election Survey* (ANES) reinforces findings from our survey research data regarding Americans low assessments of Hillary Clinton and Donald Trump. As seen in Fig. 7.5, 64% of respondents indicated that the phrase "Hillary Clinton is honest" did not describe her well, while 58% of respondents said the same of Donald Trump. The ANES data also reveals that nearly 60% of Americans did not find Donald Trump knowledgeable and only 27% said the phrase "Donald Trump is even-tempered" described him well. Interestingly, despite his categorization as the populist in the race, far fewer respondents thought Donald Trump cared about people (53%) compared to Hillary Clinton (63%).

Another interesting finding from the ANES data regards emotions respondents reported feeling about the two candidates. Respondents were asked about several emotions felt in response to the candidates such as proud, angry, and afraid and were asked to specify whether the

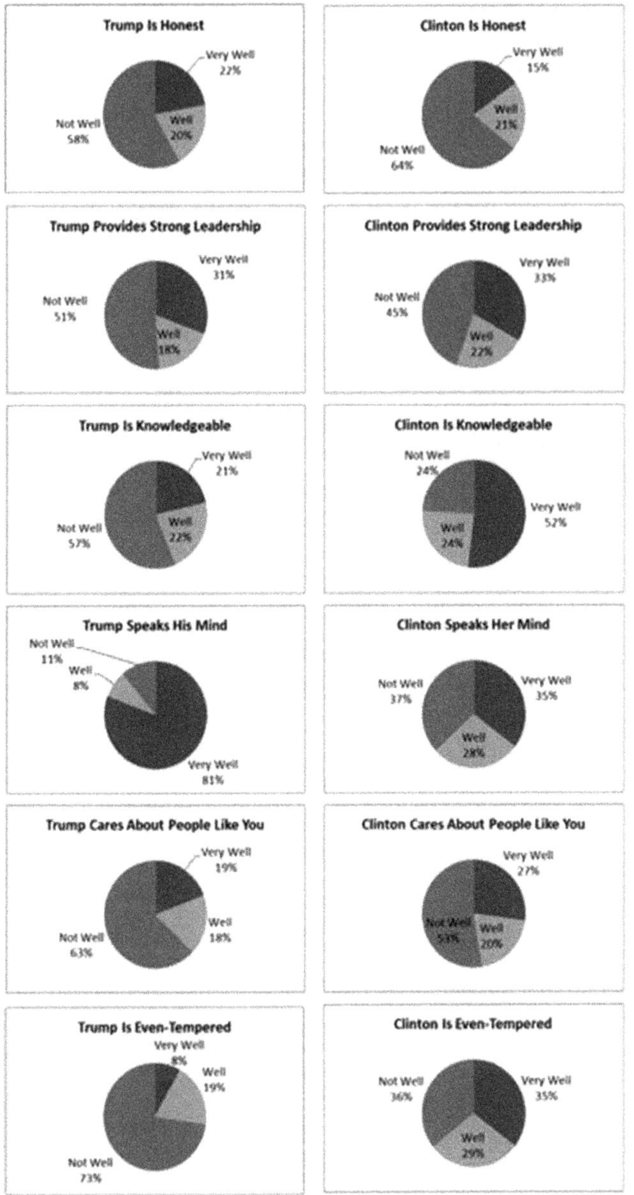

Fig. 7.5 Trump vs. Clinton candidate characteristics

candidate made them feel the emotion "never," "some of the time," "about half of the time," "most of the time," or "always." As Fig. 7.6 shows, 72% of respondents reported that Donald Trump made them feel "afraid" at least some of the time, 78% said they made him feel "angry" at least some of the time, and 82% said he made them feel "disgusted" at least some of the time. Less than 50% of respondents said he made them feel "hopeful" or "proud" at least some of the time. Views of Clinton were not much better. 62% of respondents reported she made them "afraid" at least some of the time, 71% reported she made them "angry" at least some of the time, and 68% reported feeling disgusted by Clinton at least some of the time. Clinton outperformed Trump slightly in the positive categories—earning 56% for "hopeful" and 53% for proud.

Evaluations of partisan voters of their own candidates reveal just how pervasive negative assessments of both Clinton and Trump are. Mean feeling thermometer scores of self-identified Democrats for Clinton and self-identified Republicans for Trump from the ANES were only in the 60s, surprisingly low given that partisans tend to view their own candidate quite favorably. For example, in the same survey, Obama's mean feeling thermometer score among self-identified Democrats was 76—13 points higher than Clinton's mean. In the 2012 version of the ANES, Obama's mean thermometer score from self-identified Democrats was 83, and Republican nominee Mitt Romney enjoyed a mean rating of 74 from his fellow Republicans.

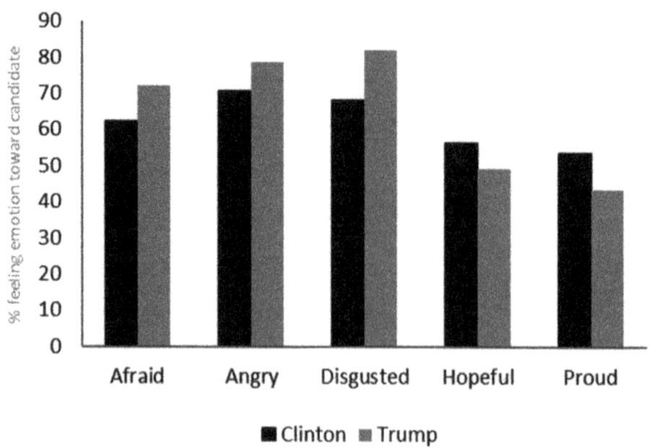

Fig. 7.6 Emotions toward 2016 nominees

Partisans also behave abnormally in 2016 when assessing their own candidate's character. When asked about Clinton's honesty, 38% of self-identified Democrats reported that the phrase "Clinton is honest" did not describe her well, and 49% of Democrats reported that she made them feel "angry" at least some of the time. On the other side of the aisle, 84% of Republicans said the phrase "he is even-tempered" described Trump poorly, and more than half of Republicans (54%) reported being afraid of their own nominee. To have such large portions of your own party's supporters afraid of you (in Trump's case) or angry at you (in Clinton's case) is unusual, to say the least. Even ideologues had deep reservations about their party's nominee. 56% of extremely liberal respondents reported that Hillary Clinton made them feel angry at least some of the time, 46% said she made them feel disgusted at least some of the time, and 39% reported she made them feel afraid at least some of the time. For Trump, 49% of extremely conservative respondents reported that Donald Trump made them feel angry at least some of the time, 40% felt afraid of him at least some of the time, and 56% felt disgusted by him at least some of the time (see Fig. 7.7). If partisans had concerns over their nominees, Independents were downright terrified. 7 out of 10 Independents reported being afraid of Donald Trump, and 6 out of 10 were angry at Hillary Clinton.

Although voters were universally negative in their assessments of the candidates' character, data from our national survey reveals a large deferential between Trump and Clinton in terms of qualification for office. As Fig. 7.8 shows, Clinton outperforms Trump on every one of the nine metrics asked about in the survey which includes questions regarding

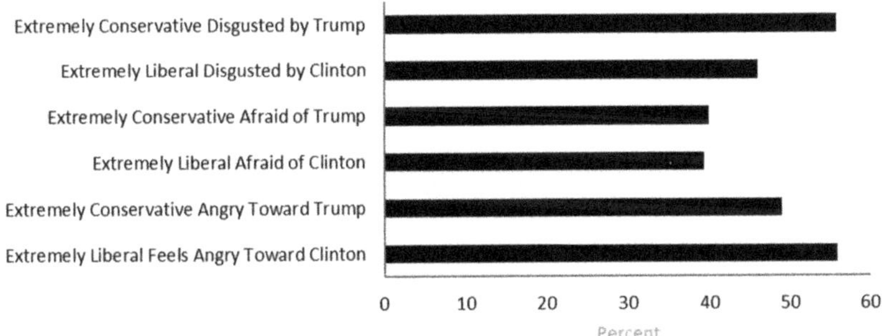

Fig. 7.7 Partisan assessments of own nominee

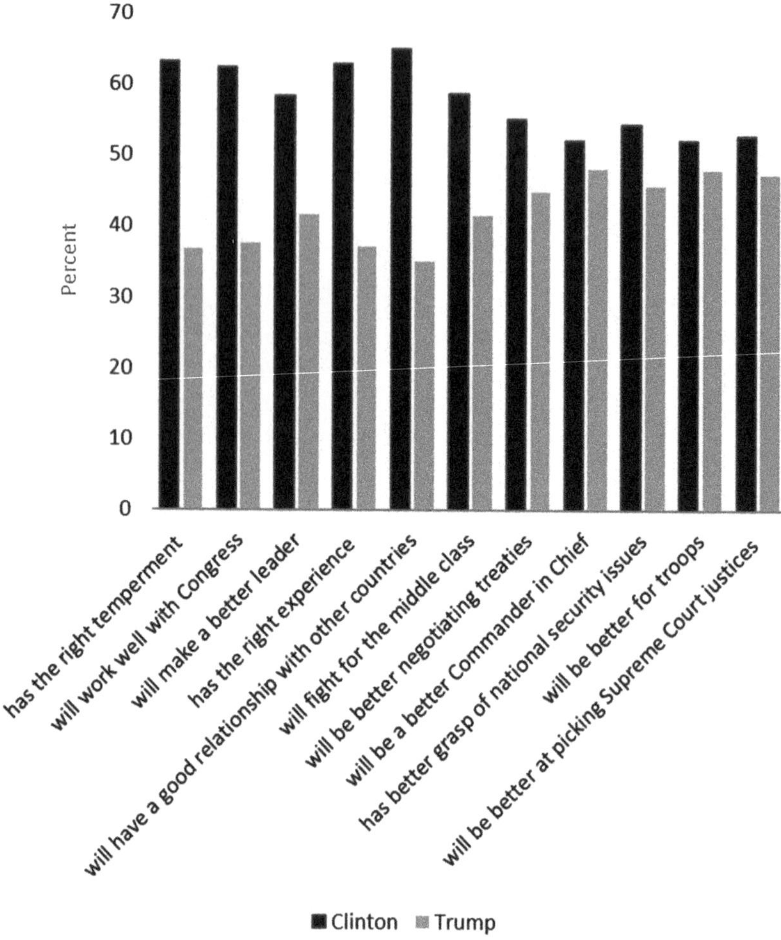

Fig. 7.8 Candidate qualifications

leadership, diplomacy, experience, temperament, grasp of national security issues, performance of the Commander-in-Chief role, and ability to negotiate treaties with other countries. For each attribute, voters were asked which candidate, Clinton or Trump, is best qualified or best suited to perform that function of the presidency. For some questions such as "who has the right experience to be president" and "who has the right temperament to be president," Clinton earns well over 60%—achievable only by drawing support from non-Democrats on that metric. Voters may have disliked Hillary Clinton and Donald Trump in nearly equal measure but clearly felt that Clinton was more qualified for office.

During the presidential primaries the media began to speculate that the unpopularity of both Clinton and Trump might encourage partisan defection. Some Bernie Sanders supporters professed to be hostile to Clinton who they viewed a part of the problem, not the solution. The 386 ANES respondents that voted for Bernie Sanders in the primary held a significantly lower mean feeling thermometer score for Clinton than Democrats who voted for Clinton: 63 points for Bernie voters compared to 76 points for Clinton voters. In most competitive primary elections the media enjoys speculating about disgruntled supporters of the losing candidate refusing to back the nominee. During the 2008 Democratic primary, there was massive speculation that disaffected Hillary Clinton voters so-called P.U.M.A.s (party unity my ass) would refuse to back Obama's general election candidacy because they felt that super delegates had been used to steal the nomination for Hillary Clinton. In the end, President Obama carried the vote of 89% of Democrats which is exactly in-line with partisan loyalty rates over the past few cycles.

Still, conditions were different in 2016. The front-runners for the nomination in both parties were uncharacteristically unpopular, the electorate usually unsettled. Media reports of the election were dominated by stories of the Never Trump movement on one side and Server Gate on the other side, and both parties were plagued with rumors of contested conventions. To get a sense of how serious the potential for third-party defection was in the electorate, my colleague and I administered a survey after the Virginia primary elections specifically designed to probe primary voters who did not support their respective party's nominee in the primary about their voting intentions for the upcoming general election.

Given the primaries were still in progress when we administered the survey in April of 2016, we expected to find some evidence of disgruntled primary voters planning to defect but overall expected that most partisans would fall in-line behind their nominee. That is exactly what we found among Democrats who voted for Bernie in the primary. Only 8% of them said they did not plan to support Hillary Clinton in the general election. The results for the Republican Party, however, were shocking; nearly 30% of Republicans who had voted for a candidate other than

Donald Trump in Virginia's Republican primary said they planned to not vote, vote for Clinton, or vote third party in the fall's general election.

As the survey was conducted during the height of the Never Trump movement, my colleague and I also included a question for Republicans as to whether they would support a contested convention to take the nomination away from Trump. This result was also surprising because nearly 30% of Republicans said they would support a contested convention. Despite the surprisingly high rates of intended defection by Republican voters who did not support Trump in the Virginia primary, my colleague and I expected that over the course of the general election, many would come home to the Republican nominee. When we began polling in late August, we were surprised to find that Virginia Republicans were still not prepared to support Donald Trump. Just 78% of Republicans indicated they would vote for their party's nominee compared to 93% of Virginia Democrats who planned to vote for Clinton. Over the course of the general election party loyalty among Republicans lagged behind their Democratic counterparts although it continued to inch up in each successive survey. In our final Virginia tracking survey which we released November 7th, Trump had managed to bring home many of his wayward partisans, increasing his share of the Republican vote to 82%. Still, this was significantly below normal party loyalty rates in Virginia. However, Virginia exit polls show that in the end, Trump earned 90% of Republican Party identifiers nationally[2] and 88% in Virginia,[3] completely in-line with other Republican nominees in the most recent election cycles. For all the unease over Trump among some Republican voters when it came time to actually enter the ballot booth and defect, Republican voters got in-line behind their party's nominee.

The public's dislike of both party's nominees is important contextually because it sets the entire context of the general election. The Clinton team knew they had a serious image problem, especially among Independent voters whose opinions of Hillary Clinton had declined sharply over the course of the Benghazi investigations. Despite anecdotal evidence of disunity in the progressive wing of the party's base, polling data found very little evidence that liberal voters would not support Clinton in the general election. Meanwhile, within the Republican electorate, there was a persistent, measurable resistance to Donald Trump. As such, the Clinton campaign saw the general election as a referendum on Donald Trump and on his brand of combative, even offensive, politics. Polls such as ours showed that Independent voters and even a small portion of Republican voters were up for grabs in 2016, and the Clinton team designed a strategy to bring them into her camp. But before we get to that, it is important to flesh out the distinctly different Trump and Clinton campaign organizations.

Notes

1. Lydia Saad, "Trump and Clinton Finish With Historically Poor Images," *Gallup*, http://www.gallup.com/poll/197231/trump-clinton-finish-historically-poor-images.aspx.
2. *Roper Center*, Cornell University, https://ropercenter.cornell.edu/polls/us-elections/how-groups-voted/groups-voted-2016/.
3. "Virginia exit poll data," *CNN Politics*, http://www.cnn.com/election/results/exit-polls/virginia/president.

CHAPTER 8

A Tale of Two Campaigns

Abstract Bitecofer conducts an examination of the Donald Trump and Hillary Clinton campaign organizations revealing a significant talent gap between the two campaign's management teams. Bitecofer shows in the 2016 presidential election the Trump campaign trailed the Clinton campaign in every metric: fund-raising, television ad buys, talent, endorsements, and infrastructure yet was victorious on Election Day. The chapter continues by analyzing the major mistakes made by each campaign and the impact they had on the race.

Keywords Presidential election · Presidential primaries · Hillary Clinton
Donald trump · Kellyanne conway · Republican · Democrat
Endorsements · Campaign advertising · Campaign money · Super pacs

With little more than a simple slogan emblazoned on thousands of red trucker hats and a charismatic and contraversial celebrity candidate, the Donald J. Trump campaign had wrangled the Republican Party's nomination away from the biggest players in Republican politics. Like a true New Yorker, he'd done it his way. However, as his primary campaign began to wind down and look toward the general election, it was clear that the Trump campaign was at a significant disadvantage in terms of talent, resources, and strategy. As part of the Republican Party's acceptance of his nomination, Trump was under pressure to professionalize his campaign team. His primary campaign manager Corey Lewandowski had

R. Bitecofer, *The Unprecedented 2016 Presidential Election*,
https://doi.org/10.1007/978-3-319-61976-7_8

little experience running a national campaign and in the party's eyes, the Trump campaign had stumbled over the nomination more than strategically maneuvered for it. Trump was also under pressure from his closest advisers, the Trump children, who disliked Lewandowski and saw him an enabler of their father's more self-destructive behaviors.

In the run-up to the convention, the Trump campaign had already hired Paul Manafort, a veteran GOP operative to oversee the delegate selection process. On June 20, 2016, Lewandowski was officially let go by the campaign,[1] and Manafort was promoted to campaign manager. The move settled Republican Party insiders who took it as a sign that Donald Trump was finally prepared to pivot for a bruising general election fight against the Clinton machine. But almost immediately, Manafort's international lobbying history and personal finances came under scrutiny and after the Republican Party removed language supporting the arming of rebels in Ukraine pressure on the campaign to fire Manafort became intense.[2] Less than two weeks from the official start of the general election, Trump fired Manafort, promoted Kellyanne Conway to campaign manager, and brought in Breitbart's chairman Steve Bannon to serve as the campaign's CEO.[3] Although an experienced strategist and pollster Conway had no experience managing campaigns, let alone a presidential campaign. Since wrapping up the nomination in May, Donald Trump had had three different campaign managers; yet another unprecedented aspect of the 2016 election.

Table 8.1 shows the leadership structure under each of the three campaign managers of the Trump campaign. During the first stage, which began when Trump first began exploring a run-in January of 2015, the campaign was run by Corey Lewandowski. Lewandowski had a thin record of electoral campaign experience. He served as a campaign manager for Senator Robert Smith's (R-NH) failed reelection bid in 2002 and as the director of Americans for Prosperity's national voter registration outfit. The talent pool of Republican campaign operatives was fairly well drained due to the size of the Republican field. Many of the Republican presidential candidates were struggling to find experienced senior staff as the most experienced operatives wanted to work with candidates that were more likely to be viable contenders for the party's nomination. Trump's candidacy was not taken seriously until he rose in the polls during the late summer of 2015. Early on, Donald Trump was also relying heavily on staffers hired out of his business *Trump International*, most of whom had no previous experience in politics.

Table 8.1 Donald Trump's evolving campaign team

Date Hired	*Name*	*Role*	*Previous Political Experience*	*Date Terminated*
Phase 1				
2/1/2015	Corey Lewandowski	Campaign Manager	Campaign Manager for failed reelection campaign of Senator Smith (NH); American for Prosperity National Voter Registration	
2/1/2015	Alan Cobb	Senior Adviser	National director of state operations for Americans for Prosperity; deputy state director of Kansas for Bob Dole's 1996 presidential campaign, senior adviser to Mike Pompeo's 2014 reelection campaign, Director of grassroots operations for the Pat Roberts (KS) 2014 reelection campaign	
2/1/2015	Roger Stone	Senior Adviser	Veteran Republican Strategist, Nixon campaign, lobbyist	8/9/2015
2/1/2015	Stuart Jolly	National Field Director	State director, Americans for Prosperity-Oklahoma, Education Freedom Alliance	4/18/2016
6/16/2015	Daniel Scavino	Director of Social Media	None	
6/16/2015	Hope Hicks	Press Secretary	None	
6/16/2015	Justin McConney	Director of New Media	None	
7/30/2015	Michael Glassner	National Political Director	Former aide to Sarah Palin in 2008 VP run, Adviser to George W. Bush 2000 campaign, Adviser Dole's 1988 and 1996 presidential campaigns	
8/25/2015	Sam Clovis	Co-Chair and Policy Adviser	Iowa Field Director for Rick Perry's campaign, conservative radio host, unsuccessful candidate for Senate	

(continued)

Table 8.1 (continued)

Date Hired	*Name*	*Role*	*Previous Political Experience*	*Date Terminated*
11/9/2015	Katrina Pierson	National Spokesperson	Unsuccessful candidate for Congress, Founder of Garland Texas Tea Party, Assisted with ted Cruz' Senate campaign	
1/1/2016	Barry Bennett	Convention Strategist	Carson campaign manager, Republican strategist and consultant	
2/25/2016	Sarah Huckabee Sanders	Senior Adviser	Daughter of Mike Huckabee, field director of his 2002 reelection campaign, field director on Bush's 2004 reelection campaign	
3/2/2016	Michael Glassner (promoted)	Deputy Campaign Manager		
3/11/2016	Ed Brookover	Senior Adviser	Senior strategist and later, campaign manager for Carson, political director for RNC, NRSC, and NRCC	8/1/2016
3/11/2016	Brian Jack	National Delegate Director	Staff Assistant RNC, political analyst American Israel Public Affairs Committee	
3/21/2016	Carter Page	Foreign Policy Adviser	None	
3/21/2016	George Papdopoulos	Foreign Policy Adviser	None	
3/21/2016	Joseph Kellog	Foreign Policy Adviser	Retired US Army general	
3/21/2016	Joseph Schmitz	Foreign Policy Adviser	None	
3/21/2016	Walid Phares	Foreign Policy Adviser	Political pundit, Romney 2012 presidential campaign	
3/28/2016	Paul Manafort	Delegate Whip, Adviser	Veteran Republican Operative, Ford, Reagan, Bush and Dole campaigns, lobbyist	

(continued)

Table 8.1 (continued)

Date Hired	*Name*	*Role*	*Previous Political Experience*	*Date Terminated*
4/13/2016	Rick Wiley	Delegate Assistance	Veteran Republican operative, Executive Director for Walker campaign, political director of RNC, executive director of Wisconsin Republican Party	5/25/2016
4/25/2016	Ken McKay	Senior Adviser	Christie Campaign, Ron Johnson campaign, Rick Scott campaign, consultant	
5/4/2016	John Mashburn	Policy Director	Pro-life policy strategist, worked with Jesse Helms, Trent Lott, Tom Delay among others	
5/19/2016	Paul Manafort (promoted)	Campaign Chair and Chief Strategist		
6/5/2016	Jim Murphy	National Political Director	Dole presidential campaign, lobbyist	
6/20/2016	Lewandowsky Fired			
Phase 2				
6/28/2016	Alan Cobb (promoted)	Director of Coalitions		
6/28/2016	Michael Abboud	Communications Coordinator	Little, but from political family in Oklahoma	
6/28/2016	Jason Miller	Senior Communications Adviser	Staff assistant to Senator Gorton, Daryl Issa's political director, Jack Ryan's Senate bid	
7/1/2016	Kellyanne Conway	Senior Adviser	Chair of pro-Cruz SuperPAC, Lutz mentee, Owner The Polling Company	
7/18/2016	Omarosa Manigault	Director of African American Relations	None	
8/17/2016	Steve Bannon	Chief Executive	Executive Chairman of Breitbart News	
8/19/2016	Paul Manafort resigns over allegations of improper contact with Russia			

(continued)

Table 8.1 (continued)

Date Hired	*Name*	*Role*	*Previous Political Experience*	*Date Terminated*
Phase 3				
8/19/2016	Kellyanne Conway (promoted)	Campaign Manager		
8/26/2016	Bill Stepien	National Field Director	Managed both of Chris Christie's gubernatorial campaigns, fired over "Bridgegate."	
9/1/2016	David Bossie	Deputy Campaign Manager	Citizens United president, director of anti-Hillary SuperPAC, considered an expert in opposition research on the Clintons	
9/26/2016	Carter Page resigns over allegations of improper contact with Russia			

One ace in Trump's sleeve in the early phase of his primary campaign was the inclusion of veteran GOP operative Roger Stone as a senior adviser. Stone had a long and storied career in Republican politics and was known for being an expert at the type of hardball politics Trump admired. Stone had helped develop Richard Nixon's "law & order" campaign theme during Nixon's 1968 successful presidential campaign. He had spent the intervening years as a major player in Republican politics and partner in the influential lobbying firm he founded with Paul Manafort, Charles Black, and Peter Kelly. Initially, Stone was attracted to Donald Trump's direct rhetorical style and helped him develop the Make America Great Again campaign slogan (recycled from Ronald Reagan's 1980 campaign) and combined it with Nixon's law and order theme. However, Trump's behavior toward Megyn Kelly at the first Republican debate, and subsequent attacks against her, frustrated Stone who saw them as distractions from Trump's messaging. Stone had confronted Donald Trump about his behavior toward Megyn Kelly which was blatantly misogynistic and attracting negative press even in conservative media outlets. Trump defended his actions and pointed to unscientific polls on the *Drudge Report* showing him as the winner of the debate as evidence that his attacks against Kelly were helping, not hurting his campaign. That evening Trump went onto *CNN* and continued to trash Kelly against Roger Stone's advice. In Stone's opinion, Lewandowski and other senior staff were "yes men" willing to let Trump destroy his own candidacy rather than challenging his behavior.[4] On August 8, 2015, Roger Stone left the campaign.

With Stone stepping away from the campaign, there was very little experience at the top of the Trump campaign. As Trump continued to rise in the polls throughout the fall, the campaign began having an easier time bringing experienced operatives on board. Despite an unconventional approach to the early primaries, Trump had a strong showing in the Iowa Caucus and absolutely dominated the New Hampshire and South Carolina primaries, and the Nevada Caucus. As his delegate count increased, he was able to pull in more talent from his former competitors as they withdrew from the race. He picked up Mike Huckabee's daughter Sarah Huckabee Sanders as press secretary and Ben Carson's campaign manager Ed Brookover as a senior strategist. Brookover had served as the political director for the Republican National Committee as well as their two congressional committees—the National Republican Senate Committee (NRSC) and the National Republican Congressional Committee (NRCC). Bringing him into the campaign established a much-needed connection to the national party. Trump also elevated Michael Glassner to Deputy Campaign Manager. Glassner had helped run Sarah Palin's vice presidential campaign and played a critical role in helping her become a national brand after leaving the Alaska governorship.[5]

As the primaries reached the halfway point and the national party began to quietly explore options for a brokered convention, Trump hired veteran Republican operative and lobbyist Paul Manafort to serve as an adviser and to oversee the campaign's efforts to seat Trump-friendly delegates in order to prevent any attempts at a coup at the party's nominating convention in July. After Ted Cruz outmaneuvered them at the Colorado Caucus, the campaign had to play catch up after largely ignoring the delegate selection process up until that point. Although technically brought into oversee the delegate selection, Manafort was also brought in as an effort to begin to professionalize the campaign in preparation for the general election. As the national party began to seriously consider Trump as the party's nominee to square off against Clinton, they began to put pressure on Donald Trump to let Lewandowski go.

The pressure to fire, Lewandowski increased heading into the summer. In the late spring, Trump committed a series of gaffes including comments accusing the judge presiding over the Trump University lawsuit of bias because of his Mexican ancestry (Judge Curiel was born in Indiana). Despite drawing widespread condemnation from fellow Republicans, including House Speaker Paul Ryan, Trump continued to assert that Judge Curiel should be removed from the case because of his ethnic heritage; which as Speaker Paul Ryan put it "is the textbook definition of racism."[6] The party, as well as Trump's children, was pressuring Trump to hire a seasoned professional to run the campaign going forward. The Trump's children saw Lewandowski as an enabler and they blamed him for Trump's inability to pivot after securing the Republican nomination in April. The campaign had already brought in Paul Manafort to whip delegates and help professionalize the campaign. Now Trump was under pressure to push Lewandowski out to allow Manafort control of the campaign.[7]

Paul Manafort, a consummate Washington Insider, butted heads with Lewandowski from the beginning. The Republican National Committee saw Manafort's hiring as a sign that despite Trump's combativeness against the party in the primary and the party's not-so-secret efforts to derail his candidacy, he was ready to assume his role as the party's leader and begin to transition his campaign so it could be competitive in the general election. Known for the premium he places on loyalty, Trump pushed back on getting rid of Lewandowski. Instead, Trump elevated Manafort to be the campaign chair and chief strategist while leaving Lewandowski as campaign manager. For a couple of months, the campaign operated under a dual leadership structure until Trump finally relented and let Lewandowski go on June 20, 2016.[8]

Despite his expertise, Paul Manafort brought a new set of issues with him to the campaign. Consulting work he'd done for a close ally of Russian President Vladimir Putin and pro-Russia Ukrainian President Viktor Yanukovych fell under scrutiny by the media.[9] As the media dug further into Manafort's past, the *Associated Press* discovered a $10 million contract between Manafort and a Russian oligarch and close friend of Putin named Oleg Deripaska.[10] Questions about Manafort's relationship with Russia continued in the weeks leading up to the convention. Manafort's ties with Russia, along with another member of the campaign, Carter Page, began to raise questions about the motivations for Trump's unusually conciliatory tone to Putin during the Republican primary.

As the party's platform committee convened at the national convention in July, things reached a fever pitch. The final platform put out by the party did not include language supporting the arming of rebels in Ukraine to fight the Russian occupation of Crimea; something foreign policy hawks in the party were keen to include. Rumors swirled that Trump's team had pushed to soften the language behind the scenes and had amended the statement from "providing lethal defensive weapons" to "providing appropriate assistance."[11] The changes to the official position on Ukraine unsettled some Republicans and became fodder for the national press; who continued to dig into Manafort's background in Eastern Europe and in Russia. After more than two months of escalating revelations, Manafort resigned from the Trump campaign on August 19, 2016. Just two weeks before the traditional start of the general election the Trump campaign was leaderless.

Given the timing Trump moved quickly, elevating Kellyanne Conway from an advisory role to his new campaign manager. Conway had joined the team in July to advise Trump on women's issues because of her background running a polling firm that conducted market research on women for corporate clients. Conway had no experience managing a major political campaign, let alone a national presidential campaign. Within days of the taking the helm, Conway proved herself to be an accomplished surrogate, representing the campaign on most of their high-profile media engagements.

Conway's strategy was to professionalize the campaign, but not the candidate. She was fond of explaining her strategy as "letting Trump be Trump" while the surrogates would play the role of the cleanup crew by explaining to the media "what Trump really meant." Over the next few weeks, a system emerged. The candidate would do an interview, say something outlandish on the stump, or tweet something controversial, and the campaign would immediately follow up with surrogates to refine the message. Conway was particularly skilled at deflection and adept at refining Trump's message into easily digestible sound bites. During the campaign, the media could not get enough of Conway, mentioning her name 7535 times between the day she assumed management of the campaign and the inaugural according to a search of the *TV News Archive*.

In terms of management of the campaign, Conway sought to address serious deficiencies in the Trump campaign's organization and infrastructure by outsourcing many functions traditionally managed internally by the campaign to the Republican National Committee. Part of this was due to necessity. The Trump campaign was months behind the Clinton campaign in terms of infrastructure and at the time, poorly resourced. On the other hand, the Republican National Committee had spent the years after Obama's 2008 campaign designing a similar, data-driven system for congressional races. The Trump campaign was able to tap the RNC's voter targeting infrastructure as well as their expansive network of volunteers and paid staff.

The Trump campaign faced other obstacles. The momentum the campaign had gained from the Republican National Convention had been squandered by Trump's feud with the Khan family. The feud, particularly Trump's insistence on continuing it even after a massive backlash, had once again left the party doubting Trump's ability to pivot. The campaign's fund-raising numbers since the primary were dismal. Federal Election Commission (FEC) disclosures for May revealed the campaign was essentially broke; they had entered the month with just over $2 million dollars cash on hand and had raised a paltry $5.6 million.[12] They would be starting the month of June with just a little over $1 million dollars in the coffers, but with a new partnership with the Republican National Committee and a costly digital fund-raising system modeled after Sanders' system designed to channel small-donor donations into the campaign. In August, just after management passed over to Conway, fund-raising improved dramatically; bringing in $90 million dollars between the campaign and its joint committees. Still, the haul was significantly less that the Clinton campaign's record-setting $143 million that month, adding to her already significant fund-raising advantage.[13] The Trump campaign would be forced to catch up quickly.

In terms of organization, the Clinton campaign team couldn't have been more different. The early momentum behind her candidacy gave her campaign access to top-tier talent, and there was no change in senior management positions between the primary election and the general election. Clinton chose Robby Mook as her campaign manager. Mook had risen to prominence as a talented Democratic Party operative through his work at the Democratic National Committee as well as his success running Terry McAuliffe's 2013 campaign for Virginia Governor, a close Clinton ally. Mook had also worked on Hillary Clinton's 2008 primary campaign as the state director for Nevada, Indiana, and Ohio; three states Clinton had carried over Obama. Along with Mook Clinton also brought in John Podesta; Bill Clinton's former Chief of Staff and Founder of the *Center for American Progress*, a liberal think tank based in D.C. to serve as the campaign's chair. Along with Mook and Podesta, Clinton also hired several Obama campaign alums including Joel Benenson who served as Obama's pollster. As shown in Table 8.2 virtually everyone serving in key positions within the campaign were veterans

Table 8.2 The Clinton campaign organization

Name	*Role*	*Previous Political Experience*	*Election*
John Podesta	Campaign Chairman	Bill's former Chief of Staff, President and Founder Center for American Progress, Counselor to Obama, Chairman of Hillary for America PAC	both
Robby Mook	Campaign Manager	Hillary Clinton 2008, Jeanne Shaheen 2008, Terry McAuliffe 2013, Executive director Democratic Congressional Campaign Committee	both
Joel Benenson	Chief Strategist and Pollster	Obama's Pollster,	both
Amanda Renteria	Political Director	Legislative aide Senator Feinstein, Chief of Staff Senator Stabenow	both
Huma Abedin	Vice Chair	Aide to Hillary Clinton as 1st Lady and Senator, Clinton 2008, Deputy Chief of Staff for Clinton Secretary of State	both
Jim Margolis	Media Adviser	Reid, Boxer, Baucus, and Warner Senate campaigns, Obama 2008 and 2012, Kerry 2004	both
Jennifer Palmieri	Communications Director	Obama's White House Communications Director, Bill Clinton White House, Edwards 2004 and 2008	both
Dennis Cheng	Finance Director	None (from Clinton Foundation)	both
Cheryl Mills	Senior Adviser	Clinton 2008, Bill Clinton White House, State Department	both
Jake Sullivan	Senior Policy Adviser	Clinton 2008, Obama 2008, Director of Policy Planning State Department, National Security Adviser to Vice President Biden	both

(continued)

Table 8.2 (continued)

Name	*Role*	*Previous Political Experience*	*Election*
Marlon Marshall	Director of State Campaigns and Political Engagement	Kerry 2004, Obama 2008, Obama 2008 and 2012, National Field Director Democratic Congressional Campaign Committee	both
Maya Harris	Senior Policy Adviser	Center for American Progress, ACLU	both
LaDavia Drane	Congressional Liaison	Obama 2008	both
Charlie Baker	Chief Administrative Officer	Democratic strategist, Senior Adviser Kerry 2004	both
Mandy Grunwald	Senior Media Consultant	Clinton 1992, Clinton 2008	both
Karen Finney	Senior Spokesperson and Strategic Communication Adviser	MSNBC Host, Director of Communications Democratic National Committee	both
Teddy Goff	Senior Digital Adviser	Obama 2008 and 2012	both
Stephanie Hannon	Chief Technology Officer	None (Former Google Executive)	both
Katie Dowd	Digital Director	Clinton State Department, Clinton Foundation	both
Jenna Lowenstein	Deputy Digital Director	Vice President of Digital Engagement Emily's List	both
Adam Parkhomenko	Director of Grassroots Engagement	Founder Ready For Hillary SuperPAC	both
Jeremy Bird	Field Consultant	Obama 2012	both
Mitch Stewart	Field Consultant	Obama 2012	both
Lori D'Orazio	Deputy Labor Campaign Director	Sanders 2016, AFL_CIO, United Auto Workers	GE Only
Michele Gilliam	Deputy Labor Campaign Director	Sanders 2016, Transport Workers Union	GE Only
Kunoor Ojha	Youth Outreach Director	Sanders 2016	GE Only

of national-level campaigns except for Clinton's most-trusted adviser Huma Abedin, whose history with Hillary Clinton came mostly from her tenure at the State Department and a close personal friendship.[14]

Recounting the formation of Clinton's campaign staff in *Shattered*, Jonathan Allen and Amie Parnes reveal that Mook had taken pains to position himself for the campaign manager position early, laying the groundwork in 2014. Although he was not the only candidate considered for the position, Mook had an important advantage; he had the endorsement of David Plouffe, President Obama's 2008 campaign manager. Despite his well-known personal dislike of Hillary, Plouffe had created a preliminary framework for Clinton which had served as a signal to other Obama alum that Clinton was the heir apparent to Obama's legacy. Mook advocated for a hybrid management structure which would funnel most of the decision-making power his way, but with Podesta's involvement, it was never clear where the chain of command ended (Allen and Parnes 2017). The issue was compounded by the influence of Clinton's longtime aide and personal friend Huma Abedin. Abedin, who Allen and Parnes write served as Clinton's gatekeeper and adviser, came to the campaign with two complications: her role in the email server scandal as Secretary Clinton's assistant as well as her marriage to former congressman Anthony Weiner whose embarrassing Twitter scandal had turned him into a national punchline. The authors describe a power struggle between Mook and Podesta as well as between Mook and Abedin which often resulted in subpar decision-making. Mook was wary of Abedin's involvement in the campaign and thought she clouded his candidate's judgment. Of course, he had no way of knowing then emails forwarded by Abedin to Weaver from Clinton's unsecured private server would surface less than two weeks before Election Day and dramatically alter the race. Although always illuminating, campaign tell-all books such as *Shattered* don't offer much insight into why a campaign won or loss. And especially for the losing campaign, these types of accounts should always be taken with a grain of salt because losing campaigns always overstate largely inconsequential issues such as clashing personalities and power struggles at the expense of elements with more profound impacts.

Although the internal power struggles and a lack of centralized decision-making almost certainly complicated things, Clinton's experienced campaign staff, along with their very experienced candidate, made few tactical errors and ran a highly effective organization. Clinton's fund-raising operation had been dominant throughout the primary. Although Sanders' campaign made headlines after earning more success than predicted, they never really came close to the fund-raising performance of the Clinton operation. At the conclusion of the primary Clinton and her supporting SuperPACs raised \$334.9 million dollars to the Sanders campaign's \$229.1 million—an advantage of more than \$100 million dollars. Although most of that advantage came from outside groups, the Clinton campaign itself also outraised the Sanders campaign by close to \$10 million dollars.[15]

For the general election, the Clinton team would face a Trump campaign that had never run a proper fund-raising operation. Trump raised just $67.1 million dollars during the primary, including a $45 million dollar loan from the candidate himself, and almost nothing from outside groups.[16] Summer fund-raising was a disaster; the campaign was essentially broke coming into August. Although they went on to raise $90 million that month as the Republican Party began to coalesce around their nominee, they had a deficit of millions, and the Clinton machine was raking in the money.

The Clinton campaign raised a staggering amount of money in August 2016 coming out of the party's convention at the end of July. At $143 million, her August haul brought in $50 million dollars more than her competitor and would be the first month of an entire cycle of fund-raising dominance. According to an analysis by *Bloomberg Politics*, using data from the Federal Election Commission Hillary Clinton would go on to raise $973.2 million dollars herself, combined with another $217.5 million dollars from SuperPACs supporting her candidacy; a combined total of $1.19 billion dollars.[17] It was the most ever raised and spent on a single candidate, although 2012 would continue to hold the record for the most expensive race ever with both President Obama and Republican challenger Mitt Romney exceeding a billion dollars.[18] As Fig. 8.1 shows, Trump's total fund-raising lagged far behind Clinton. Although Republican presidential candidates always outperformed Democratic presidential candidates in outside money, this was not the case in 2016. Clinton more than doubled Trump's SuperPAC

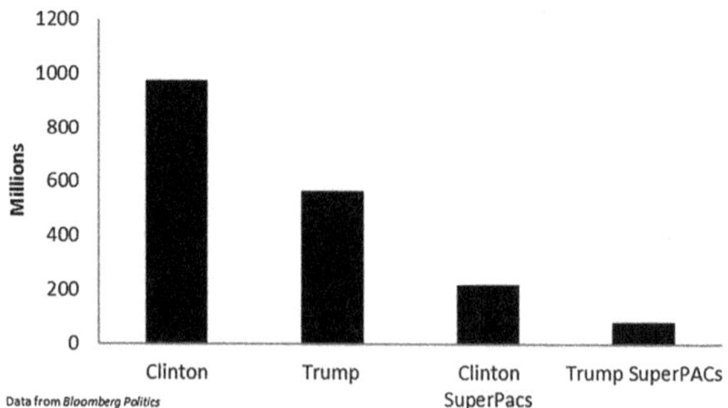

Fig. 8.1 Total fund-raising in the 2016 presidential election

support. The main SuperPAC supporting Hillary Clinton *Priorities USA Action* set a new record for fund-raising and spending by a SuperPAC since they first emerged in 2010 after the controversial *Citizens United* Supreme Court decision that legalized unlimited outside spending on elections.

Like all SuperPACs, *Priorities USA Action* raised the bulk of their money from big money donors: 89% of their donations came from just 42 people donating $1 million dollars or more.[19] A major factor in Clinton's outside spending dominance was the reluctance many big money donors had to support Trump's candidacy. One of the most prolific Republican SuperPAC donors, the Koch Brothers, led the resistance against Trump in the Republican primary[20] and declined to support him financially in the general election. Instead, they focused their attention and money on down-ticket congressional races endangered by the presence of Trump at the top of the ticket; a strategy that ended up paying huge dividends on Election Day when congressional Republicans preserved their House and Senate majorities.

The fund-raising advantage enjoyed by the Clinton campaign allowed them to dwarf Trump's campaign in terms of television advertising. Another analysis by *Bloomberg Politics* examines television ad spending using Kantar Media/CMAG data and finds that over the course of the campaign Clinton outspent Trump 3–1 on television advertising overall and outspent him every month in every state except for Colorado, Virginia, Michigan, and Wisconsin.[21] Postmortem, the decision not to go on the air in Michigan and Wisconsin surely haunts the Clinton campaign, states she lost by a combined 33,452 votes. Not only did Clinton's team elect to stay off the air in those two Rust Belt states, the Trump campaign was on the air; spending $2.4 million in Wisconsin and about $100,000 in Michigan. A report using the Kantar Media/CMAG data shows Clinton outspent Trump by more than $20 million dollars over the final two weeks of the campaign. She outspent him two to one in Ohio and Pennsylvania but lost both states soundly. She also outspent him in other key swing states like Florida and North Carolina. Unlike in previous presidential elections, ad spending had little relationship to vote share in these critical states.

The Clinton team also enjoyed a significant infrastructure advantage over the Trump campaign. After failing to build up much of an infrastructure in the primaries, the Trump campaign had to rely largely on the Republican National Committee's field operations for their voter targeting and GOTV efforts.[22] The heavy reliance on the RNC isn't uncommon for Republican presidential candidates; Romney's campaign had done so in 2012. Since the 2012 cycle, the RNC had focused sharply on building up their digital infrastructure which had failed unexpectedly on Election Day in 2012. Part of the digital upgrade involved improving their ground game capabilities which had proven their worth with surprising success in the 2014 congressional midterms. Like in 2016, the polls in 2014 had been off. Heading into Election Day, the Republicans were expected to lose several competetive Senate races. Instead, they enjoyed their second wave election of Obama's presidency picking up nine Senate seats and taking control of the Senate for the first time since 2006. Overall turnout was much lower than predicted, especially among Democratic voters. The Republican Party's newly minted GOTV strategy powered by data analytics software company i-360 had exceeded expectations, and it would only get better two years later in the 2016 presidential cycle. The technological disadvantage the Republicans had faced since 2008 was gone. The RNC was primed to help the Trump campaign mobilize their voters for the 2016 cycle.

Still, the nearly total lack of campaign infrastructure in key states like Florida and Ohio as the general election campaign began in earnest worried Republicans. The Clinton campaign was able to retain staffers in primary states that would also be battleground states.[23] Local media in swing states began to report unstaffed Trump field offices with one reporter in Colorado uncovering a twelve-year-old running a field office in Jefferson County.[24] The *Boston Globe* analyzed the two campaign's organization in New Hampshire revealing a huge discrepancy. While the Clinton campaign had 27 field offices staffed by at least 100 paid staffers the Trump campaign had just 10 with only 50 paid staffers.[25] As rumors of an understaffed Trump campaign gained steam *fivethirtyeight* conducted an analysis of the two campaigns' total infrastructure finding that the Clinton campaign had more than double the amount of field offices overall. The only two battleground states the Trump campaign out-organized the Clinton campaign in were Wisconsin and Pennsylvania, both of which would serve critical roles in Trump's victory. Like their decision to not to run television ads in those states, in hindsight the Clinton team surely regrets not devoting more infrastructure and GOVT resources to Wisconsin, Michigan, and Pennsylvania. Of course, resource allocation strategies are largely driven by polling and those states had not been competitive at any point of the general election. On average, Clinton had a 6% lead in Wisconsin and other than a brief window coming out of the Republican National Convention, Pennsylvania never got closer than 4 points. In fact, the polling so robustly favored Clinton in Wisconsin and Michigan that many political pundits were critical of the Trump campaign's decision to devote time and resources there.[26] Only after the election was it obvious to the media that the Clinton campaign was negligent for not focusing squarely on protecting the so-called Blue Wall.[27]

There was one important resource in which the Trump campaign outperformed the Clinton campaign: candidate visits. Trump's endurance on the stump was impressive, although it may also have compounded his issues with gaffes on the stump and his controversial behavior toward the traveling press corp. Trump was everywhere; sometimes holding 3 large-venue rallies a day. The day before Election Day he held 5 rallies (Sarasota, Florida, Raleigh, North Carolina, Scranton, Pennsylvania, Manchester, New Hampshire, and Grand Rapids, Michigan) in front of some 33,000 voters[28] (incidentally, he would go on to win all five of those states). Figures 8.2 and 8.3 show just how to dominate Trump was in terms of campaign appearances. Between August 1st and Election Day, Trump held 120 campaign rallies while Hillary Clinton held just 47. The two campaigns also differed in where they chose to send their candidates. While Clinton's visits were clustered almost entirely in the most competitive swing states, the Trump campaign sent their candidate to a broader array of states including safe Republican states like Texas and Mississippi and even solidly blue Oregon.

Data from Fair Vote, Visualization generated for author by Keith Russel and Associates

Fig. 8.2 Donald Trump campaign events (8/1/16–11/7/16)

Fig. 8.3 Hillary Clinton campaign events (8/1/16–11/7/16)

The Clinton campaign's disadvantage in campaign appearances largely disappears once appearances by big name surrogates are factored in. As seen in Fig. 8.4, while Trump was able to deploy his vice presidential pick Mike Pence, he had virtually no other nationally recognized campaign surrogates to help him on the stump. Meanwhile, the Clinton campaign was introducing a new term to the American politics vernacular: super surrogates. Although her own vice presidential pick didn't fall into the super surrogate category, Clinton had three surrogates at her disposal who were more popular than the candidate herself and who had national profiles. Along with Senator Elizabeth Warren Hillary Clinton had President Barack Obama, First Lady Michelle Obama, and former opponent Bernie Sanders stump for her; drawing large crowds wherever they went. Deploying her team of surrogates, Clinton was able to campaign in multiple swing states simultaneously. Donald Trump was infatiguable, but he was also only one person (see Fig. 8.5).

In addition to these important differences between the two campaigns, they also differed in terms of the amount of mistakes they made, as well as the types of mistakes they made. Every presidential candidate and their campaign make mistakes. Some mistakes are apparent in real time. Others only reveal themselves in hindsight. Some famous mistakes made by earlier presidential candidates include Michael Dukakis' response to a question about the death penalty at one of the 1988 presidential debates. A well-known and vocal-death penalty opponent, Dukakis was asked, "Governor, if Kitty Dukakis were raped and murdered would you favor an irrevocable death penalty for the killer?" Dukakis' matter-of-fact

Fig. 8.4 Donald Trump and Mike Pence campaign events (8/1/16–11/7/16)

Fig. 8.5 Hillary Clinton and her "Super Surrogates" campaign events (8/1/16–11/7/16)

no, and immediate launch into his prepared answer on the death penalty struck viewers as dispassionate, an image the candidate was already battling (Burton et al. 2015: 171).[29] Another famous debate mistake was the mannerisms of Al Gore in his first debate against George W. Bush in the 2000 election. At several points in the debate, Gore signed heavily in response to claims made by Bush and even rolled his eyes once or twice. Although such behavior may seem inconsequential after the 2016 presidential debates, at the time it was seen as rude, and by some voters, immature and helped Bush gain momentum.

Not all mistakes come from debates. They are often made at fund-raisers with party elites and exposed by opposition researchers tasked with surveilling the opponent. During the 2008 election, Barack Obama tried to explain small-town Pennsylvanians to a group of wealthy donors at a fund-raiser in San Francisco. Attempting to explain eroding support from white working-class rural voters for the Democratic Party he said, "|y|ou go into these smalls towns…the jobs have been gone for 25 years and nothings replaced them…|a|nd it's not surprising then that they get bitter they cling to guns, or religion, or antipathy toward people who aren't like them…"[30] Those comments elicited quick reprisals from his opponent John McCain and particularly from vice presidential nominee Sarah Palin.[31] In fact, they would haunt him for the entire course of his presidency.

The 2012 cycle also produced a major fundraiser gaffe, this time for Republican candidate Mitt Romney. Recorded surreptitiously by a bartender Romney made this comment to a room full of wealthy donors: "|t|here are 47% of the people who will vote for the president no matter what … who are dependent upon government, who believe that they are victims. … These are people who pay no income tax. … and so my job is not to worry about those people. I'll never convince them that they should take personal responsibility and care for their lives."[32] The video, recorded in May but released in September, became the focal point of the Obama campaign's strategy against Romney. Both the Obama and Romney gaffes were devastating because they reinforced perfectly the narratives their opponents were attempting to paint of them. For Obama, it was the idea that he was a liberal elitist, a godless, Ivy-league educated celebrity who looks down at middle-America.[33] For Romney, it was that he was a heartless capitalist and out of touch of average Americans.[34]

Sometimes candidates say things that don't create an obvious issue at the time but can be weaponized by the opposition via cherry picking; using the comment without the context. Perhaps the most famous example of this comes from the 2004 presidential election between incumbent President George W. Bush and Democratic Party challenger John Kerry. Asked at a town hall to explain why he changed his vote between the initial version on new spending for the Iraq War and the final version of the bill Kerry said, "I actually did vote for the $87 billion before I voted against it."[35] The line would go on to be featured in campaign ads framing Kerry as a flip-flopper[36]; a theme so effective that many delegates at the Republican convention brought flip-flops they waved in the air at every mention of Kerry's name. As campaign consultants have learned how effective cherry picking is, especially in order to mobilize their own partisan base, the practice has become more common. In 2012 Republican ads featured this quote from President Obama: "If you've got a business—you didn't build that. Somebody else made that happen."[37] The statement seemed to affirm every negative perception conservatives have of liberals and reinforced the frame Republicans were constructing of Obama as anti-business and anti-individualism. Of course, the statement was part of a larger statement, which when included changes the statement's meaning considerably. The full statement said, "If you were successful, somebody along the line gave you some help. There was a great teacher somewhere in your life. Somebody helped to create this unbelievable American system that we have that allowed you to thrive. Somebody invested in roads and bridges. If you've got a business—you didn't build that. Somebody else made that happen. The Internet didn't get invented on its own. Government research created the Internet so that all the companies could make money off the Internet."[38]

Republicans are not the only ones eager to exploit a comment taken out of context. During the 2nd debate in the 2012 election, Mitt Romney was asked to respond to a question regarding the level of gender diversity of his corporate boards. In defending his record on gender diversity Romney made this innocent statement, "I had the chance to pull together a cabinet, and all the applicants seemed to be men… I went to a number of women's groups and said, 'Can you help us find folks?' and they brought us whole binders full of women."[39] Democrats widely mocked the statement leading it to become a part of political pop culture; even appearing as a Jeopardy category in 2015. Cherrypicked statements are hard to prevent. Almost anything from the traditional stump sounds ominous when plucked out of a larger statement. Technology, low civic knowledge in the overall electorate, and an ideological base thirsty for "red meat" have made the use of such techniques commonplace.

Of course, not all mistakes are made by the candidate and not all are internal mistakes. Sometimes mistakes are products of external events outside of the control of the candidate or their campaign. The economy might implode two months before the election, an untimely terrorist attack might cause the electorate to focus on issues that favor your opponent, or the Russian government may interfere in the election to help your opponent. What turns external events into campaign mistakes are the ways in which the campaigns respond to them. In the 2008 election John McCain decided to suspend his campaign to return to Washington D.C. for a high-profile meeting at the White House to determine how the government should respond to the collapsing banking system. McCain made a big show of the suspension and the campaign framed the decision as an example of McCain putting "Country First," the campaign's slogan. The Obama campaign responded by getting their own candidate, also a sitting senator, a seat at the table too. Both campaigns urged the media be invited to cover the meeting. The optics could not have come out worse for the McCain campaign. Stronger on foreign policy issues, within minutes, it was clear that McCain was out of his element trying to assess the complex financial aspects of the economic collapse. Through the course of the meeting, McCain was passive, more an observer than a participant. However, the junior senator from Illinois was in his element; coming off as competent and prepared. McCain had set up the entire situation to show the American people that unlike his opponent, he was ready on Day 1. Instead, it was Obama, not McCain that came out of the meeting looking presidential and receiving positive media coverage.[40] Not only had McCain looked out of his element, he had managed to neutralize his most important advantage over Obama: preparation for office. For the first time, the American people could really picture the young, first-term senator being president and the entire event had been purposely orchestrated by his opponent's campaign.

There is no such thing as a perfect campaign. Invariably, mistakes will be made. Talented staffers will later prove problematic. Commercials will be aired that fall flat or even backfire completely. Campaign resources will be deployed to the wrong state. Mistakes, forced and unforced errors, and strategic miscalculations tend to be fairly evenly distributed between presidential campaigns. Professionalized candidates running professionalized campaigns don't tend to make many mistakes and the ones they do make tend to be offset over the course of the campaign by their opponent's mistakes.

Unlike most presidential campaigns, there was no parity between the Clinton and Trump campaigns in terms of mistakes. In preparation for this book, I kept Google docs for both campaigns documenting the mistakes made by each candidate and their campaign over the course of both the primaries and the general election. By the time, the general election season hit full stride at the beginning of September right after Labor Day, the Trump mistake list already dwarfed the Clinton list, and many of the mistakes were made by the candidate himself. Table 8.3 shows the full list of mistakes made by the Trump and Clinton campaigns. On top of the many inappropriate comments and tweets made by Donald Trump, Trump's campaign made several strategic mistakes. First on the list is the influence Donald Trump gave members of his immediate family. Each skilled in business but inexperienced in politics and public service like their father, none of the Trump children had any experience in electoral politics. As such, they were unqualified to advise their father in that capacity and should never have been part of the campaign management team. Even when family members do bring experience to the

Table 8.3 Campaign mistakes

Trump Campaign General Election Mistakes	*Clinton Campaign General Election Mistakes*
Candidate's use of twitter w/o vetting	Failure to prepare for hacked email dumps
Attacks on Judge Curiel	Vice presidential pick/persuasion strategy
Family involvement with campaign	Keeping Deborah Wasserman-Schultz as DNC head
Botched vice president rollout	Ignoring Trump's scandals (Trump University and Trump Foundation)
Failure to vet Melania's convention speech	Decision to hide pneumonia diagnosis
Ted Cruz speech at convention	"Basket of deplorables" statement
Back row seating of host state's delegation	Vice presidential debate strategy
Attacks on Khan family	Bill's Obamacare gaffe
Promotion of violence at rallies	Failure to address Clinton's image issues
Failure to prepare for first debate	Not adjusting to defense posture after Comey letter
Response to Lester Holt's question about birtherism at first debate	Not preparing an acceptable answer for email server question
Debate two Bill Clinton stunt	
Suspicious physical	
Second Amendment remedy comments	
Supportive comments about Putin	
Attacks on Paul Ryan and Mitch McConnell	
The immigration pivot head fake	
Debate two Bill Clinton stunt	
Falling for Clinton's Alicia Machado trap	
Losing all 3 debates	
Calling integrity of elections into question	
Contacts with Russians	

table, it is best not to include them because their proximity and emotional ties to the candidate tends to cloud their judgment and make them more prone to mistakes. A great example of this is Bill Clinton's direct involvement in Hillary's 2008 run. Not only was Bill an ineffective surrogate for Clinton on the stump (he often caused more harm than help) his involvement in the management of the campaign contributed to the high level of infighting that plagued the campaign. Hillary Clinton did not make this mistake twice; Bill was kept away from the campaign as much as possible and only relied on as a surrogate sparingly for her 2016 run. Even with his limited role, he still committed an important gaffe on the stump that may have negatively affected the campaign in the closing weeks when he was caught on film seeming to call Obamacare "the craziest thing in the world" and "a disaster" (he was referring to the fact that only low-income workers can access the subsidies while middle-income Americans have to shoulder the whole cost of their premiums) but the cherrypicked version of the statement reinforced the Republican Party's narrative against Obamacare.[41]

Another major mistake made by the Trump campaign was the rollout of their vice presidential pick. The rollout was badly executed. Instead of building suspense as was intended, Trump's indecisiveness made the rollout chaotic and resulted in the pick being leaked to the media. Reportedly, the leaking of his choice to the media led Trump to briefly reconsider selecting Pence.[42] Over the course of a few days, the messaging from the campaign fluctuated wildly; moving from a short list of three to a long list of ten, then five, and then maybe two. Aides were telling the press that a decision had been made only to have the president simultaneously telling the media that he was still undecided.[43] Twitter feeds from Washington reporters such as Robert Costa gave a play by play that seemed to move from certainty about Pence then back into uncertainty as rumors swirled about family infighting over the pick. Citing "unnamed sources" reports alleged that Trump favored Newt Gingrich but was being pressured by his son-in-law Jared Kushner to pick Mike Pence.[44] Reporters camped out at in front of the Indiana Secretary of State's office to see if Mike Pence would show up in time for that day's deadline to remove himself from the Indiana ballot for his reelection campaign from governor. Trump finally announces (via Twitter, of course) his selection of Pence for Vice President at 10:50am on July 15th to little fanfare.[45]

Also, included in the Trump campaign's list are the two major mistakes at the Republican National Convention previously highlighted: the decision to give Ted Cruz a speaking role and then failing to vet his speech and the use of language taken from Michelle Obama's 2008 convention speech for Melania Trump's 2016 speech. The party conventions are meant to serve as coming-out parties for the nominees. Extensive planning goes into the convention with a careful eye toward how the convention will come across to a television audience. Mistakes at conventions are exceedingly rare and are usually the result of some unforeseen complication. Both of these mistakes were completely preventable (there should never be a speech given by the candidate or campaign's surrogates that is not vetted first!) and turned what should be a week of stage-managed headlines for the candidate and for the party into controversies the media pounced on. An additional mistake was the sitting of Ohio's delegation in the back of the convention hall in order to get back at Governor Kasich. Had Trump lost Ohio his treatment of the Ohio delegation would almost certainly have come under scrutiny.

Another mistake was Trump's partial pivot on immigration reform, which produced a couple of a curious couple of weeks in August, right as Kellyanne Conway took over the campaign. It started on August 20th when Trump met with the newly convened *National Hispanic Advisory Council*. Rumors leaked that during the meeting Trump had hinted that he was open to some form of legal status for non-criminal illegal immigrants. The Trump team pushed back on the rumors, but the rumors gained steamed because of changes in Trump's tone and rhetoric toward immigration suddenly found their way into his stump speech. This was followed by a media interview in which Kellyanne Conway answered the interviewer's question regarding the candidate's support for a deportation force by saying it was "too be determined." Combined with the rumors and softened tone, Conway's comments set off a flurry of negative coverage in right-wing outlets leading to widespread speculation that Trump planned to turn his back on hard-line immigration reform proponents. Campaign surrogates pushed back, assuring voters that nothing had changed regarding Trump's position on immigration.[46]

On August 31st Trump traveled Mexico, ostensibly to pressure Mexican President Enrique Peña Nieto on the border wall. The public portions of the visit went smoothly, concluding with a subdued joint press conference with Peña Nieto in which both claimed to be looking forward to their partnership should Trump prevail in the election.[47] When reporters asked Donald Trump if they had discussed who would pay for the wall, Trump responded that it "hadn't come up."[48] Facing swift backlash he told his supporters that actually, he had delivered an ultimatum on paying for the wall to the Mexican president. Peña Nieto quickly refuted the claim saying he had made it clear to Trump that Mexico would not be paying for the wall. [49] The trip to Mexico was scheduled to conclude with an event in Phoenix, Arizona that was billed as a speech on immigration. Given the softening rhetoric, the rumors of a pivot, and Trump's decision to avoid discussing the border wall in his meeting with Peña Nieto political observers expected the Arizona speech would be the coming out party for a refined, less divisive immigration position that would be more palatable to a general election audience. The choice of Phoenix, Arizona for the speech was seen as the perfect staging for revealing a softened approach.

Speaking to a crowd of thousands at the Phoenix Convention Hall, Trump opened the speech with kind words toward Peña Nieto, noting their discussion of what Trump characterized as his great love for the people of Mexico and an acknowledgment of the close relationship the U.S. and Mexico. He then went on to characterize the current immigration system as one that serves the interests of "wealthy donors, political activists, and powerful politicians" over the interests of average Americans. He framed opposition to comprehensive immigration reform as stemming from "decent, patriotic people from all backgrounds" concerned about their "jobs, wages, housing, schools, tax bills, and living conditions." Here was the pivot everyone was waiting for. Trump would soften his tone if not his policies. Ten minutes later as Trump was announcing his plans to create a Mass Deportation Task Force within Immigration Control Enforcement (ICE), the media was scratching their heads. Why spend more than two weeks softening your tone (to the great dismay of your most ardent supporters) only to double down on the harsh rhetoric in a prime-time speech carried live by every cable news channel?

The Trump campaign was also committed mistakes that were related to external events. Certainly, the most notable of these was the *Access Hollywood* video. As noted earlier, the *Access Hollywood* video was an unmitigated disaster for Donald Trump; leading to withdrawn endorsements and new fuel to the fire about the sexual assault allegations that first arose in *The New York Times* during the Republican Primary. Trump's response to the video was dismissive, certainly nothing one would expect from a political candidate. And the mistake culminated with the campaign's decision to bring women from Bill Clinton's past to the second presidential debate to rattle Hillary Clinton which resonated with the Republican base but no one else.

Another external event mistake was the timing of the Trump University lawsuit, which after years of litigation was finally moving toward a court date. Instead of doing everything he could to keep the lawsuit out of the national headlines (such as settling the suit before running for president), Trump ensured blanket coverage of the lawsuit in May by publically attacking the federal judge overseeing the case after the judge refused to dismiss the case.[50] Trump accused the judge of incompetence, arguing to anyone who would listen that the judge's decision was biased because of his Mexican ancestry. As noted earlier, the comments were met with condemnation by his fellow Republicans and were used by his competitor as yet more evidence that Donald Trump was unfit to be president. Although candidates cannot control external events, they can control how they respond to them and for both of these events; Trump's response caused additional headaches for his campaign.

Finally, there are the mistakes made by the candidate himself; mistakes no other candidate seeking to be a serious contender for a major elected office would ever dare make. In the annals of history, there is no candidate that comes close to being comparable to Donald J. Trump. Although charismatic, Trump's style of communication, rhetoric, and behavior presents a sharp depature from presidential candidates of the past. Any one of Trump's controversies should have ended his candidacy and would have certainly done so for any of his Republican opponents. Despite these mistakes, Trump won first the Republican primary and then the general election but he won despite himself, not because of himself. Given the resonance of his populist message, the preference of the electorate for an outsider who could bring change, and his celebrity if Donald Trump had behaved in a more traditional and refined manner it is quite possible that he would have won the popular vote along with the Electoral College.

The Clinton campaign also made mistakes; the most consequential of which was only obvious in hindsight and will be examined in the next chapter. The most egregious mistake Clinton herself made was a direct result of a mistake made by her campaign team. On September 9th while speaking at a fundraiser (where else?!) Clinton made this statement, "I know there are only 60 days left to make our case—and don't get complacent, don't see the latest outrageous, offensive, inappropriate comment and think, well, he's done this time. We are living in a volatile political environment. You know, to just be grossly generalistic [sic], you could put half of Trump's supporters into what I call the basket of deplorables. Right? The racist, sexist, homophobic, xenophobic, Islamaphobic—you name it. And unfortunately there are people like that. And he has lifted them up. He has given voice to their websites that used to only have 11,000 people—now 11 million. He tweets and retweets their offensive hateful mean-spirited rhetoric. Now, some of those folks—they are irredeemable, but thankfully they are not America."[51]

The comments came in the middle of a two-week period in which Clinton seemed to be under the weather. Her voice, often strained from the rigor of the stump, turned downright raspy. She had developed a cough. Trump began to attack Clinton over her stamina on the stump, boasting about his own endurance and tendency to sleep only a few hours a night. Of course, all this did was invite media attention into the strange circumstances surrounding his own medical records (see Table 8.3). The Trump campaign seized on Clinton's so-called "basket of deplorables" comment, telling his supporters that Clinton found them to be deplorable, unredeemable people. Like Clinton's "woman cards" during the primary after Trump accused her of using her gender to advance her candidacy "basket of deplorables" became a rallying cry among Trump supporters. It was the perfect narrative to push back on Clinton's attacks against Trump and to seize the moral high ground.

Two days later on September 11th at the service at the 9/11 memorial Clinton suddenly disappeared. Video emerged of Clinton being whisked into her SUV, appearing to stumble as she got in.[52] The media tracked her to daughter Chelsea's apartment and camped out. Speculation was wild, especially on right-wing media sites like *Breitbart*, which had published numerous conspiracy stories about Clinton's supposed health issues ever since a fall in 2012 during her tenure as Secretary of State caused by dehydration which had resulted in a concussion.[53] Clinton had testified at the first Benghazi hearing while still recovering from that concussion, a grueling process in the best of health.

Nevertheless, right-wing conspiracy sites had spent the intervening years propagating conspiracy theories about her health, including that she had sustained permanent brain damage.

The incident finally forced the Clinton campaign to disclose what they should have disclosed a week earlier: Hillary Clinton had pneumonia. She would need a couple of days off of campaigning to give the antibiotics time to kick in. Given the persistent rumors of poor health being propagated via conservative media and the attacks by Trump on her stamina, the decision to hide the pneumonia diagnosis and keep her on the campaign trail is baffling; especially coming from a team of seasoned professionals. To be sure, the decision to hide the diagnosis and have her power through was motivated by a consideration that every woman reading this will relate to. As the first female presidential nominee taking sick days would be seen as weakness and the campaign was no doubt trying to avoid negative headlines. That being said, the way they chose to handle the situation not only led to a week of problematic headlines culminating in her well-documented episode at the memorial, it almost certainly contributed to her deplorable gaffe at the fundraiser.

Another unforced error was the failure of her campaign team to prepare her for the most inevitable debate/interview question in history: was her use of a private email server a mistake? There was only ever one right answer to that question, and the Clinton team either failed to convince her to give it or they failed to prep her to give it. Either way, the mistake falls on the campaign team. Although she had been cleared of legal ramifications for her use of a private email server during the beginning of her term as Secretary of State, she had been sternly admonished by FBI Director James Comey about the incidental transmission of some data that would retroactively be determined to contain classified information. Clinton had never believed the scrutiny she received from the private server was fair, let alone the calls from some Republicans to imprison her for it. A campaign strategist's job is to convince the candidate to do things they do not want to do when doing so is in their best interests. Instead, her team indulged her; allowing her to go first through the Democratic primary and then into the general election giving the response she wanted to give rather than the response she needed to give.

As such, whenever she was asked about the server, she tended to respond with complex explanations defending why she used the server before conceding that she "wished she hadn't used a private server."[54] Not only was the explanation too long, it was not sufficiently supplicant. Right or wrong, what the public demanded was contrition, not excuses. Voters wanted Clinton to throw herself on their mercy and ask for forgiveness, and the campaign team's job was to convince her it was the only path forward.

Despite the fact that their candidate was only slightly less disliked than Donald Trump, the Clinton team did almost nothing to address her public image issues. Aside from the effort at the convention to personalize her, the general election strategy completely ignored Clinton's considerable negatives; banking on the fact that Donald Trump's were worse. This was a major strategic mistake and highlights the blind spot Clinton's inner circle had toward their candidate who they, of course, liked immensely. In the summer before the election, the Clinton team should have been focused on a national rebranding of Hillary Clinton. Her image issues were twofold. Perceptions of her character had been severely eroded via the Benghazi investigations, and the Clinton campaign should have made an effort to refocus the narrative of her time as Secretary of State which by that time had been reduced to her response to the attacks in Libya and her reliance on a private server. But Clinton also had a major branding issue within the progressive wing of the Democratic base and the campaign made little effort to address it. Instead, they ignored the issue until the final weeks of the general election and then relied on a few campaign events by Bernie Sanders to erase months of residual anger and suspicion.

Of course, the Clinton campaign faced something never seen before in American politics: a coordinated attack by a hostile foreign enemy. The Russian attacks on the Clinton campaign were bold and executed perfectly. Although at the writing of this book there has not been evidence that they were able to invade voting systems to change votes, their activities almost certainly had effects on voting behavior. Discontent among Bernie Sanders supporters was exasperated by the release of the DNC emails and as revealed later, fake news planted by the Russians. The Russian attacks were also preventable. In September of 2015, FBI Special Agent Adrian Hawkins left a message at the Democratic National Committee to inform them that they had been hacked by a Russian cyber espionage team; the FBI had nicknamed "The Dukes." The message was received by a low-level staffer, who made a half-hearted investigation into the system but otherwise, failed to follow up on it.[55]

"The Dukes" spent the next seven months mining data from the DNC; including thousands of internal emails. They also went after other targets, including Clinton campaign chair John Podesta whose account was compromised after a staffer forwarded a phishing email;

giving it an aura of authenticity.[56] The White House was informed of the attacks as well as concerns that associates of the Trump campaign were having suspicious contacts with Russian agents. Although the White House didn't exactly sit on the reports (the attacks against the DNC were disclosed to the media), they also didn't pursue them with gusto. After eight years in office, the president had grown weary of endless attacks questioning his motives. A ten-minute chance run-in on a tarmac between Bill Clinton and then Attorney General Loretta Lynch had been turned into a scandal of epic portions. President Obama knew that an aggressive response to the Russian hacking would be framed by Republicans as an effort to "steal" the election, and he had no appetite for the fight. Of course, President Obama was also banking on Hillary Clinton's victory. Like most members of the political class, Trump's victory seemed impossible after months of outlandish, offensive behavior that left him consistently behind in the polls. Investigations would be opened, but discreetly. Despite informing Congress about additional emails in the server investigation, Director Comey did not inform Congress of an on-going counterintelligence investigation into the Trump campaign's possible collusion with the Russian government and the information was not leaked to the public, at least not then.

The Russians weaponized the emails they stole from Podesta and the DNC and deployed them strategically to inflict damage on Clinton.[57] They made use of WikiLeaks, long an enemy of the U.S. government, to disseminate the emails. As previously discussed, the first release was timed for the start of the Democratic National Convention and designed to increase disunity between the party and the Clinton campaign and disaffected Bernie Sanders supporters. In mid-October, WikiLeaks began to release emails stolen from Podesta; claiming to have thousands and promising to release them bit by bit over the next few years. The Podesta releases were mostly geared toward getting the headlines off of Trump's *Access Hollywood* scandal, sowing distrust among key staffers in the Clinton campaign by revealing office gossip and depressing Clinton's support among Sanders supporters[58] Although any effect from the email releases cannot be independently measured it almost certainly exasperated tensions that already existed between the mainstream of the party and the progressive wing. Of course, there was nothing the Clinton campaign could do to prevent the releases, but there were steps they could have taken to reduce their impact. Despite the inevitability of the releases the campaign chose to be reactive rather than proactive, waiting until the release before the convention to push Debbie Wasserman-Shultz out failing to get ahead of information that was bound to come out from the Podesta emails. In sports, the best offense is a good defense. In politics, the best offense is never playing defense. By failing to get out ahead of the email leaks the Clinton campaign allowed the Russian saboteurs control of the narrative and perhaps more importantly, the timing of the release of damaging information.

Notes

1. Maggie Haberman, Alexander Burns, and Ashley Parker, "Donald Trump Fires Corey Lewandowski, His Campaign Manager," *The New York Times*, https://www.nytimes.com/2016/06/21/us/politics/corey-lewandowski-donald-trump.html.
2. Nolan D. McCaskillm Alex Isenstadt, and Shane Goldmacher, "Paul Manafort resigns from Trump campaign," *Politico*, http://www.politico.com/story/2016/08/paul-manafort-resigns-from-trump-campaign-227197.
3. Peter Jacobs and Mazwll Tani, "Donald Trump reshuffles campaign, names Breitbart chairman acting CEO," *Business Insider*, http://www.businessinsider.com/steve-bannon-kellyanne-conway-donald-trump-campaign-managers-2016-8.
4. Marc Cuputo, "Sources: Roger Stone quit, wasn't fired by Trump in campaign shakeup," *Politico*, http://www.politico.com/story/2015/08/sources-roger-stone-quit-wasnt-fired-by-donald-trump-in-campaign-shakeup-121177.
5. For data on Trump's campaign team see https://ballotpedia.org/Donald_Trump_presidential_campaign_staff_hiring_timeline,_2016.
6. Heather Caygle, "Ryan: Trump's comments 'textbook definition' of racism," *Politico*, http://www.politico.com/story/2016/06/paul-ryan-trump-judge-223991.
7. Meghan Keneally, "Reviewing ex-manager Paul Manafort's rise and fall in the Trump campaign," *ABC News*, http://abcnews.go.com/Politics/reviewing-manager-paul-manaforts-rise-fall-trump-campaign/story?id=46304065.
8. For data on Trump's campaign team see https://ballotpedia.org/Donald_Trump_presidential_campaign_key_staff_and_advisors,_2016.
9. Brian Naylor, "Meet Paul Manafort, The Washington Insider Running Trump's Campaign," *NPR*, http://www.npr.org/2016/07/16/486085582/meet-paul-manafort-the-washington-insider-running-trumps-campaign.

10. Meghan Keneally, "Ex-Trump campaign manager Paul Manafort had multimillion-dollar contract with Russian oligarch, AP says," *ABC News*, http://abcnews.go.com/Politics/trump-campaign-manager-paul-manafort-multimillion-dollar-contract/story?id=46297528.
11. Josh Rogin, "Trump campaign guts GOP's anti-Russia stance on Ukraine," *The Washington Post*, https://www.washingtonpost.com/opinions/global-opinions/trump-campaign-guts-gops-anti-russia-stance-on-ukraine/2016/07/18/98adb3b0-4cf3-11e6-a7d8-13d06b37f256_story.html?utm_term=.07014e5380e8.
12. View Trump's FEC filing here http://docquery.fec.gov/cgi-bin/forms/C00580100/1079423/.
13. Louis Nelson, "Trump raises $90 million in August, trailing Clinton," *Politico*, http://www.politico.com/story/2016/09/trump-august-fundraising-totals-227847.
14. Data for Clinton campaign staff here https://ballotpedia.org/Hillary_Clinton_presidential_campaign_key_staff_and_advisors,_2016.
15. "Which Presidential Candidates Are Winning the Money Race," *The New York Times*, https://www.nytimes.com/interactive/2016/us/elections/election-2016-campaign-money-race.html.
16. https://www.nytimes.com/interactive/2016/us/elections/election-2016-campaign-money-race.html.
17. Bill Allison, Mira Rojanasakul, and Brittany Harris, "Tracking the 2016 Presidential Money Race," Bloomberg Politics, https://www.bloomberg.com/politics/graphics/2016-presidential-campaign-fundraising/july/public/index.html.
18. Kenneth P. Vogel, Dave Levinthal, and Tarini Parti, "Obama, Romney both topped $1B," *Politico,* http://www.politico.com/story/2012/12/barack-obama-mitt-romney-both-topped-1-billion-in-2012-084737.
19. Paul Blumenthal, "Hillary Clinton's Super PAC Has Raised More Money Than Any Super PAC Ever Nearly all of the money has come from seven-figure donors.," *HuffPost*, http://www.huffingtonpost.com/entry/hillary-clinton-super-pac_us_5812833ce4b0990edc303558.
20. Katie Forster, "Koch brothers lead billionaire resistance against Donald Trump," *Independent*, http://www.independent.co.uk/news/world/americas/koch-brothers-donald-trump-clash-resistance-conservative-billionaires-network-us-president-charles-a7560706.html.
21. Ken Goldstein, John McCormick, and Andre Tartar, "Candidates Make Last Ditch Ad Spending Push Across 14-State Electoral Map," *Bloomberg Politics*, https://www.bloomberg.com/politics/graphics/2016-presidential-campaign-tv-ads/.

22. David A. Graham,"There Is No Trump Campaign," *The Atlantic*, https://www.theatlantic.com/politics/archive/2016/06/there-is-no-trump-campaign/486380/.
23. Kenneth P. Vogel, Ben Schreckinger, and Eli Stokols, "Trump campaign in disarray," *Politico,* http://www.politico.com/story/2016/04/donald-trump-campaign-staff-disarray-221557.
24. Naomi Lim, "Meet the 12-year-old behind Trump's campaign in Jefferson County, Colorado," *Politico*, http://www.cnn.com/2016/08/22/politics/weston-imer-12-year-old-donald-trump-campaign-colorado/index.html.
25. James Pindell, "Clinton's N.H. infrastructure dwarfs Trump's operation," *Boston Globe*, https://www.bostonglobe.com/metro/2016/10/27/clinton-operation-leaves-trump-dust/2J1SufLUOx472FsKIJnpTN/story.html.
26. John Cassidy, "Why Is Donald Trump in Michigan and Wisconsin?" *The New Yorker*, http://www.newyorker.com/news/john-cassidy/why-is-donald-trump-in-michigan-and-wisconsin.
27. Edward-Issac Dovre, "How Clinton lost Michigan—and blew the election," *Politico,* http://www.politico.com/story/2016/12/michigan-hillary-clinton-trump-232547.
28. Data from Fairvote Candidate Tracker http://www.fairvote.org/presidential_tracker.
29. Nia-Malika Henderson, "8 unforgettable presidential debate blunders," *CNN Politics*, http://www.cnn.com/2016/09/26/politics/presidential-debate-mistakes-history/index.html.
30. Mayhill Fowler, "Obama: No Surprise That Hard-Pressed Pennsylvanians Turn Bitter," *HuffPost*, http://www.huffingtonpost.com/mayhill-fowler/obama-no-surprise-that-ha_b_96188.html.
31. Jeff Zeleny, "Opponents Call Obama Remarks 'Out of Touch'," *The New York Times*, http://www.nytimes.com/2008/04/12/us/politics/12campaign.html.
32. View Mitt Romney's 47% comment here https://www.youtube.com/watch?v=M2gvY2wqI7M.
33. View john McCain's Celebrity commercial here https://www.youtube.com/watch?v=KOrmOvHysdU.
34. Brett LoGiurato, "This Devastating New Obama Ad Uses Mitt Romney's '47 Percent' Comments As A Soundtrack," *Business Insider*, http://www.businessinsider.com/obama-ad-47-percent-romney-singing-campaign-middle-class-2012-9.
35. See the John Kerry gaffe here https://www.youtube.com/watch?v=esUTn6L0UDU.

36. See the Kerry flip-flopper ad here https://www.youtube.com/watch?v=pbdzMLk9wHQ.
37. See Romney's "You Didn't Build That" commercial here https://www.youtube.com/watch?v=Z83oQ3d-BgQ.
38. *Fact Check*, http://www.factcheck.org/2012/07/you-didnt-build-that-uncut-and-unedited/.
39. See Mitt Romney's "binders full of women" statement here https://www.youtube.com/watch?v=OX_AN4w3da8.
40. Henry Paulson Jr.,"When Mr. McCain Came to Washington Inside the White House meeting where Obama called McCain's bluff: 'I could see Obama chuckling'," *The Wall Street Journal*, https://www.wsj.com/articles/SB10001424052748704022804575041280125257648.
41. Froma Harrop, "No, Bill Clinton Did Not Call Obamacare Crazy'," *RealClear Politics*, https://www.realclearpolitics.com/articles/2016/10/27/no_bill_clinton_did_not_call_obamacare_crazy_132167.html.
42. Kelly O'Donnell, "Trump Wavered on Pence Pick After News Leaked: Sources," *NBC News*, http://www.nbcnews.com/politics/2016-election/trump-wavered-pence-pick-after-news-leaked-sources-n610651.
43. Zeke J. Miller, and Alex Altman, "Behind The Scenes Drama as Donald Trump Picks Mike Pence," *Time*, http://time.com/4409330/donald-trump-mike-pence-vice-president-2/.
44. Stephen Collinson, "Trump pick shows power of family brain trust," *CNN*, http://www.cnn.com/2016/07/14/politics/donald-trump-mike-pence-vice-president-children/index.html.
45. Amber Philips, "The craziest 24 h of Donald Trump's campaign so far," *The Washington Post*, https://www.washingtonpost.com/news/the-fix/wp/2016/07/15/the-craziest-24-hours-in-donald-trumps-campaign-so-far/?utm_term=.4901d27a6fcf.
46. Ben Kamisar,"Trump's immigration pivot: A timeline," *The Hill* http://thehill.com/blogs/ballot-box/presidential-races/293313-trumps-immigration-pivot-a-timeline.
47. Joshua Partlow, Sean Sullivan, and Jose DelReal, "After subdued trip to Mexico, Trump talks tough on immigration in Phoenix," *The Washington Post*, https://www.washingtonpost.com/politics/trump-lands-in-mexico-for-last-minute-meeting-with-president-pena-nieto/2016/08/31/6e1a9f8c-6f8f-11e6-8533-6b0b0ded0253_story.html?utm_term=.0c215b34b26c.
48. Candace Smith, Morgan Winsor, and Meghan Keneally, "Trump Says He 'Didn't Discuss' Border Wall Payment With Mexican President," *ABC News*, http://abcnews.go.com/Politics/donald-trump-holds-joint-press-conference-mexican-president/story?id=41770165.

49. "Stephen Collinson and Jeremy Diamond, "Mexican president disputes Trump over border wall payment discussion," *CNN Politics*, http://www.cnn.com/2016/08/30/politics/donald-trump-enrique-pea-nieto-mexico/index.html.
50. "Donald Trump Attacks Federal Judge Involved In Trump University Case," All Things Considered, *NPR* http://www.npr.org/2016/05/31/480183253/donald-trump-attacks-federal-judge-involved-in-trump-university-case.
51. Angie Drobnic Holan, "In Context: Hillary Clinton and the 'basket of deplorables'," *Politifact*, http://www.politifact.com/truth-o-meter/article/2016/sep/11/context-hillary-clinton-basket-deplorables/.
52. Ian Schwartz, "RAW: Clinton Stumbles And Falls, Escorted Into Van After Abruptly Leaving 9/11 Memorial," *RealClear Politics*, https://www.realclearpolitics.com/video/2016/09/11/video_clinton_stumbles_and_falls_escorted_into_van_after_abruptly_leaving_911_memorial.html.
53. Mark Mazzetti and Michael Gordan, "Clinton is Recovering from Pneumonia," *The New York Times*, http://www.nytimes.com/2012/12/16/us/politics/hillary-clinton-concussion.html.
54. Mike Lyons, "On defense: Questions for Clinton and Trump at CINC forum," *The Hill*, http://thehill.com/blogs/pundits-blog/defense/294528-on-defense-questions-for-clinton-and-trump-at-cinc-forum.
55. Eric Lipton, David Sanger, and Scott Shane, "The Perfect Weapon: How Russian Cyber power Invaded the U.S.," *The New York Times*, https://www.nytimes.com/2016/12/13/us/politics/russia-hack-election-dnc.html.
56. https://www.nytimes.com/2016/12/13/us/politics/russia-hack-election-dnc.html?_r=0.
57. https://www.nytimes.com/2016/12/13/us/politics/russia-hack-election-dnc.htm?_r=0l.
58. Tara McKelvey, "WikiLeaks email hack shows Clinton aides infighting," *BBC News*, http://www.bbc.com/news/world-us-canada-37614486.

References

Allen, Jonathan, and Amie Parnes. *Shattered: Inside Hillary Clinton's Doomed Campaign*. New York: Crown, 2017.

Burton, Michael John., William J. Miller, and Daniel M. Shea. *Campaign Craft: The Strategies, Tactics, and Art of Political Campaign Management*. Santa Barbara, CA: Praeger, 2015.

CHAPTER 9

What (Really) Happened

Abstract Bitecofer demonstrates that the Clinton campaign's choice to prioritize a persuasion electoral strategy over a base mobilization strategy in the 2016 presidential election cost Hillary Clinton the election. The nomination of Donald Trump by the Republican Party presented the Clinton campaign with a unique opportunity to court Independent voters and disaffected Republicans. Their persuasion approach was cemented with the selection of Tim Kaine, a centrist senator from Virginia, over progressive firebrand Senator Elizabeth Warren. The Clinton campaign structured their entire campaign message as a referendum on Donald Trump's fitness for office. Not only did their strategy fail to win over Independents but it also further isolated many Bernie Sanders voters who defected in large numbers to cast ballots for third-party and write-in candidates.

Keywords Presidential election · Presidential primaries · Hillary Clinton Bernie Sanders · Donald Trump · Republican · Democrat Defection · Third party · Tim Kaine · Persuasion · Mobilization

In order to explain why the Clinton campaign came up short on Election Day, it is important to move beyond singular aspects of the campaign and look instead at the campaign's overall strategic approach. Campaign

R. Bitecofer, *The Unprecedented 2016 Presidential Election*,
https://doi.org/10.1007/978-3-319-61976-7_9

visits, resource allocation, and ad buys are all tactics used to execute a broader strategy. Most explanations offered to explain the results of the 2016 presidential election focus purely on tactics. While tactics are certainly important and can have substantial impacts on campaigns, they should never be mistaken for strategy. Tactics without an overarching strategy produce suboptimal outcomes. Campaigns need a strategic framework through which they decide what tactics to use to win the campaign. Campaign strategy involves decisions about which issues to emphasize, what positions to take on issues, how to attack the opposition, and how to optimally allocate resources (Sides et al. 2015). When I advise candidates running for political office, the first question I ask them is are you interested in running for office or winning office. Tactics are what you use to run for office, strategy is what you need to win office.

Coming into June 2016, the Clinton campaign was in an enviable position. Never in her wildest dreams did Hillary Clinton expect to be gearing up for a general election contest against Donald Trump. No doubt when considering this moment since leaving the Obama administration, she expected to be competing against Jeb Bush, Chris Christie, or perhaps Marco Rubio. Maybe they would get really lucky and draw Ted Cruz; a right-wing ideologue with limited appeal in the broader electorate and whom even his own Republican colleagues in the Senate disliked. As the Democratic Party's nominee, Clinton would enter the 2016 race with a embedded disadvantage: third term incumbency fatigue. After eight years of a Democratic president, voters may be predisposed to prefer the Republican nominee to make a change. As Donald Trump's dominance in the polls in the Republican primary demonstrated staying power, the Clinton team must have felt like they had won the lottery. The nomination of Donald Trump by the Republican Party would open a wide path to the White House for Hillary Clinton. Not since Bill Clinton's reelection campaign in 1996 had the Democratic Party started off the general election with as strong an advantage. Yes, Clinton's reputation had been severely damaged by the email server scandal, but her opponent had scandals of his own such as the Trump University lawsuit and the Trump Foundation scandal, not to mention his behavioral issues. After watching her favorability ratings collapse from the 60s to the high 40s over the course of 2015, the Clinton campaign knew she had a likability issues. But there was one person the electorate liked even less, and he was at the top of the other party's ticket.

Over the two months since wrapping up the Democratic primary the campaign had been considering the best strategic approach for the general election. The American electorate is comprised of two types of voters: partisan voters that need to be mobilized to turn out to vote on Election Day and reliable non-partisan voters who show up at the ballot box for every election, but must be persuaded to support your candidate over the opponent. Unfortunately, the same things that mobilize base voters to turnout to vote can negatively impact a campaign's ability to attract persuadable voters. Base voters need to be mobilized with ideological issue positions and strident rhetoric known as "red meat" against the opposition. Persuasion voters are looking for moderation in both tone and temperament. These voters tend to get turned off by the very same campaign tactics that excite the party's base. Every candidate in a competitive general election faces this conundrum and must develop a strategic plan that accounts for both types of voters.

To read Johnathon Allen and Amie Parne's Clinton campaign tell-all book *Shattered: Inside Hillary Clinton's Doomed Campaign*, the Clinton campaign stumbled into their pick of Tim Kaine, a senator from Virginia, as their pick for vice president. According to the authors, the decision ultimately came down to synergy; Hillary wanted a partner that would be compatible in terms of policy and pragmatism. Tim Kaine had a reputation as an amiable Democrat; well respected by most of his Republican colleagues and extremely popular in his home state of Virginia which at the time of the decision was still a battleground state. Also under consideration was Elizabeth Warren, who proved her loyalty by endorsing Clinton over Sanders in early May and then hitting the stump hard for the campaign. Warren quickly proved to be an effective attack dog, going hard after Donald Trump in both her stump speech and via Trump's favorite medium Twitter. Although selecting Elizabeth Warren would help shore up support among progressives who supported Bernie Sanders in the primary, it wasn't clear that she would always have Clinton's back in the way that Joe Biden had faithfully served President Obama. Like many politicians, Clinton placed a high premium on loyalty and she just wasn't sure she could fully trust Warren.

While these aspects about the vice presidential pick were surely considered, the decision to pick Tim Kaine was motivated by strategy not assessments of loyalty. Picking Tim Kaine was a product of the campaign's decision to try to capitalize on the Republican Party's nomination of Donald Trump. Despite growing ideological polarization in

American politics, the nomination of Trump presented what was almost surely a once in a lifetime opportunity for Democrats. Coming out of June 2016, *fivethirtyeight's* presidential forecasting model gave Clinton a nearly 70% chance of beating Donald Trump in the general election. Their forecasting model, like others, depends largely on polling data, although *fivethirtyeight* also offered a more nuanced model that also considered historical external factors shown to affect presidential vote outcomes such as the state of the economy. Even the more nuanced model showed Clinton as a heavy favorite, and the Clinton campaign was certain of two things: Trump wouldn't be making the pivot Republicans were hoping for, and he would continue to generate controversy.

State-level polls in competitive states were even more reassuring. While Clinton had many paths to the 270 Electoral College votes she needed to win the White House, Trump only had a few, and all of them required him to flip several Obama states just to become competitive. Outside of the Republican base, few Americans saw Donald Trump as qualified to be president. Never before had a party put forth a nominee the majority of Americans saw as behaviorally and temperamentally unfit to hold the office. As demonstrated in Chap. 6, even self-identified Republicans had deep reservations about Trump. Of course, these same voters were no fans of Clinton. Some downright hated her. She was the second most disliked nominee in history, beaten only by her opponent. Still, in survey after survey, one theme was consistent: Voters saw her as well-qualified for the presidency.

The campaign knew they had a problem with the progressive wing of the party's base. There would be bridge building efforts of course, but the campaign believed that the specter of a Trump presidency would be motivation enough to bring these voters back into the fold. The Clinton campaign had a rare opportunity to not only win the presidential election, but to do so in a landslide large enough to win back the Senate and severely erode the Republican majority in the House of Representatives. All they needed was the right electoral strategy; one that would bring in Independents and maybe even draw in some college-educated white Republican women. Disaffected Republicans were looking for justification to defect from the Republican ticket, and the Clinton team's strategy needed to make them feel safe to do so. They were offended by Trump but more than a little wary of Clinton. Her favorability ratings among Independents mirrored those of Republican identifiers. Those that couldn't be pulled over might at least be pushed into voting for one of the two conservative third-party candidates: Gary Johnson or Evan McMullin. In order to avoid further frustrating progressive voters by triangulating back to the center on issues, the Clinton campaign structured their persuasion messaging almost entirely on their opponent. They would make the election a referendum on one thing: Donald J. Trump.

Like all nominees before them, Clinton and Trump would face tough decisions regarding who to select as their running mate. The vice presidential selection is used strategically to achieve different goals (the first of which should always be to do no harm). It can be used to “balance” the ticket in terms of experience or ideology. Mitt Romney’s selection of Paul Ryan in 2012 allowed the ticket to pull in disaffected Republican base voters who had fought hard to direct the nomination away from Romney to a more conservative candidate during the primaries. Ryan’s reputation as a budget hawk satisfied conservatives but Ryan was also of the establishment, someone who would not drive away Independents. When Barack Obama selected Joe Biden as his running mate in 2008, he wasn’t only looking for chemistry, he was looking for someone seasoned to balance out the experience differential between himself and John McCain. Meanwhile, McCain’s selection of Sarah Palin, then a completely unknown governor of Alaska, was motivated by a desire to offset the historic nature of Obama’s nomination as well as to add energy to an otherwise boring ticket. The selection of Dick Cheney by Texas Governor George W. Bush in 2000 was made to buff up the ticket’s foreign policy credentials as they ran against an incumbent vice president. In 1992, Bill Clinton’s selection of Al Gore was unorthodox. Rather than picking a running mate that brought something to the ticket that Clinton himself lacked, his selection of Tennessee Senator Al Gore was a double down. The Democratic Party’s ticket would be made up not just of one, but of two southern white moderate males. It was a pure persuasion strategy aimed at recapturing white working-class voters who had drifted over to the Republican Party during the Reagan years. Dubbed the Clinton Model (Sides et al. 2015, 140), Bill Clinton’s persuasion strategy won Democrat’s the largest share of white voters since Carter’s 1976 election and almost certainly led to his victory.

For the Trump campaign, the running mate needed to bring political experience to the ticket and be free of scandal. More importantly, the pick needed to be willing to tolerate the nominee’s antics. A number of prominent Republicans such as Governors John Kasich and Nikki Haley were quick to take their own names out of consideration.[1] Both of Trump’s initial top picks came with complications. Chris Christie and Newt Gingrich had supported Trump much more quickly than other establishment Republicans. Christie endorsed Trump after exiting the race at the end of February, stumping with him at the same time the Never Trump movement was emerging.[2] But Christie was bogged down in his own scandal over his role in shutting down the lanes on the George Washington Bridge over a political feud with the mayor of Fort Lee.[3] He was also disliked by Trump's son-in-law Jared Kushner because he had successfully prosecuted Kushner's father when he was a U.S. district attorney.[4] Gingrich was another possibility. As a former Speaker of the House, Gingrich brought needed experience to the ticket but he would also bring more confrontational politics and controversies for the campaign to defend.

Also under consideration was Governor Mike Pence of Indiana. Pence was attractive because he was a strident social conservative likely to bring in those evangelicals who supported Cruz over Trump in the Republican primary. The presence of Pence on the ticket sent a signal to the Republican base that Trump was not just giving lip service to socially conservative policies, while also signaling to the Republican Party establishment that he was willing to work with them on a conservative agenda despite his sometimes inconsistent positions. Pence was also attractive because his mild-mannered Midwestern demeanor was the polar opposite of Donald Trump's grandiloquent style. Pence was also a skilled deflector, capable of defending his running mate without creating new headaches. For Pence, joining a ticket that was seen by many as certain to fail and perhaps even be career suicide accomplished two things. First, it allowed him to avoid running for reelection in Indiana. Though not upside down on his favorable/unfavorable ratings, Pence wasn't particularly popular[5] and was likely to face a tough challenge from a well-financed Democrat because of his controversial support of a religious freedom law that had briefly led to massive corporate boycotts and backlash in Indiana until it was amended a few months later to include language explicitly prohibiting discrimination based on sexual orientation.[6] Joining Trump's ticket, even if it failed, brought another advantage: It would give Pence the national profile needed to launch his own bid for president in 2020. Besides, if they somehow won the race, Pence would be second in line to the presidency behind a man who seemed predisposed for self-destruction. Altogether, not a bad place to be.

For the Clinton campaign, the selection of Hillary Clinton's running mate was more complex. First and foremost, the running mate needed to be likable to offset Clinton's serious image issues. With the pick of her running mate, the Clinton team would cement which general election strategy, persuasion or base mobilization, would be their predominant approach. Under the persuasion approach, the Clinton team needed a moderate running mate with a reputation for collegiately and bipartisanship. They had the perfect candidate in mind: Tim Kaine of Virginia. A former governor of Virginia and a current senator, Kaine was universally liked and enjoyed strong favorability ratings. At the time of the selection, Virginia was a critical swing state. After years of choosing Republicans on the presidential ballot, Virginia had broken for the Democrats for the first time in decades in 2008 when Obama won the state handily and again in his 2012 reelection. The Democrats were keen on keeping Virginia blue, and the elevation of Tim Kaine onto the ticket was certain to help them achieve that goal. Despite being a sitting senator, Kaine's seat offered another important advantage: The vacancy would be filled by appointment by the Democratic governor and close Clinton ally Terry McAuliffe which would allow a new Democrat to run for the seat as the incumbent in the 2018 cycle.

The other option was to use the selection of Clinton's running mate to prioritize their base mobilization efforts and reach out to disaffected Bernie Sanders voters. At the end of the primary calendar, the Democratic base was deeply divided. Despite the fact that Hillary Clinton had already secured the pledged delegates she needed to win the nomination Bernie Sanders refused to concede; promising his supporters he would fight all the way to the convention floor. Sanders' refusal to drop out of the race and gracefully concede angered the Clinton team but there wasn't much they could do about, especially because of Hillary Clinton's own refusal to concede to Obama until the floor of the convention during the 2008 primary. However, once off the campaign trail passions cooled and the Sanders campaign abandoned their contested convention plans. Bernie Sanders officially endorsed Hillary Clinton on July 12, two weeks before the start of Democratic National Convention.[7]

Although turnout in the Democratic primary exceeded turnout in the Republican primary as it usually does, there was evidence that the Republican base was far more energized than the Democratic Party's base. Donald Trump received more votes in the Republican primary than any other Republican in history. Turnout on the Republican side increased significantly over its 2008 and 2012 numbers, coming in at

14.8% up from 9.8% in 2012 and 11% in 2008. Overall total primary turnout was lower than 2008, the last time both parties had open primaries (28.5% compared to 30.4) but still very strong. However, strong turnout was driven by increased turnout on the Republican side, Democratic turnout decreased by 5% from its 2008 rate.[8] Some voters were "Feeling the Bern" but there was little evidence of a revolution brewing in the party's turnout data.

Given the enthusiasm gap and the populist nature of Trump's candidacy, the vice presidential pick could be used to select a progressive Democratic to excite the progressive wing of the Democratic base. The Clinton team had several strong options for running mates with solid progressive bona fides. They could go with Sanders himself, but the fact that he was a self-described socialist made him a dangerous pick despite his popularity with progressives and millennials because both make up only small portions of the overall electorate. Bernie Sanders enjoyed high favorability ratings throughout the presidential primaries, but he had also never faced a negative ad blitz. With Sanders on the ticket, the Republicans would make his embrace of socialism a major issue. Elizabeth Warren would be a better pick because she was just as liberal as Bernie Sanders but was also seen as a more mainstream Democrat; especially after her endorsement of Clinton over Sanders as the primaries wrapped up in June.[9] If Clinton was the consummate Washington Insider Warren was the consummate outsider, despite her status as a sitting senator. Over her tenure in the Senate, she had given President Obama grief over Wall Street friendly legislation and cabinet picks. When assessing her as a running mate, Clinton feared that Warren's ideological rigidity might cause her to undercut Clinton if the policies she advanced were not progressive enough. Hillary wanted to be sure her vice president would have her back the way that Joe Biden had covered faithfully Obama's even when he disagreed with him (Allen and Parnes 2017).

Another option was Cory Booker, the junior senator from New Jersey. Although less well known to the broader electorate, Booker was well-liked by the progressive wing of the party and brought with him a compelling personal narrative from his time serving as the mayor of Newark. During his tenure as mayor, Corey Booker developed a reputation as a "man of the people." He had fought hard to win the mayor's office from a political machine, winning on his second attempt and a documentary had been made to chronicle his first try. He had also once run into his neighbor's burning house to carry his constituent to safety.[10] Booker offered another advantage: Not only was he a progressive Democrat, he was also an African American. His selection could galvanize progressives while simultaneously encouraging African American voters to keep up the record high turnout that helped elect Obama twice.

Finally, the campaign could go with Senator Sherrod Brown of Ohio. Senator Brown offered two advantages. Most importantly, Brown won and kept his Ohio Senate seat by embracing anti-free trade economic populism that was especially attractive to Rust Belt voters (as well as Bernie Sanders voters). Sherrod Brown had long been a vocal opponent of NAFTA and had fought hard against President Obama's efforts to approve the TPP trade deal. As a Midwesterner and sitting senator in Ohio, Brown would also give the Clinton campaign an important advantage in the most critical of swing states as well as shore up the Blue Wall of Wisconsin, Michigan, and Pennsylvania who together gave the Democrats a massive structural advantage in the Electoral College.

Ironically, all of the people on Clinton's short list of progressive running mates came with the same complication and it was an important one. As they were all sitting senators, pulling one to join the presidential ticket could leave the Democrats short a Senate seat in an election cycle where control of the chamber was up for grabs and may well come down to a tie to be broken by the vice president. Even the most generous forecasting models gave the Democrats just 50 Senate seats. This complication was most problematic for Sherrod Brown. Picking Brown meant that Ohio's Republican Governor John Kasich would fill the seat with a Republican and perhaps cost the Democrats their chance at a Senate majority. On top of that, the trend of Ohio toward the Republican Party could mean losing that critical state for the long term. Picking Cory Booker presented a similar conundrum. Although down to his final year in office, Republican Governor Chris Christie would choose Booker's replacement, again costing the Democrats possible control of the Senate, at least through the next election.

Only two candidates on the short list could be pulled from the Senate without costing the Democratic Party an opportunity to take back their Senate majority: Elizabeth Warren and Tim Kaine. Although Massachusetts was also controlled by a Republican governor, state law there requires a special election to fill the seat. Still, elevating Warren wasn't without some risk because of Massachusetts' habit of electing Republicans to statewide office. Despite going for Barack Obama by 23 points in 2012 and nearly 26 points in 2008, solidly blue Massachusetts had elected two Republicans to statewide offices during the same time period: Scott Brown to the Senate in a 2010 special election (the first Tea Party victory) and Charlie Baker as governor in 2014. Before becoming the 2012 Republican nominee Mitt Romney also served as governor in Massachusetts from 2003 to 2007. Pulling Elizabeth Warren to join the ticket meant no guarantee the seat would stay with the Democrats. This wasn't an issue for Tim Kaine. Virginia's Democratic governor would fill the seat with a Democrat. By picking Kaine, Democrats preserved their chances to control the Senate. Ultimately, the decision came down to Kaine or Warren; Persuasion or base mobilization. Picking Elizabeth Warren would isolate moderates and right-leaning Independents, effectively ending the campaign's hopes to expand the Electoral College map and perhaps costing the party gains in the Senate. What the campaign couldn't know was that by not picking Warren and prioritizing outreach to the middle of the electorate, they were further isolating the progressive wing of the party's base and cementing a loss on Election Day.

On July 23, just two days before the start of the Democratic National Convention, Hillary Clinton announced her selection of Senator Tim Kaine of Virginia as her running mate. Despite attempts to brand him as a progressive Democrat, Kaine was a pragmatic centrist. Also, like Clinton, he had flip-flopped on TPP. The pick of Kaine delighted mainstream Democrats, who saw Kaine as a bridge builder. Of course, the same things mainstream Democrats liked about Tim Kaine earned his nomination a collective yawn from progressive Democrats.[11] Still, despite the grousing from progressives, the team still believed they would come around to supporting the party's ticket.

After failing in the primary to develop an inspiring campaign slogan (they went with I'm With Her), for the general election the Clinton team settled on Stronger Together, which would mean different things to different voters. To disaffected Sanders voters—many of them political Independents—the slogan would encourage them to put aside their ideological differences and come together to support the Democratic Party's ticket if only to stop Trump. To right-leaning Independents and moderate Republicans, the slogan would constrast sharply with Trump's divisive rhetoric while reinforcing the notion that the Democratic Party's tent was big enough to include them too. To mainstream Democrats, the slogan invoked the communitarianism that lies at the heart of liberal orthodoxy (Marietta 2012) and contrasted sharply with Trump's claim at the Republican convention that "he alone could fix" the problems plaguing the country.

Despite a rocky start to the Democratic National Convention that may have led to some early second-guessing on the Kaine pick, the decision to go with Kaine and to reach out to the middle of the electorate was vindicated almost immediately. The modest polling bounce Clinton got from the convention was enhanced by Trump's decision to attack the Khan family, a Muslim Gold Star family who spoke about their son's sacrifice to highlight Trump's divisive rhetoric about Muslims (Gold Star is a term used to describe parents, siblings, or children of service members killed in combat). Over the course of the next few days, Trump came after the Khan family relentlessly.[12] The incident reaffirmed the Clinton team's belief that Trump not only wouldn't pivot for the general election, but *couldn't* pivot because he lacked the self-control.

The Clinton campaign's messaging strategy focused almost exclusively on Donald Trump's tempermental and behavorial issues. Like Obama in his 2012 reelection campaign, they would saturate the airwaves over the summer with negative ads. By the time, the Trump campaign finally came on air with a $4 million dollar ad buy in just four swing states (Ohio, Florida, North Carolina, and Pennsylvania) at the end of August the Clinton campaign had already spent $60 million dollars on television ads,[13] most of which were negative ads attacking Trump for his contraversial behavior. One of their most effective ads was titled *Our Children Are Watching*. It showed young children watching clips of Trump saying offensive comments.[14] Another ad targeted military voters, featuring WWII veteran Joel Sollender watching clips of Trump insulting U.S. generals and Senator John McCain, a Vietnam veteran and P.O.W.[15] An ad by the SuperPAC supporting Clinton *Priorities USA* highlighted Trump mocking a disabled reporter.[16] In September, the campaign dropped their most effective ad: *Mirrors*.[17] The ad showed images of young women staring at themselves in the mirror overlaid with Trump's most disparaging comments about women. Though effective with everyone, the ad specifically targeted fathers with daughters whom the campaign hoped would think of their own daughters and personalize the disparaging comments.

All told about 90% of the negative ads run against Donald Trump by the Clinton campaign were ads that focused purely on personal characteristics rather than on policy issues or a mix of personal characteristics and policy issues (Fowler et al. 2016). In the postmortem, the campaign got hammered for not airing more policy-focused ads. By focusing almost exclusively on Trump's personal shortcomings, Clinton failed to make a policy case against him, particularly on economic issues. But

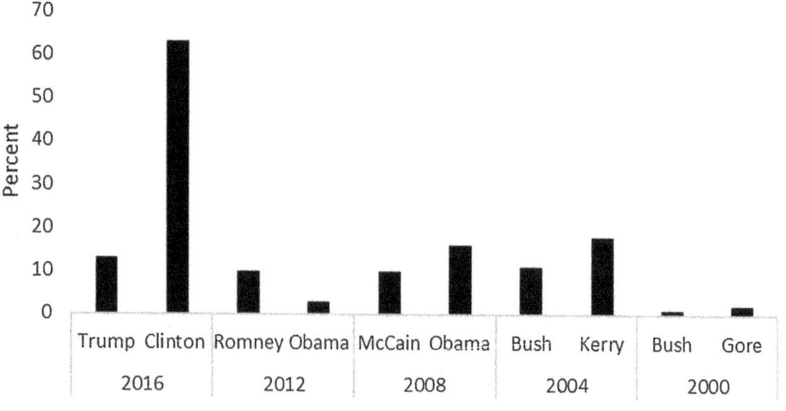

Data from Fowler, Ridout, and Franz 2016

Fig. 9.1 Personal attack ads by cycle

the downplaying of policy was intentional, not a mistake. As part of their persuasion strategy, the Clinton team needed to avoid triggering the ideological predispositions that come with policy discussions. Reminding right-leaning Independents and moderate Republicans that they better align with the Republican Party along policy dimensions would be counterproductive to their efforts to recruit them.

The dominance of the persuasion strategy in the Clinton campaign's messaging is most striking when you compare Clinton's advertising with advertising conducted in previous presidential cycles. In their analysis of campaign advertising, Fowler et al. (2016) separate ads into three categories: personal ads, policy ads, and ads that mix elements of both. The distribution of policy ads, personal ads, and mixed ads shows the Clinton campaign is a major outlier. When considering all types of ads run by the Clinton campaign, 63% were negative personal ads. As Fig. 9.1 shows, no other campaign between 2000 and 2016 comes close to the level of reliance on negative character attack ads as the Clinton campaign in 2016. Where the Clinton team focused on personal characteristics, the Trump ad strategy focused heavily on policy: about 70% of all ads. About 13% of the ads run by the Trump campaign were negative character attack ads against Clinton.

Over the course of the general election, the Clinton team built their case against Trump. Every time Trump would gain some traction in the polls, some gaffe or scandal would kill his momentum and expand

Clinton's lead. After Labor Day, the closest Trump got to Clinton in the *RealClear Politics* poll aggregator was in the middle of September when he pulled almost even with her for a few days, just before the first presidential debate on September 26. Trump's weak performance in that debate caused him to slide in the polls. That slide was compounded a few days later with the slide from the release of the *Access Hollywood* tapes on October 7 which left him at an average 5–6 point disadvantage for most of October.

At the state level (where the election is ultimately decided via the Electoral College), the Clinton team had every reason to believe their strategy was working. The 2016 cycle had eleven battleground states heading into the general election: New Hampshire, Pennsylvania, Virginia, North Carolina, Florida, Ohio, Michigan, Wisconsin, Iowa, Colorado, and Nevada. However, polling in Virginia, Pennsylvania, Michigan, Wisconsin, and Colorado heavily favored Clinton and by mid-October, Virginia, Colorado, and Wisconsin were no longer considered to be competitive. The Clinton team largely pulled out of Virginia and Colorado and stopped running ads in those states. The inclusion of those three states into Clinton's column gave her 238 Electoral College votes.

Over the course of the election, Trump lost ground rather than gained it. As the general election hit its stride, the battleground map expanded to at least theoretically include Arizona and Georgia. In September, the Clinton campaign began to add staff to Georgia, even purchasing a small ad buy there. They ran a customized ad titled *Sacrifice* which used statements Trump made about knowing more about ISIS than U.S. generals, calling the generals incompetent, and arguing that despite having never served in the military, he had made sacrifices for his country too by becoming a multi-millionaire real estate developer.[18] The ad featured images of disabled veterans including former Georgia Senator Max Cleland; a double amputee Vietnam veteran.[19]

In October, the Clinton team began flirting with investing resources in Utah and Arizona, two more solid red states. Utah was proving problematic for Donald Trump because of the influence of Mitt Romney and the presence of Independent candidate Evan McMullin on the ballot. McMullin was outpolling Trump in the state, buoyed by strong support from fellow Mormons. Although the Clinton team never invested much into these traditional Republican strongholds, as Donald Trump tanked in the polls after the *Access Hollywood* video, they spent $2 million dollars on ads in Arizona. At that time, *fivethirtyeight* gave Clinton a 54% chance to carry the state although polling showed her behind largely based on assumptions of high Latino turnout due to a backlash to Trump's immigration rhetoric. The campaign also dispatched some of their surrogates including First Lady Michelle Obama, Bernie Sanders, and Chelsea Clinton to hold rallies there.[20] Gaining traction in traditional red states validated the campaign's persuasion strategy. Their outreach to the middle of the electorate by deemphasizing issues and making the election a referendum on Trump was working.

The choice of the persuasion approach was also being reaffirmed by major newspaper endorsements. Table 9.1 shows a comparison of endorsements by major newspapers between 2012 and 2016. Of the forty-five newspapers included, Clinton received 87% of their endorsements. Donald Trump received just one endorsement from the *Las Vegas Review-Journal.* Even Libertarian Party nominee Gary Johnson outperformed Trump, picking up three. Hillary Clinton flipped thirteen papers from Romney, including an endorsement from the *Arizona Republic.*[21] It was the first time in the paper's 126 year history it endorsed the Democratic

Table 9.1 Major newspaper endorsements 2012 vs. 2016

Newspaper	*2016 Endorsement*	*2012 Endorsement*
New York Times	Clinton	Obama
Los Angeles Times	Clinton	Obama
New York Daily News	**Clinton**	**Romney**
Washington Post	Clinton	Obama
Houston Chronicle	**Clinton**	**Romney**
Arizona Republic	**Clinton**	**Romney**
Dallas Morning News	**Clinton**	**Romney**
San Francisco Chronicle	Clinton	Obama
San Diego Union-Tribune	**Clinton**	**Romney**
Sacramento Bee	Clinton	Obama
Baltimore Sun	Clinton	Obama
South Florida Sun-Sentinel	**Clinton**	**Romney**
Cincinnati Enquirer	**Clinton**	**Romney**
Akron Beacon Journal	Clinton	Obama
Chicago Sun-Times	Clinton	None
Charlotte Observer	Clinton	Obama
Tampa Bay Times	Clinton	Obama
Hartford Courant	Clinton	Obama
Columbus Dispatch	**Clinton**	**Romney**
Alabama Media Group	Clinton	None
Denver Post	Clinton	Obama
The Salt Lake Tribune	Clinton	Obama
The Des Moines Register	**Clinton**	**Romney**
The Omaha World-Herald	**Clinton**	**Romney**

(continued)

Table 9.1 (continued)

Newspaper	*2016 Endorsement*	*2012 Endorsement*
Minneapolis Star Tribune	Clinton	Obama
Boston Globe	Clinton	Obama
Cleveland Plain Dealer	Clinton	Obama
Fort Worth Star Telegram	**Clinton**	**Romney**
Honolulu Star-Advertiser	Clinton	Obama
Kansas City Star	Clinton	Obama
Newsday (NY)	**Clinton**	**Romney**
Louisville Courier-Journal	Clinton	Obama
Miami Herald	Clinton	Obama
The Star-Ledger (NJ)	Clinton	Obama
Orlando Sentinel	**Clinton**	**Romney**
Philadelphia Inquirer	Clinton	Obama
St. Louis Post-Dispatch	Clinton	Obama
San Antonio Express-News	Clinton	Obama
San Jose Mercury News	Clinton	Obama
Seattle Times	Clinton	Obama
Chicago Tribune	Johnson	Obama
Detroit News	**Johnson**	**Romney**
Richmond Times-Dispatch	**Johnson**	**Romney**
USA Today	**Not Trump**	**None**
Las Vegas Review-Journal	Trump	Romney

Data from *Mother Jones*
Bold Indicates Party Switch

Party's nominee and they received numerous death threats in response.[22] Their endorsement came with a scathing indictment of Donald Trump in which they argued without equivocation that Trump was not qualified to be president.[23] The *Cincinnati Enquirer* endorsed their first Democrat in nearly a century by arguing that Donald Trump's poor impulse control presented a national security risk. Other notable Clinton endorsements include *The Dallas Morning News* who cited Trump's use of what they called "xenophobia, racism, and misogyny" to play on people's fears, and the *San Diego Union-Tribune* who also had never endorsed a Democrat. *The San Diego Union-Tribune* cited the collapse of Venezuela under Hugo Chavez and issued this dire warning justifying their endorsement of Clinton writing, "Trump could be our Chavez." Even the *USA Today*, who never before participated in the endorsement game, felt the need to weigh in against Trump. Keeping with tradition, they didn't make an endorsement but they implored their readers to "vote, just not for Trump."[24] The effort by conservative editorial boards to derail their own party's nominee underscores the tremendous apprehension many Republicans had about Donald Trump. Heading into the final 2 weeks of the campaign, the Clinton team had every reason to be confident that their strategy was working exactly as planned.

Then on October 28, ten days from Election Day, the American electorate woke up to this alarming headline in *The New York Times*: "New Emails Jolt Clinton Campaign in Race's Last Days."[25] Then FBI Director James Comey sent a letter to Congress advising them that the bureau had uncovered additional emails that may be related to Hillary Clinton's server recovered from Anthony Weiner's laptop. Weiner was embroiled in a new crisis, an investigation into inappropriate sexual conduct with a minor. During a search of his laptop, investigators had uncovered emails from Abedin that originated from Clinton's private server. Abedin had forwarded the emails to her husband for printing.

The FBI does not ordinarily inform Congress of ongoing investigations. The Justice Department, which oversees the FBI, also has an explicit rule prohibiting employees from interfering in elections requiring employees to refrain from doing anything that can be construed as interference. As Congress and the American public would only find out after the election, the FBI was actively investigating the Trump campaign for possible collusion with the Russian government in relation to their sabotage efforts against the Clinton campaign. Later, in testimony before the Senate's Intelligence Committee's hearing on his firing by President Trump in May 2017, former Director Comey was asked to explain why he felt compelled to make the additional emails public, but not the investigation into Trump's campaign. Comey defended his decision by citing his promise to immediately inform Congress of any new developments in the email server case. He worried that failing to disclose the discovery before the election could tarnish the reputation of the agency should Clinton win and the emails later produce evidence of wrongdoing.[26]

The Clinton campaign was left reeling from the disclosure. Comey's letter advised Congress that there were thousands of emails and the review may not be completed before the election, now less than ten days away. The Clinton campaign pushed back hard against Comey's decision to go public and demanded that the review be fast-tracked, especially after learning that his letter to Congress occurred before any review of the emails for relevancy to the server case. Seven days later, Director Comey advised Congress that the review of the emails had been completed and revealed nothing to change their earlier conclusions. The investigation was reclosed.[27] It was 3 days before Election Day.

In her first public statements on the election in May of 2017 at the *Women for Women International Summit*, Hillary Clinton acknowledged mistakes made by the campaign but attributed her surprise loss on Election Day mainly to two culprits: the Comey letter and Russian interference. Clinton told Christiane Amanpour "[i]f the election had been held on October 27th, I would be your president."[28] The remarks were met with skepticism among the media who prefer the *Shattered* narrative, which places the blame for the loss on Hillary Clinton herself.

Although met with skepticism, the effect of Russian sabotage and negative headlines in the wake of the Comey letter almost certainly affected voters' evaluations of Hillary Clinton, even if they didn't directly lead to her loss. Polling provides some evidence that Clinton was in a stronger position before the Comey letter was revealed than she was in after. As Fig. 9.2 shows, on October 28, the day the letter was revealed to the public, Clinton held leads in eleven of the twelve competitive states, including states that had flipped back and forth between Clinton and Trump over the course of the election such as Iowa and Florida. In some states such as North Carolina, Nevada, and Arizona, Clinton loses her lead over Trump in the first few days after the email revelation and then stays behind him through Election Day. Of course, all three states had been volatile throughout the election. In Nevada, the lead had changed two times previously. In Florida, the lead changed three times and spent long periods tied. Still, in other states that Clinton had led in for long periods of time, Clinton fell behind Trump suddenly. In New Hampshire, Clinton led Trump for sixty straight days, most of that time well outside the margin of error. Then, on October 30, Clinton's lead disappears and she and Trump basically inverse their standings in the polls. In North Carolina, Clinton had led Trump since October 3 but fell behind him there as well in the days after the revelation. In Nevada, Clinton had the lead over Trump for 48 days until suddenly losing her lead on November 1.

Even in states in which Clinton maintained her lead, there is a decline in her poll standings that correlates with the announcement of the investigation. Polls in Virginia, Michigan, Pennsylvania, and Colorado all narrow after October 28 although each remained in Clinton's favor. In these states, polling had been remarkably stable through October, a month that was packed with significant campaign events such as the

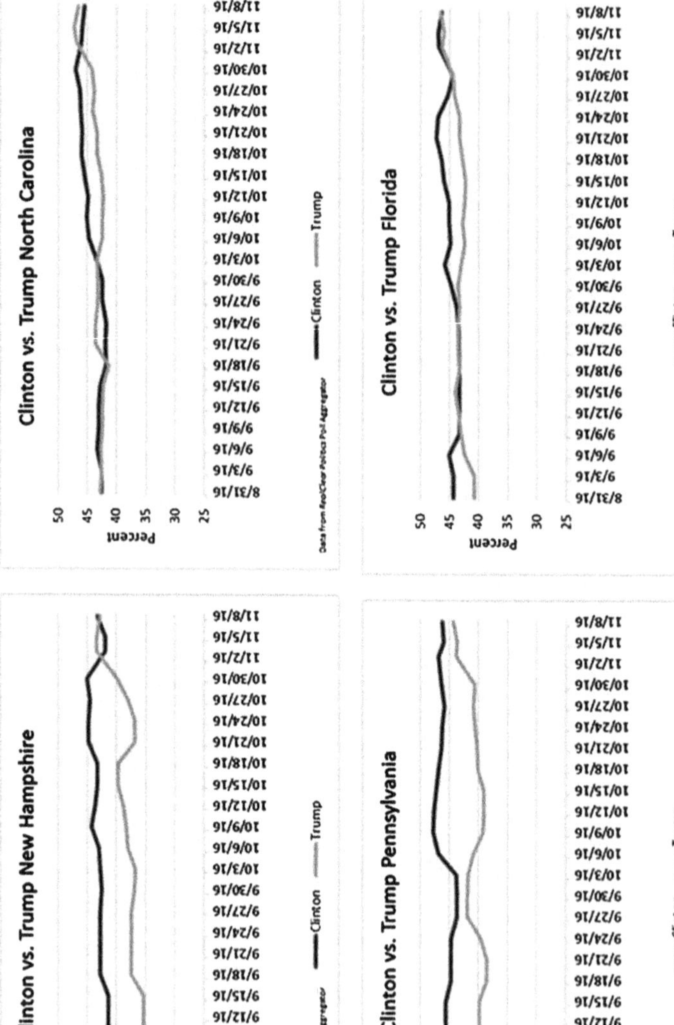

Fig. 9.2 Battleground state polls

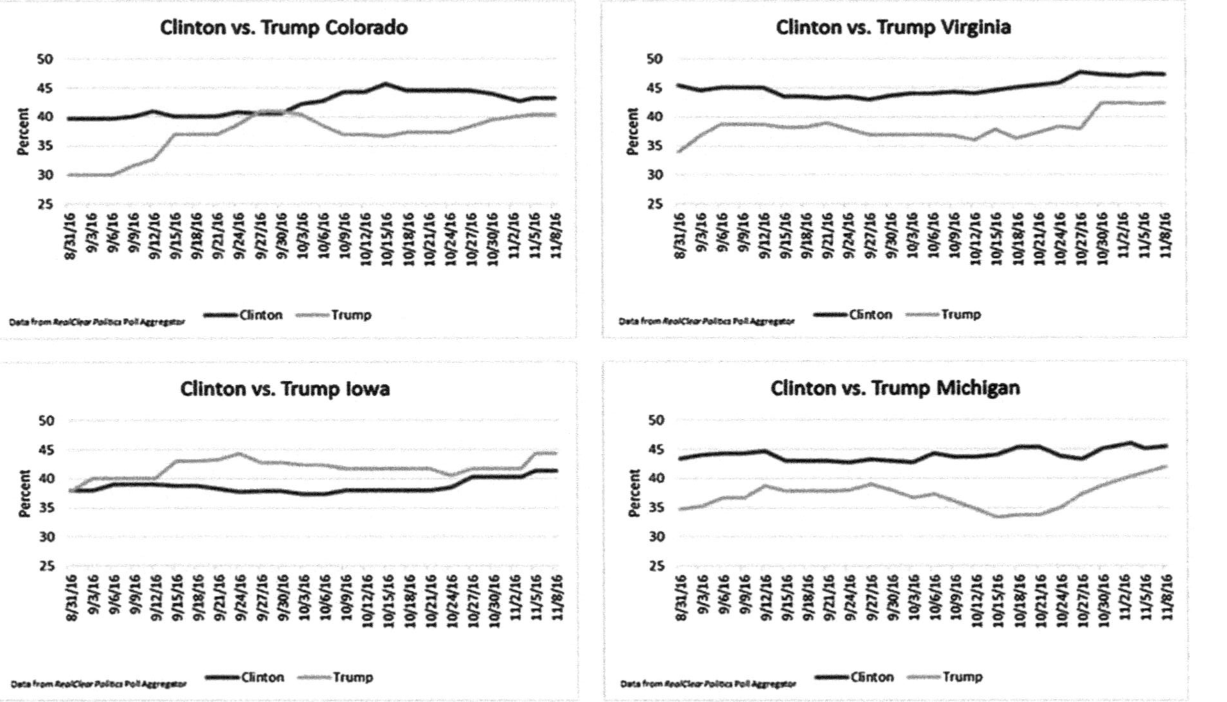

Fig. 9.2 (continued)

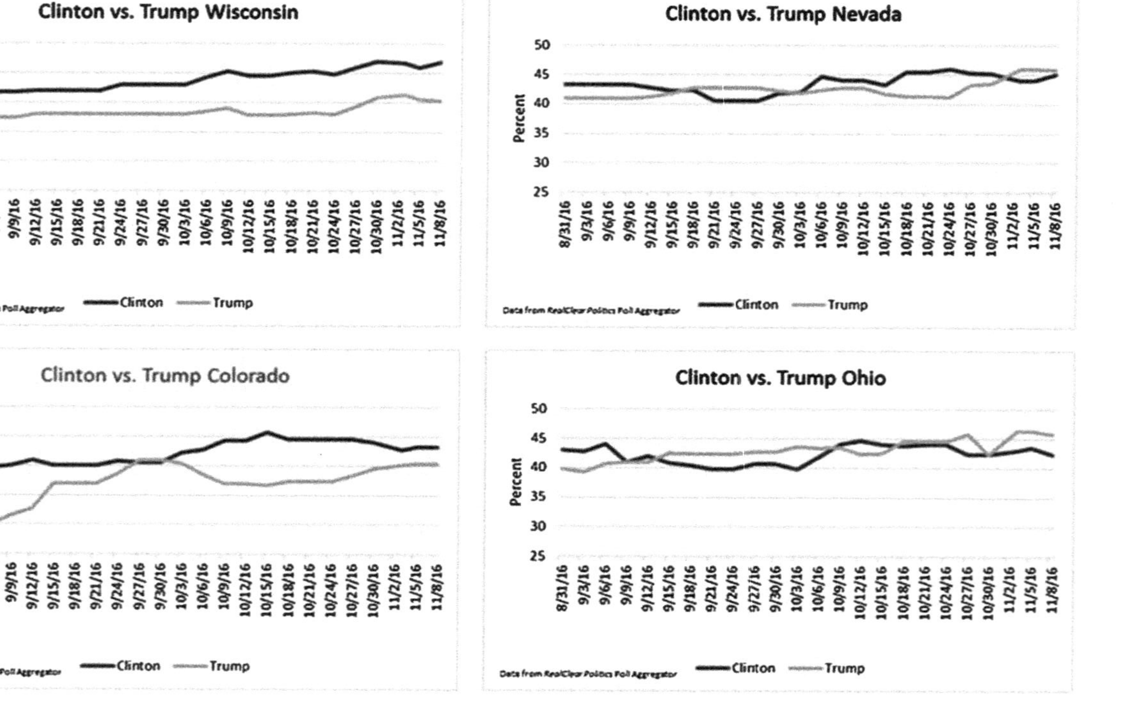

Fig. 9.2 (continued)

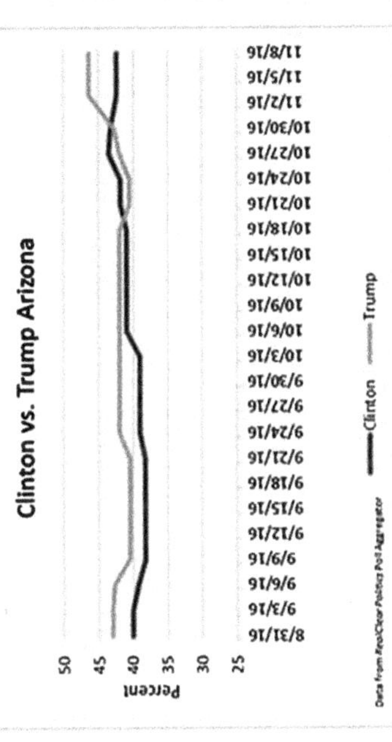

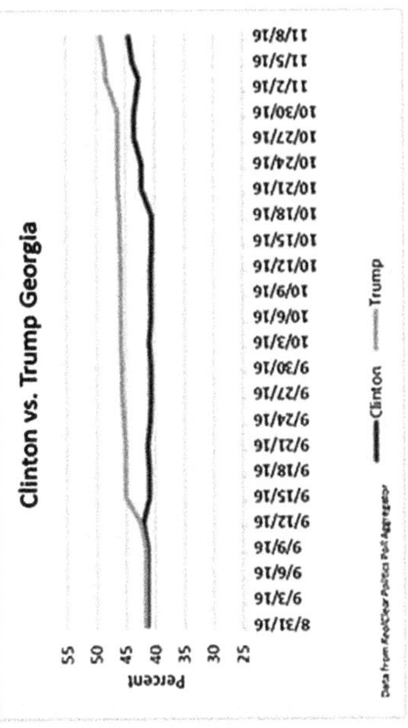

Fig. 9.2 (continued)

second and third debates as well as the *Access Hollywood* video release; the biggest scandal to ever drop during an American presidential campaign.

But correlation is not causation and it's not only possible, it is likely, that other factors were affecting the polls during the closing two weeks of the campaign. Presidential campaigns tend to narrow in the final days leading up to the election. This is usually a product of undecided voters coming off the fence and finally making a choice. In 2016, there was an added element of uncertainty. The 2016 presidential election displayed the highest rates of third-party defection in a presidential election since the 1992 presidential election between Bill Clinton and incumbent Republican President George H.W. Bush. Defection rates in that election cycle were usually high because of the presence of Independent candidate Ross Perot who earned 18.9% of the popular vote despite having formally withdrawn from the race in July only to reenter it in October (Brewer and Maisel 2015 299). Although far more modest, 5.7% of the ballots cast in the 2016 presidential election went to either one of the third-party tickets or to write-ins; more than three times the amount cast for third-party candidates or write-in candidates in 2012 and more than double the 2.7% defection rate in the historic 2000 presidential election.

Table 9.2 shows the national defection rate as well as state-level defection rates for both the 2012 and 2008 cycles. Every single state (+ Washington D.C.) saw an increase in voter defection rates with some states producing huge increases such as Utah which gave 21% of its vote to Independent (and home state) candidate Evan McMullin. The average third-party defection rate in the battleground states was 5.5%, states that tend to be decided along the narrowest of margins. Changes in the polls in the closing two weeks might have been affected by movement of these voters from one of the two major party candidates to one of the third-party candidates or vice versa.

Even with polls narrowing, heading into the last three days before Election Day, the Clinton team was on solid footing. Most national polls showed Clinton with leads either at or above the margin of error, and the *RealClear Politics* aggregator showed Clinton with a 3.2% overall advantage for the popular vote. Critical state polls such as Pennsylvania, Michigan, Wisconsin, Virginia, and Colorado also gave Clinton leads above the margin of error. Winning those states, along with safe Democratic states like California and New York, Clinton would have 265 of the 270 Electoral College votes she needed to win the election. All

Table 9.2 Third party defection rates 2012 vs. 2016

State	*2016 Defection*	*2012 Defection*	*Change*
Alabama	3.55	1.09	+2.46
Alaska	12.17	4.39	+7.78
Arizona	6.20	1.76	+4.44
Arkansas	5.77	2.55	+3.22
California	6.65	2.65	+4.1
Colorado	8.59	2.38	+6.21
Connecticut	4.51	1.23	+3.28
Delaware	5.19	1.42	+3.77
D.C.	5.45	1.81	+3.64
Florida	3.16	0.87	+2.3
Georgia	3.60	1.22	+2.38
Hawaii	7.74	1.61	+6.13
Idaho	13.24	2.84	+10.4
Illinois	5.42	1.67	+3.75
Indiana	5.26	1.94	+3.32
Iowa	7.11	1.84	+5.27
Kansas	7.29	2.29	+5
Kentucky	4.79	1.70	+3.09
Louisiana	3.46	1.64	+1.82
Maine (A.L.)	7.30	2.75	+4.55
Maryland	5.76	2.13	+3.63
Massachusetts	7.18	1.84	+5.34
Michigan	5.23	1.07	+4.16
Minnesota	8.64	2.39	+6.25
Mississippi	1.94	0.92	+1.02
Missouri	5.10	1.85	+3.25
Montana	8.08	2.95	+5.13
Nebraska (A.L.)	7.55	2.17	+5.38
Nevada	6.58	1.97	+4.61
New Hampshire	6.41	1.63	+4.78
New Jersey	4.01	1.03	+2.98
New Mexico	11.71	4.17	+7.54
New York	4.48	1.48	+3
North Carolina	4	1.26	+2.76
North Dakota	9.81	2.98	+6.83
Ohio	4.75	1.64	+3.11
Oklahoma	5.75	0	+5.75
Oregon	10.84	3.62	+7.22
Pennsylvania	4.36	1.44	+2.92
Rhode Island	6.70	2.05	+4.65
South Carolina	4.39	1.35	+3.04
South Dakota	6.73	1.35	+5.38
Tennessee	4.57	2.24	+2.33

(continued)

Table 9.2 (continued)

State	*2016 Defection*	*2012 Defection*	*Change*
Texas	4.53	1.44	+3.09
Utah	27.0	2.47	+24.53
Vermont	13.05	2.46	+10.59
Virginia	5.87	2.54	+3.33
Washington	10.63	2.54	+8.09
West Virginia	5.07	2.17	+2.9
Wisconsin	6.32	1.29	+5.03
Wyoming	9.83	3.54	+6.29
US Total	**5.73**	**1.73**	**+4**

she would need to add to her total to win the 2016 presidential election was one additional swing state (other than New Hampshire, which only has four votes). *Sabato's Crystal Ball* predicted, she would bring home around 322 total Electoral College votes[29] and the final forecasting model run by Nate Silver at *fivethirtyeight* on the morning of Election Day gave Clinton a 71.4% probability of winning the election.[30]

The candidates' schedules over the final two weeks of election reflect Clinton's polling advantage in the swing states overall and particularly her strength in the Midwest. Figure 9.3 presents a map of Clinton's campaign events in the final ten days of the campaign. She made three appearances in North Carolina and eight in Florida; the two states that appeared the most competitive coming down the stretch. Despite media reports to the contrary, the Clinton team did not ignore the Midwest in the final weeks of the campaign. Spooked by the attention being given to the Midwest by the Trump campaign and the narrowing in the polls, Clinton held two rallies in Michigan and five in Pennsylvania during the final week of the campaign. Additionally, the campaign deployed their so-called super surrogates to the Midwest. President Obama, Bernie Sanders, and Bill Clinton all held events there as well as multiple events for Tim Kaine.

Figure 9.4 shows the combined effort Hillary Clinton and her surrogates put into the competitive states. Although events were held in the Midwest, the campaign devoted the bulk of their attention to states that polling showed to be the most competitive such as North Carolina, New Hampshire, Nevada, and Florida. Hillary Clinton held eight events in Florida and three events in North Carolina in the final ten days of the

Fig. 9.3 Hillary Clinton campaign appearances (final 10 days)

Fig. 9.4 Hillary Clinton and super surrogates campaign events (final 10 days)

campaign, and the super surrogate team saturated those states including a rally Clinton held with Michelle Obama in North Carolina.

All told, in the final ten days of the campaign, Clinton held 27 campaign events and Trump held 35. Figure 9.5 shows Trump's appearances by state over the closing ten days of the campaign. Overall, Donald Trump was more varied in where he spent his time. He held only six events in Florida compared to Clinton's eight. Just after the Comey letter was released, Trump started holding a series of events in Michigan, leading many pundits to question the strategy. Of course, after he carried the state on Election Day most people assumed that internal polling or some other type of internal information had tipped the campaign off to a changing landscape in the state. Whether or not that is the

Fig. 9.5 Donald Trump and Mike Pence campaign events (final 10 days)

case strategically, the Trump team *needed* to devote resources to the Midwest in order to have any chance at all of winning the election. One of the main reasons he was given so little prospect of winning the election was the complicated Electoral College formula he needed to reach 270 Electoral College votes compared to Clinton. In order to have any chance at winning the election, the Trump team had to break off at least one of the Blue Wall states plus carry Ohio so it is no surprise that the Trump campaign focused so much of their time and attention to the Midwest.

A clear strategic mistake the Clinton campaign made in the days just before the election was the campaign's refusal to concede Iowa and Ohio to Donald Trump and redirect those resources to shore up support in the other Midwest states. Although polling in Wisconsin held steady through Election Day (which makes the results in WI especially surprising), polling in Pennsylvania and Michigan narrowed significantly in the final week of the campaign and should have been recognized as an early warning sign. By then, it should have been obvious to the Clinton team that they were going to lose Ohio. They had been running behind Trump there for most of the general election, failing to gain traction even during the height of the *Access Hollywood* scandal. She also steadily struggled in Iowa where the race widened even further in Trump's advantage after the Comey letter. Despite this, the campaign continued to devote a lot of their resources into the two states. Holding Iowa and Ohio for the Democrats was crucial to her plan of expanding the Electoral College map. As part of the expansion plan, the campaign also diverted resources to Arizona. Flipping Arizona was always a long shot; predicated primarily on hopes of an unprecedented mobilization of Latino voters who the campaign hoped would be activated by Trump's divisive rhetoric and by his border wall and deportation policies. Ultimately, Arizona would break for Trump 48% to Clinton's 45%. Compared to 2012 in which Arizona went for Romney 53% to Obama's 44%, the Democrats did make solid gains. However, it did not come from Latino voters. Clinton underperformed Obama's share of the Latino vote in 2012 by 11 points, earning 61% although she exceeded his vote share in 2008 where he only received 56% of the Latino vote. Instead, Clinton's gains came from college-educated voters. Romney carried 58% of college-educated voters in 2012, whereas Trump took just 51%. Voter turnout in the state between 2012 and 2016 was virtually unchanged.[31]

Examining Donald Trump's campaign activity during the final ten days of the election reveals that the Trump campaign recognized they would carry Ohio and Iowa. While Clinton and her team were blanketing the states, Trump held just one rally in Ohio and two in Iowa. Between herself and her surrogates, Clinton saturated Ohio and Iowa over the same time period, holding six events in Iowa and six events in Ohio. Trump ended up carrying Ohio decisively, by seven points, and Iowa by almost nine points. Team Clinton also saturated North Carolina (15 visits) and Florida (17 visits) only to lose both. The irony is that they didn't need any of those states to win the election. If the Clinton campaign held the Blue Wall (MI, WI, and PA), then Clinton could lose North Carolina, Ohio, and Florida to Trump and still win the election provided she carry Colorado, Nevada, New Hampshire, and Virginia, all of which she went on to win. By trying to expand the Electoral College map and not adjusting their strategy once the race started to narrow in the final week, the Clinton campaign allowed the Blue Wall to not only crack, but to shatter.

A final warning sign the Clinton team failed to heed was their candidate's inability to get above 45% in the national poll aggregator over the course of the general election. Trump's rise and fall in his polling average never translated into large gains for Clinton. For most of the election cycle between 15% and 20% of the electorate was unaccounted for in Clinton and Trump's national polling averages. At its most competitive point between September 15 and September 20, Trump and Clinton's combined polling average was just 81.6%, leaving nearly 19%

of the electorate either undecided, supporting a third-party candidate, or refusing to answer the ballot question on the survey. Heading into the final two weeks of the campaign, about 12% of the electorate was still not reflected in the two party vote share. In comparison with the 2012 election, there was never a point in the general election in which more than 10% of the vote was not reflected in Romney and Obama's vote share, and during the final two weeks, around 95% of the vote was accounted for between the two of them. On November 6, 2012, just 3.1% of the aggregate average was missing from the major party vote share.

The unusually high rate of vote share not going to the two party's nominees largely escaped unnoticed by the media and ostensibly by the campaigns, but it should have dominated the conversation during those closing weeks. With so much of the vote choice unaccounted for by the head-to-head between Clinton and Trump, the status of the race was consistently misinterpreted. Although Hillary Clinton led Donald Trump consistently for weeks; with more than 15% of the electorate undecided or planning on defection, there really was no way to predict what would happen on Election Day. In the final days, Johnson was pulling about 4.7% and Stein was pulling 1.9%. Combined with Clinton's 45.5% and Trump's 42.2%, around 6% of the vote remained unaccounted for heading into Election Day. Contrary to the high level of certainty of a Clinton victory being presented by the media and generated by the forecasting models, the electorate was unusually unsettled. Anything could happen.

Why the Persuasion Campaign Failed

They say that hindsight is 20/20. Nowhere is that more true than in political campaigns. The losing campaign of a competitive race wakes up the day after the election with sudden clarity as to what went wrong and what they should have done differently. For Robby Mook and Hillary Clinton, "the day after" must have been especially painful because there was so little for the campaign to point at to explain her stunning loss. The Clinton campaign had outperformed their opponents in terms of fund-raising, advertising, campaign organization, and candidate performance. They had led their opponent throughout the entire course of the general election, something no other nominee has done in the past two decades. Logistically, the campaign had been close to perfect. But there was one critical mistake that only became apparent in the aftermath of the election. In crafting their general election strategy, the campaign had forgotten an enduring adage of Democratic politics: Democrats fall in love, Republicans fall in line. The persuasion campaign the Clinton team ran in the 2016 presidential election relied on inversing that adage. The Clinton campaign had conducted the nearly perfect execution of the wrong campaign strategy, and the mistake cost Hillary Clinton the election.

The persuasion strategy failed for two key reasons. The first reason is that high levels of ideological polarization in the electorate have left few persuadable voters and have made it extremely unlikely that partisans will defect because of the high premium that is placed on partisan control of the government. American voters have become increasingly partisan over the past few decades and more ideologically extreme. For the persuasion strategy to work, two things had to be achieved: Party loyalty rates among Republicans had to decline at least a few points below their average of 90% from the last few elections, and Hillary Clinton needed to come close to splitting Independent voters with Donald Trump, at least in the critical swing states. Because men are more likely to identify as Independents than women and because Independents are predominately white, the Republican nominee tends to outperform the Democratic nominee among Independents. Clinton didn't need to win Independents per se, but she had to make significant inroads with them.

There are only two election cycles in which partisans defected from their party's nominee in high numbers: The 1980 election when so-called Reagan Democrats defected to support Republican candidate Ronald Reagan and 1992 and 1996 when some Republican voters defected to support Bill Clinton. In that race, Clinton, an incumbent governor of Arkansas, reached out to working-class voters with a now famous messaging strategy coined by Democratic strategist and Clinton operative James Carville: "the economy stupid." The campaign's focus on economic issues popular with conservative voters persuaded them to flip over to Bill Clinton, helping him win the election. But the persuadable electorate of the 1990s had long ago been replaced with an ideologically sorted electorate consistently loyal to their party. Figure 9.6 shows party loyalty rates in each presidential election since 1952. Since the turn of the millennium party loyalty rates have averaged 89.2% for Democrats and 91.4% for Republicans. In 2016, 89% of Democrats cast ballots for Hillary Clinton and 90% of Republicans did the same for Donald Trump. The Clinton campaign's efforts to court Republicans wary of Donald Trump failed. Campaigns reinforce underlying partisanship (Polsby et al.

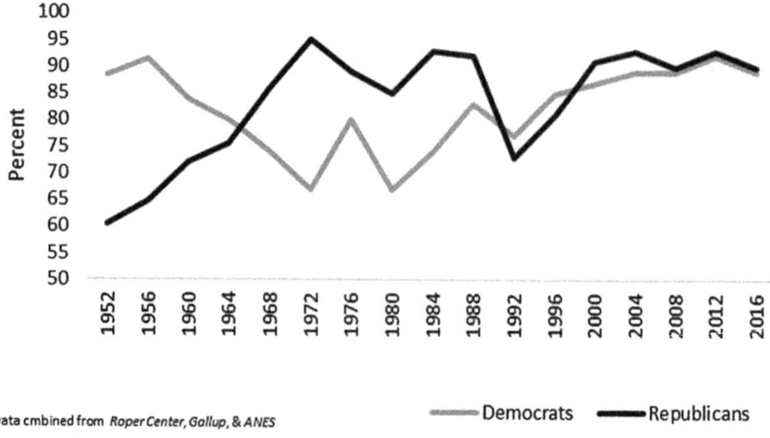

Fig. 9.6 Party loyalty in Presidential Elections

2016, 135), even if they are constructed not to. At the end of the day, even wary Republicans voted for their own party's nominee.

Although the Clinton team hoped to bring in some disaffected Republican voters, the persuasion strategy's main target was Independent voters. The Clinton team expected her to be highly competitive among Independents despite her own image issues among them. Although carrying the Independent vote doesn't necessarily mean winning the election, the Independent vote can be determinative in critical swing states. Part of what makes a state competitive is a robust number of Independent voters in the electorate. This causes an increase in competition between the parties. The influence of Independent voters in battleground states is contingent on their portion of the electorate such as in Ohio in 2012 when Romney won Independent voters by ten points but the state was still carried by President Obama because of strong Democratic turnout. In that cycle, 38% of the Ohio electorate were Democrats compared to just 31% who were Independent and 31% who were Republican. Independent voters are most influential in New Hampshire because on average 44% of New Hampshire voters identify themselves as Independents.

Most people who identify themselves as Independents admit to leaning toward a party when they are pressed. The "true" portion of the electorate that insists they do not align with a party is somewhere between 12% and 20%. Research finds that most Independents

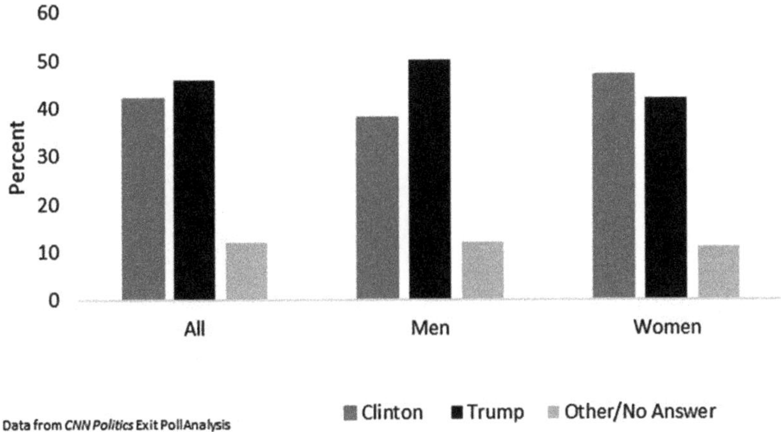

Fig. 9.7 Independent voters nationwide

are actually closet partisans, they behave like weak partisans (Keith et al. 1992) and there is little difference in policy preferences between Independent leaners and weak partisans.[32] Although the number of Independents has steadily increased over time, much of that growth comes from weak partisans who are fleeing the damaged brands of the parties in the polarized era.

Ultimately, Clinton ended up losing the Independent vote nationally to Donald Trump by six points (42%–48%). Much of the third-party/write-in defection came from Independent voters who comprised 31% of the electorate. Although only 3% of Democrats and 4% of the Republicans reported defecting to a third-party candidate, 12% of Independent voters voted for a third-party or write-in candidate. People who identified as liberal or moderate were also more likely to defect. About 6% of liberals and 8% of moderates reported voting for a third-party candidate or a write-in candidate.

Clinton carried Independent women by 5% (47–42%) but lost Independent men to Trump by 12 points (see Fig. 9.7). She failed to carry Independent voters in any of the 11 competitive states. Figure 9.8 shows Clinton's best state among Independents was New Hampshire, where she managed to merely tie Donald Trump. All told she lost Independent voters by an average of nine points in the battleground states. The loss was driven by male Independents. As Fig. 9.9 shows,

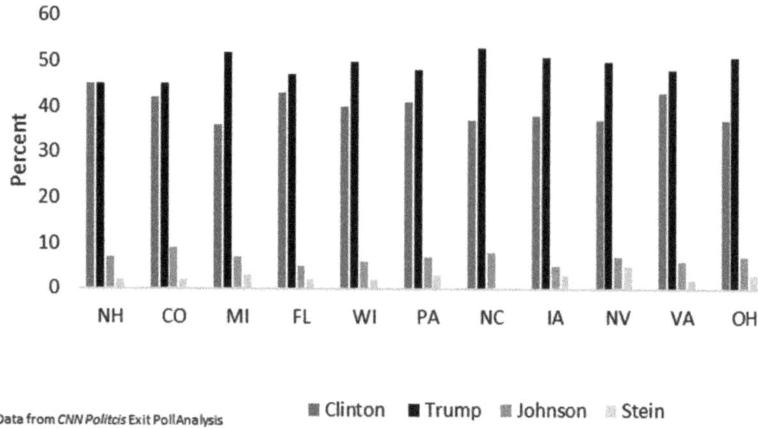

Fig. 9.8 Independent voters by swing state

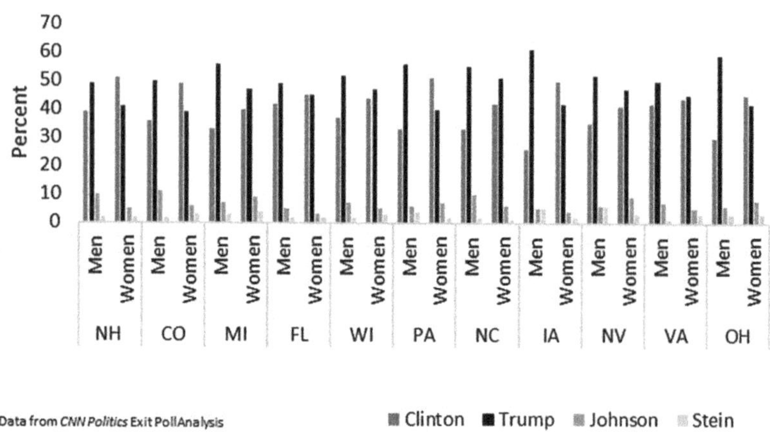

Fig. 9.9 Swing state independent voters, by gender

Clinton beat Trump among female Independents in some, but not in all states. Clinton lost female Independents by seven points in Michigan, three points in Wisconsin, nine points in North Carolina, six points in Nevada, and one point in Virginia. She won female Independents in Pennsylvania by 11 points but lost male Independents by 23 points,

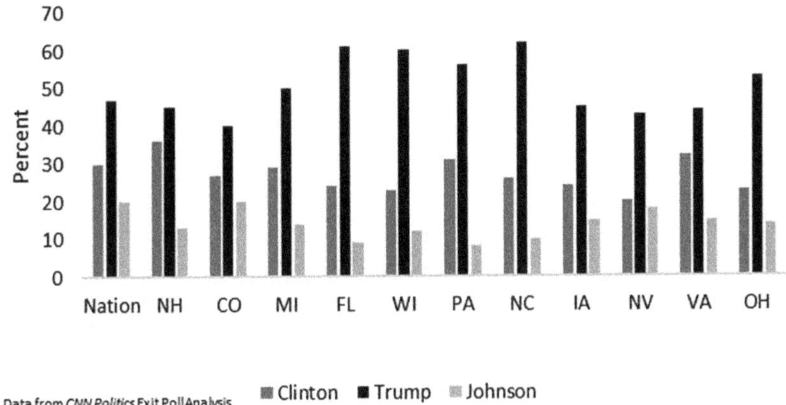

Fig. 9.10 Vote choice of those with unfavorable views of both candidates

more than offsetting any advantage from winning female Independents. She performed poorly among male Independents in swing states in one region in particular: the Midwest. She lost male Independents in Pennsylvania and Michigan by 23 points, in Ohio by 29 points, and in Wisconsin by 15 points.

The election results in the swing states reveal that the campaign's persuasion effort failed miserably, especially among voters who reported having unfavorable views of both candidates. Trump outperformed Clinton among those voters on average by 23 points. As Fig. 9.10 shows, she lost these voters by 37 points in Wisconsin and Pennsylvania, 36 points in North Carolina, 30 points in Ohio, and 21 points in Iowa and Florida, all states she failed to carry. The entire crux of the Clinton campaign's messaging strategy was focused on convincing voters that disliked Clinton and Trump that Trump was worse and yet, those voters completely rejected Hillary Clinton. If the Comey letter had an effect, it would most likely be among these voters.

After the election, much was made about Hillary Clinton's failure to carry the vote of white women. Nationally, Clinton lost white voters by 20 points, 37%–57%. As Fig. 9.11 shows, the Republican nominee always outperforms the Democratic nominee among white voters. The only times since the southern realignment and collapse of the New Deal coalition that the Democratic Party has done well with white voters has been

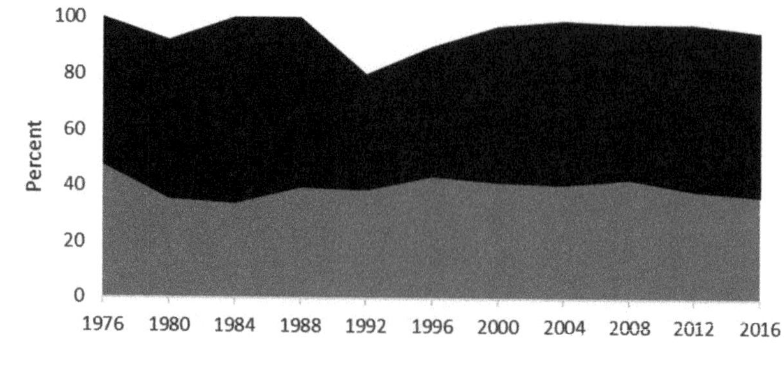

Fig. 9.11 White vote, by party

when the nominee is from the South. In 1976, Jimmy Carter, a governor (and peanut farmer!) from Georgia only underperformed Gerald Ford among white voters by four points. The Democratic Party lost the white vote by wide margins in both of Reagan's elections in 1980 and 1984 as well as the election of George H.W. Bush in 1988. Bill Clinton (another southern governor) bought the party a temporary reprieve among white voters in 1992 and 1996. In those cycles, Clinton came within two points of the Republican nominee in 1992 (it should be noted that Ross Perot was on the ticket) and within two points in his 1996 reelection campaign. After that, the white vote returned to post-realignment stasis giving George W. Bush a 13 point margin in 2000 and a 17 point margin in his 2004 reelection. Barack Obama lost the white vote by 12 points in 2008 and by 20 points in his 2012 reelection. As such, Clinton's loss by 21 points was typical for Democratic Party nominees since 2000. The party's issues with white voters existed well before the 2016 cycle.

Although Clinton did not make gains among white voters overall, the Clinton campaign's persuasion strategy was effective with one subgroup of white voters: college-educated women. As Fig. 9.12 shows, Clinton outperformed Donald Trump nationally among white college-educated women by seven points (51–44%) and carried them in seven of the eleven battleground states by an average of 14 points. She ended up carrying three of these states: Virginia, New Hampshire, and Colorado,

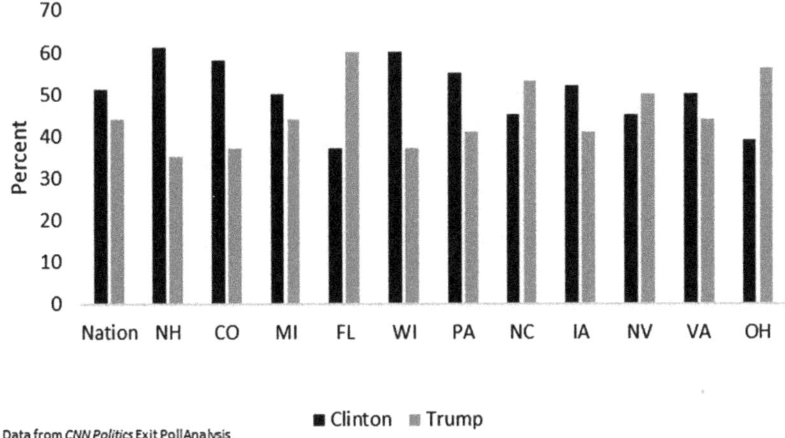

Fig. 9.12 Vote choice of white college-educated women

all states with higher than average rates of college education. Despite carrying the vote of white, college-educated women in Michigan and Pennsylvania, she lost college-educated white men by wide margins: 22 points in Michigan and 17 points in Pennsylvania. Interestingly, Clinton tied Trump among white college-educated men in Wisconsin (46% each) and won white college-educated women by 23 points but still lost that state. Although Clinton lost the vote of all white women to Trump by nine points (43% to Trump's 52%), most of the loss was powered by non-college-educated women, whose voting habits more closely resemble the votes of men than they do of their college-educated peers. Clinton lost non-college educated white women voters nationally by 27 points, nearly the same margin Clinton lost white men by (31 points).

It is hard to fault the Clinton team for believing their persuasion strategy would be effective. Although Independents have favored Republicans in recent cycles, moving Independents into the Democratic Party's column was not without recent precedent. In his 2008 run against John McCain, Barack Obama carried Independent voters nationally by eight points, the first Democrat to do so since Bill Clinton carried them in 1996. But the 2008 election occurred in the midst of an economy collapsing under the tutelage of the Republican Party. Despite having Donald Trump on the other side of the ticket, the Clinton campaign

Table 9.3 Third party defection in the democrat's blue wall

	Johnson	*Stein*	*McMullin*	*Other*	*Total Defection*	*Loss Margin*
Michigan	172,136	51,463	8177	19,126	250,902	10,704
Pennsylvania	146,715	49,941	6472	65,176	268,304	44,292
Wisconsin	106,674	31,072	11,055	38,729	187,530	77,744

faced a different electoral context. Although the economy had recovered under Obama and unemployment was low, a Clinton win meant a third term of Democratic Party control of the White House during a time period where the electorate craved change. This, combined with the high levels of distrust voters had of Hillary Clinton, it is no surprise that the Clinton campaign strategy failed to win over enough Independents to carry the battleground states she needed for an Electoral College victory via her persuasion strategy.

If the Clinton campaign had elected to emphasize base mobilization over persuasion, she almost certainly would be the President of the United States. Clinton's Electoral College loss came down to less than 77,744 votes spread over three Midwestern states out of the 136,669,237 total ballots cast in the 2016 election. Hillary Clinton lost the election for one reason, third-party defection, especially in the so-called Blue Wall. As Table 9.3 shows, Clinton could have carried both Michigan and Pennsylvania on just the ballots cast for Green Party candidate Jill Stein and could have carried Wisconsin with the Stein vote combined with votes for write-in candidates. With Michigan, Pennsylvania, and Wisconsin in her column, along with the other states she ended up winning, she would have beaten Donald Trump in the Electoral College 278–260. The 2016 defection rate in Wisconsin was nearly five times higher than the 2012 defection rate. In 2012, just 1.29% of voters cast ballots for someone other than Barack Obama or Mitt Romney. In 2016, 6.32% of Wisconsinites defected from the two party nominees. Defection rates were also five times higher in Michigan and three times higher in Pennsylvania. All told twelve states were decided by less than 5%. New Hampshire broke for Clinton by .37%, Florida for Trump by 1.20%, Maine for Clinton by 2.96%, Minnesota for Clinton by 1.52%, Nevada for Clinton by 2.42%, Colorado for Clinton by 4.91%, and Arizona and North Carolina for Trump by 3.55% and 3.66%, respectively. In all of them except for North Carolina, third-party defection rates exceed the vote margin between Trump and Clinton, and in some cases greatly.

With lower third-party defection from liberal voters, Clinton's popular vote margin would have also increased. Although Clinton carried California by 4.2 million votes, another 400,000 went to Jill Stein and write-in candidates. In total, just over 1.4 million votes were cast for the Green Party ticket across the country. Another 1.5 million were cast for write-in or "other" candidates. Unfortunately, because states don't tend to record the name of write-in candidates, it is not possible to estimate what portion of them went to Bernie Sanders. Nor is it possible to estimate the portion of the 4.5 million votes cast for Gary Johnson that might have gone for the Democratic ticket. Because Johnson is a Libertarian who takes liberal positions on social issues and neo-conservative positions on economic issues, it is not likely that he picked up many liberal voters but he most likely received some support for them.

What factors impacted defection rates among the fifty states? Although all states experienced an increase in defection rates over other recent cycles (including 2000), there is significant variation between states on the size of the increase. The states with the three highest rates of defection have obvious explanations for them. Utah's defection rate of 27% is a function of the inclusion of Independent candidate Evan McMullin on the ballot. Idaho's 13% defection rate is most likely because of McMullin as well. Although he is from Utah, Idaho and Utah are neighboring states and both have very high rates of Mormonism. The third highest defection rate was in Vermont and is due to write-in ballots cast for Senator Sanders.

In order to understand the overall increase in third-party defection as well as the significant variation in the amount of defection between states, I specify a linear regression model with each state's percent of third-party or write-in defection as the dependent variable. Given the acrimony of Sanders supporters toward Hillary Clinton and the unease some Republicans felt toward Donald Trump's fitness for office, it is expected that states that Bernie Sanders carried in the Democratic primary and states that didn't go to Donald Trump in the Republican primary will have higher rates of defection than states that supported Clinton and Trump in the primary. Because voters in swing states are usually aware of the heightened importance of their vote and are courted heavily by the two major party candidates, it is expected that swing states will have lower rates of defection than other states.

Table 9.4 Effect of Sanders primary support on defection rate

Third Party Defection	*Defect*
swing	0.147
	(−1.61)
sanders state	17.97*
	(2.63)
Indie	1.086
	(1.22)
nonwhite	0.960
	(−1.19)
collegegrad	1.123*
	(2.11)
N	51

Exponentiated coefficients; z statistics in parentheses * $p < 0.05$, ** $p < 0.01$, *** $p < 0.001$

The results of the analysis are presented in Table 9.4. States that supported Bernie Sanders in the primary are more likely to produce higher defection rates than states that supported Hillary Clinton. On average, Sanders states have a 2.9% higher defection rate than states that went with Clinton, and the relationship is statistically significant at the.01 level meaning that the null hypothesis (there is no relationship between a state supporting Bernie Sanders in the primary and having a higher defection rate in the general election) can be rejected with a high degree of confidence. Interestingly, there is no relationship between states that went against Donald Trump in the Republican primary and general election defection rates, nor does a state's status as a swing state effect their defection rate.

Figure 9.13 shows the sharp difference in defection rates between states that voted for Clinton in the Democratic primary and states that voted for Sanders. The mean defection rate in Clinton states was 5.19% of the electorate, while in states that supported Sanders the mean is almost double: 9.04%. The high levels of defection found in states that supported Sanders in the primary, including those that are swing states, suggest that Bernie Sanders voters were more likely to defect than other voters. Would the selection of Bernie Sanders or Elizabeth Warren as Clinton's running mate discouraged these voters from defecting? To explore the affect a progressive running mate might have had on the election, I conducted a non-scientific survey of Bernie Sanders supporters. The survey includes responses from 492 respondents who volunteered to participate in the survey.

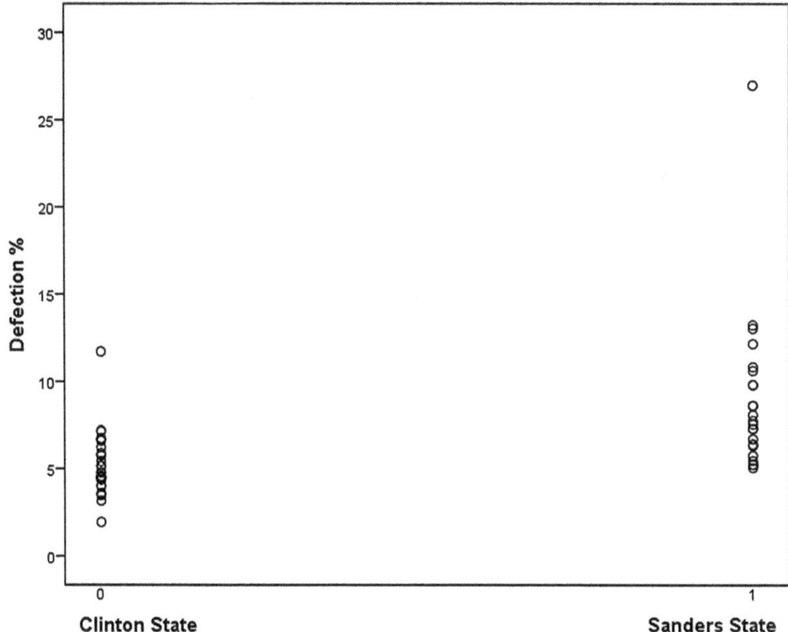

Fig. 9.13 General election defection Clinton vs. Sanders states

Respondents were recruited on Facebook group pages devoted to Bernie Sanders fans and come from all over the U.S. Respondents who voted in the 2016 presidential election were asked to identify which presidential candidate they cast a ballot for. Figure 9.14 shows that only 12% of the Sanders' supporters included in the analysis cast ballots for Hillary Clinton. About 60% reported voting for Jill Stein followed by 21% who wrote Bernie Sanders in as a write-in candidate. Only 4% reported voting for Johnson.

Of the 63 respondents who reported voting for Clinton, the vast majority (94%) indicated that they did so because they did not want Donald Trump to win the presidency rather than because Hillary Clinton had won their support (see Fig. 9.15). Sander supporters who defected from Clinton were asked to identify the main reason they did not vote for her. They were provided three options: her email server scandal, she was not progressive enough, or another reason. As seen in Fig. 9.16, half of the respondents cited "another reason," while the

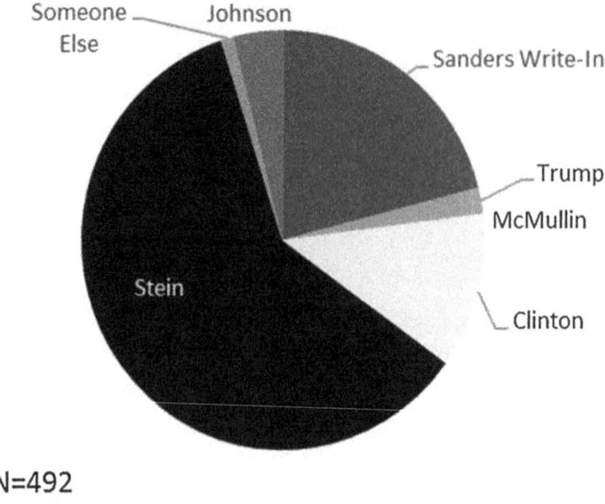

Fig. 9.14 2016 Vote choice of Sanders supporters

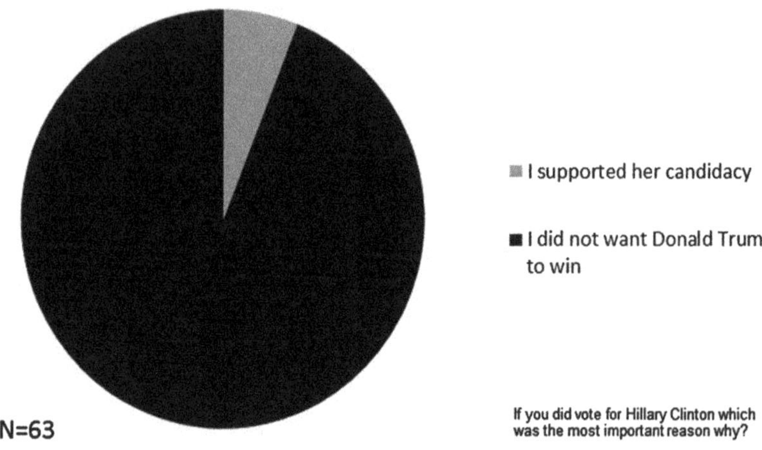

Fig. 9.15 Reason Sanders supporters voted for Clinton

other half cited that "she was not progressive enough." Just 1% said that her email server scandal affected their vote decision.

Sanders supporters that did not vote for Hillary Clinton were also asked how the selection of Bernie Sanders or Elizabeth Warren might

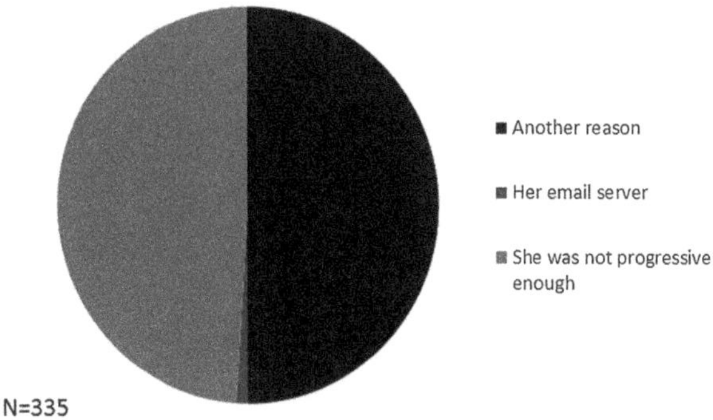

Fig. 9.16 Most important reason for defection

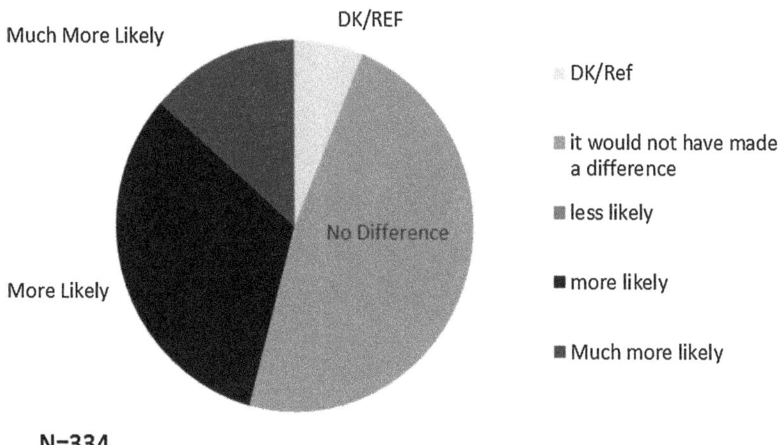

Fig. 9.17 Effect of progressive Vice President pick on defection

have affected their vote decision. Figure 9.17 displays the results. Although 46% of the Sanders supporters included in the analysis reported that it would not have made a difference to their vote an almost equal amount reported that it would have made them more likely to cast their ballot for Clinton instead. Many of the Sanders supporters that participated in the survey also made comments in the threads that accompanied the survey links. The level of vitriol directed at Hillary Clinton months after the election was surprising. Many of these voters weren't just skeptical of Hillary Clinton, many despised her. Of the 360 respondents in the survey who did not vote for Clinton and who responded to the question "If you did not vote for Hillary Clinton would you change your vote today if you could?" only five people said they would.

A word of caution: As a non-scientific poll, these data cannot be used to draw inferences regarding all Bernie Sanders supporters. Additionally, it is not possible to know what the effect of having Sanders or Warren on the ticket would have had on either these respondents or the broader population of defectors. If Bernie Sanders or Elizabeth Warren (or another progressive running mate) had been selected, it would have altered the entire strategic approach of the Clinton campaign. The Clinton team would have made base mobilization a more prominent feature of the campaign and almost certainly would have altered their messaging strategies as well as their resource allocation strategies. It is not possible to replay the 2016 election to see if a mobilization strategy would have succeeded where the persuasion strategy failed, but we do know that under their persuasion strategy Independents were not moved into the Democratic column and that liberal defection alone cost Hillary Clinton more than 1.5 million votes nationally as well as victories in the three Midwestern states that swung the Electoral College to Donald Trump. The Clinton team's failure to recognize the level of acrimony in progressive wing of the party's base and take steps to remedy it cost her the opportunity to be the first female President of the United States. Her loss was an ideological loss.

The abject failure of the persuasion strategy to win over Independents in the 2016 election raises concerns regarding the strategy's viability, at least in national elections. Of course, it is possible the persuasion strategy would have performed better with a different Democratic nominee. Even without the erosion of her favorability ratings from the email server case, Clinton was bound to face resistance from Independent voters due to the reputational aspects inherent to the Clinton dynasty. After almost 30 years in the national spotlight, few voters did not come into the 2016 election cycle without preconceived opinions of both Hillary and Bill Clinton. Although millennial voters broke for Clinton by 19 points over Trump, Clinton underperformed Obama slightly among millennial voters because voters under the age of 40 were far more likely to defect to a third-party candidate. Born in the 1980s and 1990s, these voters spent their entire lifetime with the Clinton's in the national spotlight and as a result, within the crosshairs of the Republican Party. As such, it is little wonder that so many young voters are deeply suspicious of Hillary Clinton. Additionally, it would later be revealed that millennial voters especially were targeted with anti-Clinton propaganda via social networks like Facebook and Twitter.

Still, given the high levels of anti-establishment fervor on both sides of the electorate, it is also possible that any establishment Democrat would have struggled against an anti-establishment Republican nominee. Much of the Republican Party's gains in Congress over the past six years have been powered by growing anti-establishment sentiment in the Republican electorate. First as the Tea Party, then as the Freedom Caucus, "Washington outsiders" have become increasingly influential in the Republican Party. While the populism that emerged on the right was quick to infiltrate the Republican Party, populism on the left initially emerged as a protest movement separate from the Democratic Party. However, the insurgent candidacy of Bernie Sanders in the 2016 presidential election may be a turning point in Democratic Party politics. Rather than challenging Hillary Clinton as an Independent, third party candidate Sanders ran within the Democratic system for the Democratic Party's nomination and was almost successful. Given the role that third-party defection played in Hillary Clinton's loss, it is clear that voters that embrace left-wing populism are not likely to support mainstream Democratic candidates even when the stakes are high. The Democratic Party should expect to see efforts by the progressive wing of the party to win the nomination in 2020. Given the high levels of partisan polarization in the American electorate, base mobilization strategies may be more effective than strategies that seek to expand a party's appeal. Although persuasion politics isn't dead, it is on life support. In the polarized era, its all about that base.

Notes

1. Nolan D. McCaskill "6 people who don't want to be Trump's VP," *Politico*, http://www.politico.com/blogs/2016-gop-primary-live-updates-and-results/2016/05/donald-trump-vp-refuse-222863.
2. Nick Gass, "Chris Christie endorses Donald Trump," *Politico*, http://www.politico.com/story/2016/02/chris-christie-endorses-donald-trump-219861.
3. Kate Zernike, "Chris Christie Knew About Bridge Lane Closings as They Happened, Prosecutors Say," *The New York Times*, https://www.nytimes.com/2016/09/20/nyregion/bridgegate-trial.html.

4. Gregory Krieg, "Kushner vs. Christie: The nasty Trump transition fight that goes back a decade," *CNN Politics*, http://www.cnn.com/2016/11/16/politics/trump-transition-jared-kushner-chris-christie/index.html.
5. Alicia Parlapiano, "Pence Ranks Low in Approval, but Not as Low as Trump and Clinton," *The New York Times*, https://www.nytimes.com/interactive/2016/07/14/us/politics/mike-pence-approval-rating-governors.html.
6. Tony Cook, and Tom LoBianco, "Indiana governor signs amended 'religious freedom' law," *USA Today*, https://www.usatoday.com/story/news/nation/2015/04/02/indiana-religious-freedom-law-deal-gay-discrimination/70819106/.
7. MJ Lee, Dan Merica, and Jeff Zeleny, "Bernie Sanders endorses Hillary Clinton," *CNN Politics*, http://www.cnn.com/2016/07/11/politics/hillary-clinton-bernie-sanders/index.html.
8. Drew Desilver, "Turnout was high in the 2016 primary season, but just short of 2008 record," *Pew Research Center*, http://www.pewresearch.org/fact-tank/2016/06/10/turnout-was-high-in-the-2016-primary-season-but-just-short-of-2008-record/.
9. Carrie Dean, "Elizabeth Warren Endorses Hillary Clinton on Rachel Maddow Show," *NBC News*, http://www.nbcnews.com/politics/2016-election/elizabeth-warren-endorse-clinton-rachel-maddow-show-n589236.
10. Matt Flegenheimer, "In Newark Mayor Saves Woman from Fire, *The New York Times*, http://www.nytimes.com/2012/04/13/nyregion/newark-mayor-cory-booker-saves-woman-from-house-fire.html.
11. Susan Davis and Jessica Taylor, "4 Reasons Why Progressives Aren't Thrilled With Clinton's Pick Of Kaine," *NPR*, http://www.npr.org/2016/07/23/487133679/4-reasons-why-progressives-arent-thrilled-with-clintons-pick-of-kaine.
12. Alexander Burns, "Ignoring Advice, Donald Trump Presses Attack on Khan Family and G.O.P. Leaders," *The New York Times*, https://www.nytimes.com/2016/08/03/us/politics/donald-trump-gop.html.
13. Niall Stanage, "Clinton buries Trump in negative ads," *The Hill*, http://thehill.com/homenews/campaign/292563-clinton-buries-trump-in-negative-ads.
14. You can view the ad here https://www.youtube.com/watch?v=5zO5ohGI-LM.
15. You can view the ad here https://www.youtube.com/watch?v=RaxNEzA3jRs.
16. You can view the ad here https://www.youtube.com/watch?v=D54o-Tc_4aI.

17. You can view the ad here https://www.youtube.com/watch?v=vHGPbl-werw.
18. You can view the ad here https://www.youtube.com/watch?v=sEqiNIPIPPQ.
19. Aaron Gould Sheinin, "Hillary Clinton goes on the air in Georgia with first TV ad," *The Atlanta Journal Constitution*, http://politics.blog.ajc.com/2016/09/06/hillary-clinton-goes-on-the-air-in-georgia-with-new-tv-ad/.
20. Patrick Caldwell, "A Confident Clinton Campaign Directs Resources to Arizona and Texas," *Mother Jones*, http://www.motherjones.com/politics/2016/10/hillary-clinton-arizona-texas-trump.
21. Anne Gearan, "Clinton campaign eyes 'expansion states' of Utah, Arizona and Georgia," *The Washington Post*, https://www.washingtonpost.com/news/post-politics/wp/2016/10/12/clinton-campaign-eyes-expansion-states-of-utah-arizona-and-georgia/?utm_term=.1e030eb73b89.
22. "Arizona Republic responds to death threats for endorsing Clinton," *CBS News*, http://www.cbsnews.com/videos/arizona-republic-responds-to-death-threats-for-endorsing-clinton/.
23. "Endorsement: Hillary Clinton is the only choice to move America ahead," *AZ Central*, http://www.azcentral.com/story/opinion/editorial/2016/09/27/hillary-clinton-endorsement/91198668/.
24. Pema Levy and Will Greenberg, "A Running Tally of Newspaper Endorsements in the Presidential Election," *Mother Jones*, http://www.motherjones.com/politics/2016/09/clinton-trump-newspaper-endorsements.
25. Adam Goldman and Alan Rappaport, "Emails in Anthony Weiner Inquiry Jolts Clinton Campaign, *The New York Times*, https://www.nytimes.com/2016/10/29/us/politics/fbi-hillary-clinton-email.html?_r=0.
26. "Oct. 28 FBI letter to congressional leaders on Clinton email investigation," *The Washington Post*, https://www.washingtonpost.com/apps/g/page/politics/oct-28-fbi-letter-to-congressional-leaders-on-clinton-email-investigation/2113/.
27. Matt Apuzzo, Micahel S. Schmidt, and Adam Goldman, "Emails warrant No New Action Against Hillary Clinton, FBI Director Says," *The New York Times*, https://www.nytimes.com/2016/11/07/us/politics/hilary-clinton-male-voters-donald-trump.html.
28. "'I would be your president': Clinton blames Russia, FBI chief for 2016 election loss," *The Washington Post*, https://www.washingtonpost.com/politics/hillary-clinton-blames-russian-hackers-and-comey-for-2016-election-loss/2017/05/02/e62fef72-2f60-11e7-8674-437ddb6e813e_story.html?utm_term=.bc20f791096c.

29. "The Crystal Ball's 2016 Electoral College Ratings," Sabato's Crystal Ball, University of Virginia, http://www.centerforpolitics.org/crystalball/2016-president/.
30. "Who will win the presidency?," *FiveThirtyEight* https://projects.fivethirtyeight.com/2016-election-forecast/.
31. Voting data from the US Election project available at http://www.electproject.org/2012.
32. Amy Walter, "The Myth of the Independent Voter," *Cook Political Report*, http://cookpolitical.com/story/6608.

References

Allen, Jonathan, and Amie Parnes. *Shattered: Inside Hillary Clinton's Doomed Campaign*. New York: Crown, 2017.

Brewer, Mark D., and Louis Sandy Maisel. *Parties and Elections in America: The Electoral Process*. Lanham, MD: Rowman & Littlefield, 2016.

Fowler, Erika Franklin, Travis N. Ridout, and Michael M. Franz. "Political Advertising in 2016: The Presidential Election as Outlier?" *The Forum* 14, no. 4 (2016). doi:10.1515/for-2016-0040.

Keith, Bruce E. *The Myth of the Independent Voter*. Berkeley, CA: California University Press, 1992.

Marietta, Morgan. *A Citizen's Guide to American Ideology*. 1st ed. New York: Routledge, 2012.

Polsby, Nelson W, Aaron B Wildavsky, Steven E Schier, and David A. Hopkins. Presidential Elections. 1st ed. Lanham, MD.: Rowman & Littlefield, 2016.

Sides, John, Daron R Shaw, Matthew Grossmann, and Keena Lipsitz. *Campaigns and Elections*. 2nd ed. New York, NY: W.W. Norton & Company, Inc., 2015.

Index

A
Abedin, Huma, 116, 117
Abington School District v. Schempp, 12
Access Hollywood, 86, 87, 130, 153, 162, 166
Ads, 39, 120, 124, 151–153
Amanpour, Christiane, 157
Americans for Prosperity, 106
Arizona, 51, 56, 130, 153, 157, 167, 176
Arizona Republic, 154
Ayotte, Kelly, 45, 86

B
Baker, Charlie, 116, 150
Bannon, Steve, 106, 109
Beck, Glen, 21
Benghazi, 25–27, 57, 102, 132, 134
Bernie or Bust, 4, 83
Biden, Joe, 28, 38, 84, 89, 145, 148
Binders full of women, 125
Bipartisanship, 147
Black, Charles, 110
Bloomberg Politics, 118, 119
Blue Dog Democrats, 14
Blue Wall, 89, 121, 149, 166, 167, 176
Boehner, John, 22
Booker, Cory, 148, 149
Border wall, 40, 53, 129, 130, 167
Boston Globe, 120
Breitbart, 41, 106, 132
Brokered convention, 4, 50, 77, 111
Brookover, Ed, 108, 111
Brown, Scott, 150
Brown, Sherrod, 149
Brown v. Board of Education, 11
Bush, George H.W., 162, 174
Bush, George W., 23, 107, 123, 124, 145, 174
Bush, Jeb, 32, 34, 56, 62

C
Cain, Herman, 22, 61
Campaign events, 47, 134, 157, 164, 165
Candidate mentions, 6, 48, 50, 55–57
Cantor, Eric, 21, 23, 24
Carson, Ben, 2, 32–34
Carter, Jimmy, 47, 174

R. Bitecofer, *The Unprecedented 2016 Presidential Election*,
https://doi.org/10.1007/978-3-319-61976-7

Caucus, 23, 24, 34, 35, 87, 111
Centrist, 27, 64, 65, 150
Chaffetz, Jason, 24
Cheney, Dick, 145
Cherry picking, 124, 125
Christie, Chris, 61, 142, 146, 149
Cincinatti Enquirer, 155
Citzens United v. F.E.C., 119
Civil Rights Act of 1964, 11
Civil war, 6, 21, 31, 60
Clinton, Bill, 84, 87, 135, 160, 175, 182
Clinton, Chelsea, 154
Clinton, Hillary, 1–8, 25, 35, 64, 86, 96, 122, 168, 183
Clinton Model, 145
CNN, 20
Colorado, 86, 111, 119, 120, 153, 157, 162, 167, 174, 176
Comey, James, 88, 156
Comey letter, 88, 89, 157, 165, 166, 173
47% comment, 138
Congress, 3, 12, 13, 15, 20, 22, 60, 72, 88, 135, 156, 183
Conservative, 12–15, 17, 21, 23, 26, 33, 41, 42, 99, 110, 133, 145, 146, 156, 169, 177
Contested convention, 60, 62, 102, 147
Conway, Kellyanne, 7, 106, 113, 129
Corker, Bob, 4
Costa, Robert, 40, 128
Country First, 126
Crooked Hillary, 45, 57
Cruz, Ted, 4, 32–34, 61, 62, 83, 129
Curiel, Gonzalo, 112

D
Dallas Morning News, 155
Defection, 101, 102, 162, 168, 171, 176–178, 182, 183
Delegate, 7, 35, 36, 60, 62–64, 66, 67, 69, 72–74, 76, 77, 106, 111
Delegate allocation, 35, 67, 74
Democrat, 3, 6, 15, 17, 60, 64, 65, 70, 72, 76, 89, 143, 145–150, 155, 175, 183
Democratic National Committee, 4, 63, 72, 78, 83, 114, 134
Democratic National Convention, 60, 65, 78, 82–84, 135, 147, 150, 151
Deplorables, 132
Deripaska, Oleg, 112
Diaz, Mario, 82
Dionne, E.J., 26
Distinguished party leaders, 63, 72
Divisive primary, 130
DNC emails, 134
Dole, Bob, 107
Drudge Report, 110
Dukakis, Michael, 122
The Dukes, 134

E
Earned media, 6, 41, 66
Edwards, John, 76
Egalitarian, 13
Electability, 37, 64
Electoral College, 7, 89, 131, 144, 149, 150, 153, 162, 166, 176, 182
Elite endorsement theory, 60
Elites, 35, 37, 38, 40, 54, 65, 72
Email server, 26, 56, 57, 87, 88, 117, 133, 142, 156, 179, 180, 182
Eminem, 2
Endorsements, 2, 3, 6, 8, 24, 60, 61, 72, 77, 130, 154
Engel v. Vitale, 12

Establishment, 1, 4–6, 21–25, 27, 28, 36, 38, 40, 42, 59, 61, 62, 64, 73, 74, 76, 78, 145, 146, 183
Establishment Clause, 12
Expectations, 34, 37, 66, 67, 85, 120

F
Factionalism, 31
Fake news, 42
Feel the Bern, 35
Filibuster, 22, 23
Fiorina, Carly, 13
Fivethirtyeight, 87, 120, 144, 153, 164
Flake, Jeff, 82
Florida, 4, 7, 56, 62, 86, 89, 119–121, 151, 153, 157, 164, 165, 167, 173, 176
Forecasting models, 87, 88, 149, 168
Formal primary, 21, 22, 32–34, 48, 56, 60, 72
Freedom Caucus, 22–24, 183
Freedom of Information Act, 26
Fundraising, 32

G
Gaffe, 26, 41, 124, 128, 133, 152
Gang of Eight, 23
General election, 3, 4, 7, 8, 22, 31, 37, 42, 46, 56, 57, 65, 81, 83, 90, 94, 101, 102, 105, 106, 111–114, 118–120, 126, 130, 131, 133, 134, 142–144, 147, 151–153, 166–168, 178
Georgia, 153, 174
Gingrich, Newt, 22, 128, 146
Glassner, Michael, 111
Gold Star family, 5, 151
Gore, Al, 1, 60, 73, 89, 123, 145
GOTV, 120
Gowdy, Trey, 82
Grassroots, 37
Great Recession, 20, 21, 37
Green Party, 176, 177
Growth and Opportunity Report, 23

H
Haley, Nikki, 4, 145
Hannity, Sean, 26
HBO, 13
24-hour news cycle, 6, 40, 41
House of Representatives, 2, 22, 23, 63, 72, 82, 144
Huckabee, Mike, 2, 32

I
Idaho, 177
Ideological homogeneity, 13, 16
Ideologues, 42, 99
Ideology, 16, 17, 42, 145
I'm With Her, 150
Independent, 17, 28, 35, 78, 88, 102, 153, 162, 169–171, 175, 177, 182, 183
Inglis, Bob, 21
Invisible primary, 32, 33, 35, 37, 48, 49, 55, 72
Iowa, 3, 22, 33–36, 57, 63, 66, 67, 73, 89, 153, 157, 166, 167, 173
Iowa Caucus, 2, 3, 6, 32–34, 36, 39, 40, 60, 61, 66, 72, 111
Iowa State Fair, 47
Issa, Daryl, 24

J
Javits Center, 88, 89
Jim Crow, 12
Jindal, Bobby, 2
Johnson, Gary, 145, 154, 177

K
Kaine, Tim, 8, 143, 147, 149, 150, 164
Kasich, John, 4, 34, 62, 81, 82, 145, 149
Kelly, Megyn, 49, 54, 56, 110
Kelly, Peter, 110
Kerry, John, 124
Khan, Ghazala, 84
Khan, Khirz, 84
Koch Brothers, 119
Kushner, Jared, 128, 146

L
Leaners, 17, 171
Lewandowski, Corey, 56, 105, 106, 112
Liberal, 12, 13, 15, 17, 20, 22, 41, 42, 84, 99, 102, 114, 124, 148, 150, 171, 177, 182
Libertarian, 22, 154
Limbaugh, Rush, 21, 41
Lynch, Loretta, 135
Lyndon, Johnson, 12

M
Machado, Alicia, 86
Make American Great Again!, 47
Manafort, Paul, 77, 85, 106, 110, 112
Manchin, Joe, 15
March 1st primaries, 62, 66, 69, 74, 75
Martinez, Susana, 4
McAuliffe, Terry, 147
McCain, John, 48, 56, 64, 82, 126, 151, 175
McCarthy, Kevin, 24, 26
McCaskill, Claire, 2
McMullin, Evan, 145, 153, 162, 177
Media, 1, 3, 4, 6, 20–22, 36, 37, 40–43, 46, 47, 50, 54–57, 61, 66, 68, 72, 82, 88, 89, 101, 110, 112, 113, 119–121, 126, 128–130, 132, 133, 135, 157, 164, 168
Media bias, 41, 42
Michigan, 89, 119, 121, 149, 153, 157, 162, 164–166, 172, 175, 176
Midterm cycle, 6, 14, 32, 39, 48, 120, 147, 152, 158, 167, 179
Midterm election, 120
Millennials, 37, 65, 182
Mobilization, 147, 150, 167, 176, 182, 183
Moderate, 14, 15, 21, 23, 25, 40, 147, 150, 152, 171
Momentum, 34, 35, 61, 62, 64, 66, 67, 72, 114, 123, 152
Mook, Robby, 114, 168
MTV, 13
Multiculturism, 42
Muslim ban, 55

N
NAFTA, 149
Nationalism, 6, 40
Negative ads, 151
Nevada, 36, 66, 68, 74, 86, 114, 153, 157, 164, 167, 172, 176
Nevada Caucus, 3, 36, 66, 67, 111
Never Trump, 59, 62, 77, 101, 102, 146
New Deal Coalition, 12, 173
New Hampshire, 3, 33, 34, 36, 66–68, 73, 86, 111, 120, 121, 153, 157, 164, 167, 170, 171, 174, 176
New Hampshire Primary, 32, 36, 61, 66, 67

Newspaper endorsements, 154
The New York Times, 20, 32, 42, 47, 131, 156
Nixon, Richard, 110
Nomination, 1–7, 21, 22, 27, 28, 31, 33–37, 39, 40, 59, 61–68, 70, 72–78, 83, 84, 101, 102, 105, 106, 112, 142, 143, 145, 147, 150, 183
Nominee, 4, 7, 24, 27, 31, 37, 64–66, 74, 78, 82–84, 86, 98, 99, 101, 102, 111, 118, 124, 133, 142, 144, 145, 150, 154–156, 168–170, 173, 174, 182, 183
North Carolina, 89, 119, 121, 151, 153, 157, 164, 167, 172, 173, 176

O
Obama, Barack, 5, 36, 37, 63, 64, 68, 122, 176
Obamacare, 23, 128
Obama, Michelle, 84, 122, 154, 165
Obergefell v. Hodges, 12
Occupy Wall Street, 25
Office-seeking candidates, 75
Ohio, 4, 56, 62, 81, 86, 89, 114, 119, 120, 129, 149, 151, 153, 166, 167, 170, 173
O'Malley, Martin, 28
Oregon, 121
Orlando, Tony, 2

P
Page, Carter, 112
Palin, Sarah, 42, 124, 145
Pants-on-fire statements, 42
Partisan acrimony, 8, 18, 19
Partisan blogs, 13, 20
Partisans, 7, 19, 20, 98, 99, 101, 102, 169, 171
Partisanship, 18, 169
Party dignitaries, 73
Party elites, 6, 7, 52, 54, 60, 72, 77, 124
Party insiders, 6, 7, 60, 70, 72, 76–78, 84, 85, 106
Party sorting, 13, 15, 18, 19
Party unity, 15, 83, 84, 101
Patient Protection and Affordable Care Act, 23
Paul, Rand, 32
Paul, Ron, 22, 40
Peña, Enrique, 129
Pence, Mike, 86, 122, 128, 146
Pennsylvania, 5, 86, 89, 119–121, 149, 151, 153, 157, 162, 164, 166, 172, 173, 175, 176
Perot, Ross, 162, 174
Perry, Rick, 22, 32
Personal ads, 152
Persuasion, 8, 143, 145, 147, 150, 152, 154, 169, 170, 173–176, 182, 183
Pivot, 106, 112, 114, 129, 130, 144, 151
Pledged delegate, 69
Plouffe, David, 117
Podesta emails, 89, 136
Polarization, 5, 8, 17, 19, 20, 143, 169, 183
Policy ads, 152
Policy-seeking candidates, 75
Politifact, 29, 140
Polls, 7, 22, 33, 34, 36, 51, 55, 57, 76, 83, 85–88, 94, 95, 102, 106, 110, 111, 120, 135, 142, 144, 152, 153, 157, 162, 164
Pope Francis, 13
Populism, 6, 21, 25, 28, 37, 40, 149, 183

Portman, Rob, 4, 81, 86
Pragmatism, 143
Presumptive nominee, 64, 72
Priebus, Reince, 52
Primary, 3–6, 20–24, 32, 35, 37–40, 42, 43, 46, 47, 56, 57, 59–68, 72–77, 83, 88, 101, 102, 105, 110, 112, 114, 117, 119, 120, 131–133, 142, 143, 146, 147, 150, 177, 178
  invisible, 21
Priorities USA Action, 119
Progressive, 3, 6–8, 24, 27, 28, 35–37, 65, 84, 102, 134, 135, 144, 145, 148–150, 178–180, 182, 183
Proportional allocation, 77

R

Ramos, Jorge, 48, 54
Ready for Hillary, 116
Reagan, Ronald, 169
RealClear Politics, 33, 86, 153, 162
Red meat, 125, 143
Republican, 2–8, 12, 13, 15, 17–19, 21–26, 28, 31–34, 36, 39–42, 46–48, 52, 54, 56, 57, 59, 60, 62–64, 66, 67, 69, 72–78, 81–83, 85, 87, 98, 101, 102, 105, 106, 110–112, 118–121, 124, 125, 131, 142–147, 149, 150, 152, 153, 162, 169, 170, 173–175, 177, 178, 183
Republican National Committee, 2, 4, 23, 52, 69, 81, 82, 111–114, 119
Republican National Convention, 82, 83, 114, 121, 129
Republican platform, 51
Resource allocation, 120, 142, 182
R.I.N.O.S., 21
Roe v. Wade, 12
Romney, Mitt, 4, 21, 22, 56, 94, 118, 124, 125, 150, 176
Rubio, Marco, 4, 32, 34, 56, 61, 62, 73, 75
Russia, 112, 113
Ryan, Paul, 24, 56, 87, 112, 145

S

Sabato, Larry, 40
Sanders, Bernie, 2, 3, 5, 6, 8, 28, 35, 38, 48, 64, 65, 68, 84, 122, 134, 135, 143, 147, 148, 154, 177, 178, 182
Sanders, Sarah Huckabee, 111
San Diego Union Tribune, 155
Santorum, Rick, 22, 32
Sasse, Ben, 82
SEC primaries, 62, 69, 74
Secularization, 12
Segregation, 12
Senate, 2, 8, 15, 22, 23, 62, 65, 82, 111, 119, 120, 142, 144, 148–150, 156
Senate Foreign Relations Committee, 27
Senate Intelligence Committee, 111
Social media, 13, 43
South Carolina Primary, 22, 33–36, 66, 68, 74, 76
State Department, 25, 26, 116
Stein, Jill, 176, 177, 179
Stevens, Chris, 26
Stone, Roger, 110, 111
Strategy, 8, 26, 37, 39–42, 46, 47, 57, 83, 85, 87, 89, 90, 103, 105, 113, 119, 120, 124, 134, 142–145, 147, 151–153, 156, 165, 167–170, 173, 174, 176, 182
Stronger Together, 150
Substantive endorsements, 78
Super delegate, 60, 63, 72, 73, 76, 78
SuperPacs, 32, 117–119

Super surrogates, 122, 164
Surrogates, 113, 122, 129, 154, 164, 167
Symbolic endorsements, 60, 77

T
Tactics, 142, 143
TARP, 20
Tea Party, 21–23, 25, 40, 150, 183
Third party, 88, 102
Thune, John, 86
TPP, 25, 149, 150
Trump, Donald, 3, 5–8, 28, 32–35, 40, 42, 46–48, 51, 56, 57, 62, 72, 74, 84, 87, 96, 122, 131, 142, 144, 168, 179
Trump Foundation, 142
Trump, Melania, 83, 129
Trump Train, 6, 59, 75
Trump University, 111, 131, 142
Tur, Katie, 43
Tweets, 43, 84, 127, 132
Twitter, 3, 48, 128

U
Ukraine, 106, 112
Unity Reform Commission, 78
Unprecedented, 1–5, 7, 25, 56, 59, 62, 72, 82, 89, 94, 106, 167
USA Today, 155
Utah, 153, 162, 177

V
Vermont, 28, 35, 36, 67, 177
Viability, 60, 63, 64, 67, 72, 76, 182
Vice president selection, 145
Vietnam, 12, 48, 52, 151, 153
Virginia, 15, 21, 86, 95, 101, 102, 114, 119, 143, 147, 150, 153, 157, 162, 167, 172, 174
Voting Rights Act of 1965, 11

W
Walker, Scott, 32
Warren, Elizabeth, 28, 65, 83, 84, 143, 148–150, 180, 182
Washington outsider, 40
Wasserman-Schultz, Deborah, 83
Watergate, 12
Weak partisans, 171
Weiner, Anthony, 117, 156
Wikileaks, 83, 135
Winner-take-all, 35, 67, 74, 77
Wisconsin, 47, 86, 87, 89, 119–121, 149, 153, 162, 166, 172, 173, 175, 176
Woman card, 132

Y
Yes We Can, 47
Young, Neil, 3

CPSIA information can be obtained
at www.ICGtesting.com
Printed in the USA
LVHW070832230220
647903LV00027B/1285